# A Guide to DB2

# A Guide to DB2

A user's guide to the IBM product *IBM® Database 2*
(a relational database management system
for the MVS environment)
and its companion products QMF and DXT

## C. J. Date

**ADDISON-WESLEY PUBLISHING COMPANY**

Reading, Massachusetts • Menlo Park, California
London • Amsterdam • Don Mills, Ontario • Sydney

To Ted, for obvious reasons

# Preface

The subject of this book, DB2, is an IBM program product for the MVS environment. More specifically, it is a relational database management system for MVS, which means that it is a product that allows users in that environment (both end-users and application programmers) to store data in, and retrieve data from, databases that are perceived as collections of relations or tables. It provides access to those databases by means of a relational language called SQL ("Structured Query Language").

As a name, "DB2" can scarcely be said to display much distinction—it does little to suggest the nature of the product—and the full name ("IBM Database 2") is not much better. Specifically, it does not make it clear that the product is relational, or that it supports the SQL language, or that it runs on MVS. (Furthermore, it is not even particularly accurate. The product is not a database at all; it is a database management system.) This inauspicious start, however, cannot conceal the fact that DB2 is a highly important product. Its announcement in June 1983 was a significant occasion: it placed IBM's final seal of approval on what has come to be known as *the relational approach* to database management. That approach, first proposed in 1969–70 by E. F. Codd of the IBM San Jose Research Laboratory, has slowly but steadily been gaining acceptance (both inside and outside IBM) ever since that time. DB2 is now the leading member of a family of mainline products from IBM, all of them relational, all supporting the SQL language, and all running on one of the major IBM operating systems (DB2 on MVS, SQL/DS on DOS/VSE, and SQL/DS Release 2 on VM/CMS).

As just mentioned, the relational approach was first proposed in 1969–70. The SQL language was proposed in 1974, and a major prototype implementation of that language, called System R, was built and evaluated by IBM over a period of approximately five years (1975–79). The technology developed in that prototype was then incorporated into SQL/DS, IBM's first fully supported relational product (announced for DOS/VSE in 1981 and for VM/CMS in 1983), and subsequently into DB2 (announced for MVS in 1983). System R, SQL/DS, and DB2 all have very similar externals; in particular, the SQL language is very similar across the three systems. Thus, although this book is specifically concerned with DB2, much of it applies with little change to System R and SQL/DS also. (However, references to "the SQL language" from this point forward should be taken to refer specifically to the dialect supported by DB2, unless otherwise indicated.)

The major purpose of this book is to present a detailed (and not wholly uncritical) description of the DB2 product: what it is and is not, what it is intended for, and how it can be used. The book is aimed at DP management, end-user management, database specialists (including database and system administrators, database designers, and database application programmers), DP students and teachers, and end-users or DP professionals who wish to broaden their knowledge of the database field by studying a state-of-the-art system. The emphasis throughout is on the *user* (where by "user" we mean, principally, either an end-user or an application programmer); treatment of user-oriented material, such as the SQL language, is very thorough. By contrast, details that are of interest only to system programmers or operators, such as details of system commands, are generally omitted or at best treated only sketchily. Readers are assumed to have at least a general appreciation of the overall structure, concepts, and objectives of a database system; however, knowledge of relational systems *per se* is not required.

The structure of the book is as follows. Chapters 1 and 2 present an overview of the DB2 product, showing how it fits into its environment and in outline how it works. Chapter 3 is concerned with data definition and Chapters 4–6 with data manipulation. Chapter 7 discusses the system catalog. Chapter 8 describes a special relational facility, called the view mechanism, and Chapter 9 discusses the DB2 security subsystem, showing in particular how the views introduced in the previous chapter can be used to provide security. Chapters 10–12 are concerned with application programming; among other topics, they discuss the use of the SQL language for writing application programs, and they cover transaction processing in some detail (including recovery and concurrency considerations). Chapter 13 considers DB2 storage structures. Chapter 14 describes the DB2 interactive interface (DB2I), and Chapter 15 discusses the query/report-writing front-end product called QMF (Query Management Facility). Finally, Chapter 16 summarizes the advantages of a system like DB2, discusses performance considerations, and speculates about the future of relational systems. The chapters contain a large number of worked examples and (in most cases) a set of exercises, together with answers to most of those exercises.

The book also contains several appendices, including one that addresses the question of what it means for a system to be relational, and another (fairly lengthy) that presents a practical approach to the problem of relational database design.

Some readers may be aware that I have already published a number of other books on database technology:

1. *An Introduction to Database Systems: Volume I,* Third Edition. Addison-Wesley, 1981 (referred to below as Volume I).

2. *An Introduction to Database Systems: Volume II.* Addison-Wesley, 1983 (referred to below as Volume II).

3. *Database: A Primer.* Addison-Wesley, 1983 (referred to below as the Primer).

Readers familiar with one or another of these three books will notice some family resemblances between them and the present book. They should not be misled into thinking that the material of the present book is not new. It is true that certain portions of the present book do borrow from those existing books—not unreasonably, since major portions of those books were concerned with the technology of System R, upon which DB2 is largely based. In all cases, however, the borrowed material has been updated, expanded, or otherwise considerably transformed. To be specific:

- Chapters 3–7 are a major expansion and revision of Chapters 6 and 7 of Volume I; Chapter 7 in particular also incorporates some material from Chapter 7 of the Primer.
- Chapter 8 is a considerably updated version of Chapter 9 of Volume I.
- Chapter 9 is a major expansion/revision of a small portion of Section 4.4 of Volume II.
- Chapters 10–12 are based on Chapter 8 of Volume I and a small amount of material from Chapter 3 of Volume II.
- Certain portions of Appendix B are based on Chapters 17 and 18 of the Primer.

## ACKNOWLEDGMENTS

First and foremost, it is a real pleasure to acknowledge the friendship and support I have received from Ted Codd, not only during the writing of this book but throughout my professional activities over the last several years. Like so many other people in this field, I owe my career and very livelihood to the work that

Ted originally did in the late sixties and early seventies, and I am delighted to be able to acknowledge that debt in public here. It is only fitting that this book should be dedicated to him.

Second, I would like to thank the following friends and colleagues for their assistance and encouragement throughout this project and for their constructive criticism of early drafts of the manuscript: Jnan Dash, Walt Roseberry, Phil Shaw, and most especially Sharon Weinberg. Third, I would like to express my gratitude to my excolleagues on the DB2 design and development team for their patience in dealing with my numerous technical questions; there are too many individuals involved to name them all here, but I would especially like to mention (in addition to those already identified above) my coworkers in the DB2 technical planning department: Sandy Eveland, Paul Higginbotham, Roger Reinsch, Dan Wardman, and George Zagelow. Finally, I am very pleased to acknowledge the hard work put in, at Addison-Wesley and elsewhere, by the many people directly involved in the production of this book. I hope the result does justice to their efforts.

C.J.D.

*Saratoga, California*
*September 1983*

# Contents

## CHAPTER 3
## DATA DEFINITION

## CHAPTER 4
## DATA MANIPULATION I:
## RETRIEVAL OPERATIONS

## CHAPTER 5
## DATA MANIPULATION II:
## RETRIEVAL OPERATIONS (CONTINUED)

## CHAPTER 6
## DATA MANIPULATION III:
## UPDATE OPERATIONS

## CHAPTER 7
## THE CATALOG

## CHAPTER 8
## VIEWS

## CHAPTER 12
## APPLICATION PROGRAMMING III:
## DYNAMIC SQL

## CHAPTER 13
## STORAGE STRUCTURE

## CHAPTER 14
## THE DB2 INTERACTIVE INTERFACE (DB2I)

## CHAPTER 15
## THE QUERY MANAGEMENT FACILITY (QMF)

## CHAPTER 16
## SUMMARY AND CONCLUSIONS

## APPENDIX A
## THE RELATIONAL MODEL

## APPENDIX B
## RELATIONAL DATABASE DESIGN

## APPENDIX C
## SYNTAX OF SQL DATA MANIPULATION OPERATIONS

## APPENDIX D
## SYSTEM REQUIREMENTS

# A Guide to DB2

# 1

# An Overview
# of DB2

## 1.1 INTRODUCTION

"DB2" is an abbreviation for "IBM Database 2." DB2 is a subsystem of the
MVS operating system.* More specifically, it is a *database management system*
(DBMS) for that operating system. Even more specifically, it is IBM's long-
awaited *relational* DBMS for MVS; it is a system that allows any number of
MVS users to access any number of relational databases by means of a relational
language called SQL ("Structured Query Language").

IBM's product line prior to DB2 included a nonrelational (actually hierarchical) DBMS for MVS, namely IMS, and a relational DBMS for DOS/VSE and
VM/CMS, namely SQL/DS, but did not include a relational offering for MVS.
(We shall have more to say about IMS and SQL/DS later.) In June 1983, however,
the MVS relational system DB2 was finally announced. The purpose of this book
is to describe that system.

---

*Throughout this book we shall use the term "MVS" to mean both the standard MVS
operating system (i.e., the IBM "Multiple Virtual Systems" system product) and the
extended version known as MVS/XA ("MVS / Extended Architecture"). Every reference
in the text to MVS applies equally to both versions.

1

What does it mean for a system to be relational? To answer this question properly, it is unfortunately necessary to discuss a good deal of preliminary material first. Since any such discussion would be out of place at this early point in the book, we defer it for now (see Section 1.4 and Appendix A for the details); however, we give a rough-and-ready answer to the question without that discussion, in the hope that such an answer will help to allay any apprehensions the reader may be feeling at the outset. Briefly, a relational system is a system in which:

(a)  the data is perceived by the user as tables (and nothing but tables); and

(b)  the operators at the user's disposal (e.g., for query) are operators that generate new tables from old. For example, there will be one operator to extract a subset of the rows of a given table, and another to extract a subset of the columns—and of course a row subset and a column subset of a table are both in turn tables themselves.

Fig. 1.1 illustrates these two points. The data (see part (a) of the figure) consists of a single table, named CELLAR, with three columns and four rows. Two sample queries—one involving a row-subsetting operation and the other a column-subsetting operation—are shown in part (b) of the figure. *Note:* These two queries are in fact examples of the SELECT statement of the Structured Query Language SQL mentioned earlier. SQL (usually pronounced "sequel") is the database language supported not only by DB2, but also by SQL/DS and by several nonIBM products.

The purpose of this book, then, is to provide an in-depth tutorial and reference text on the relational system DB2 (and, to a lesser extent, to its companion products QMF and DXT—see Section 1.3). It is intended for end-users, application programmers, database administrators, and more generally anyone who wishes to obtain an understanding of the major concepts of the DB2 system. It is not intended as a substitute for the system manuals provided by IBM; but it *is* intended as a comprehensive, convenient (single-volume) guide to the use of the product. As stated in the Preface, the emphasis is definitely on the user, and therefore on product externals rather than internals, although various internal aspects are discussed from time to time. The reader is assumed to have an overall appreciation of the structure and objectives of database systems in general, but not necessarily any specific knowledge of relational systems in particular. All applicable relational concepts are introduced in the text as they are needed. In addition, Appendix A provides a more formal summary of those concepts, for purposes of reference.

In this preliminary chapter, we present a brief overview of the DB2 product. In particular, we show in outline the environments it operates in, discuss some

(a)  Given table:

```
                        CELLAR   WINE          YEAR   BOTTLES
                                 ----------    ----   -------
                                 Zinfandel     77        10
                                 Chardonnay    82         6
                                 Cabernet      76        12
                                 Riesling      82         9
```

(b)  Operators (examples):

1. Row subset:          Result:  WINE          YEAR   BOTTLES
                                 ----------    ----   -------
```
   SELECT  WINE, YEAR, BOTTLES   Chardonnay    82         6
   FROM    CELLAR                Riesling      82         9
   WHERE   YEAR = 82 ;
```

2. Column subset:       Result:  WINE          BOTTLES
                                 ----------    -------
```
   SELECT  WINE, BOTTLES         Zinfandel        10
   FROM    CELLAR ;              Chardonnay        6
                                 Cabernet         12
                                 Riesling          9
```

**Fig. 1.1**  Data structure and operators in a relational system (examples)

related products briefly, and give some idea as to what is involved in creating and accessing a DB2 database. All of these topics, and of course many others, are amplified in subsequent chapters.

## 1.2   DB2 ENVIRONMENTS

DB2 is designed to work in cooperation with three other MVS subsystems, namely IMS, CICS, and TSO.* Fig. 1.2 illustrates that cooperation.

The figure can be read as follows:

1. Any given DB2 application—that is, any application program that accesses one or more DB2 databases—will execute under the control of exactly one of the three subsystems IMS, CICS, and TSO: That is, exactly one of those three subsystems will be responsible for providing certain essential system services (to

---

*In the interests of accuracy, we should make it clear that TSO is not really a "subsystem" in the special sense in which that term is used in MVS; rather, it is an integral part of MVS itself. It is possible to acquire an MVS system without IMS or CICS, but not one without TSO. But these distinctions are not significant for our purposes, and for simplicity we will regard all three—IMS, CICS, and TSO—as subsystems in this book.

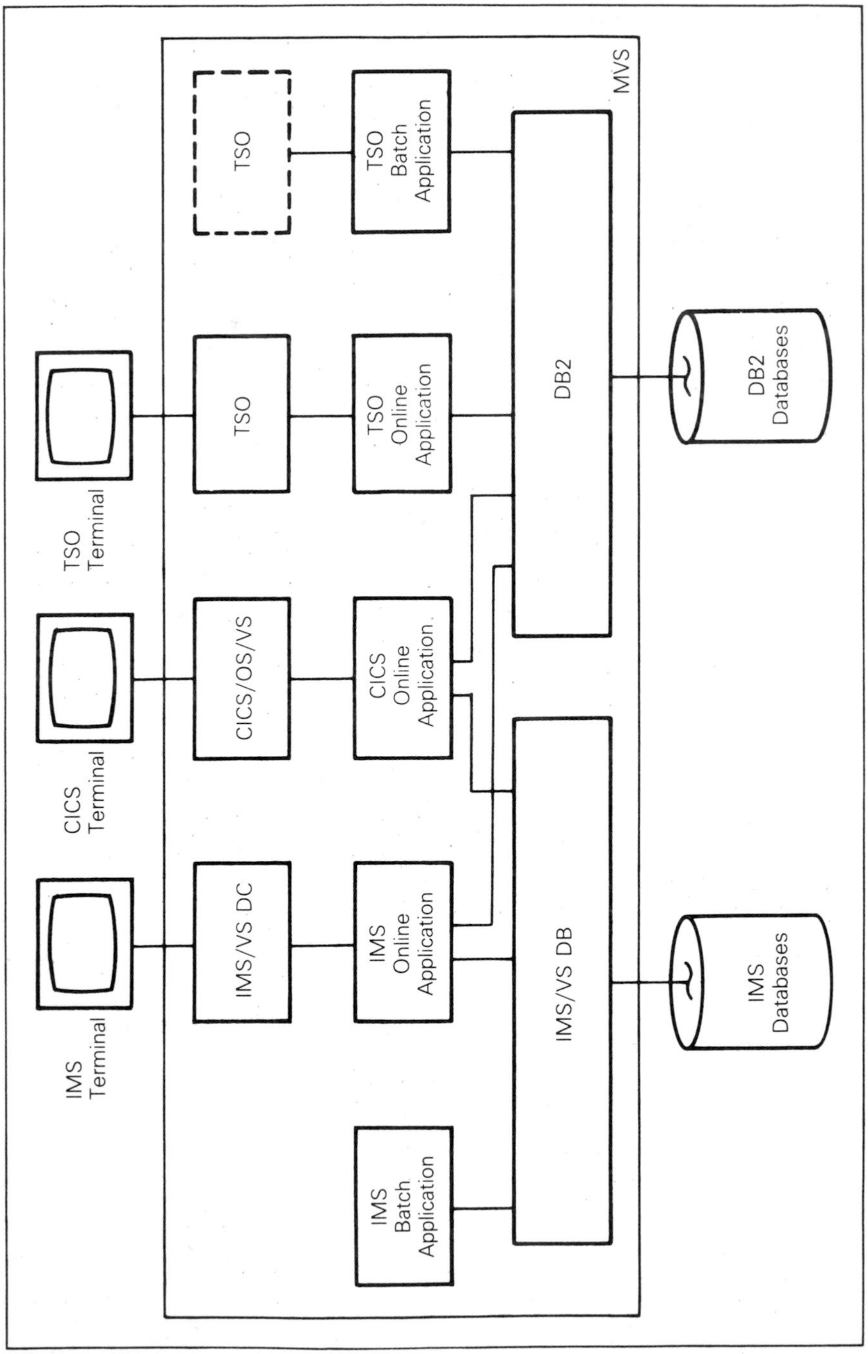

Fig. 1.2  DB2 operating environments

be discussed in Chapter 11). We can therefore divide DB2 applications into three disjoint categories, namely IMS, CICS, and TSO applications, respectively.

2. In general, any given application (DB2 or otherwise) may optionally use the data communication facilities of IMS, CICS, or TSO (as applicable) to communicate with one or more terminals. If it does, it is said to be an online application, otherwise it is said to be a batch application. DB2 applications running under IMS or CICS must be online (see point 4 below); DB2 applications running under TSO may be either online or batch.*

3. A DB2 application running under IMS or CICS (but not TSO) can optionally access one or more IMS databases in addition to its DB2 database(s).

4. A nonTSO batch application cannot access DB2 databases at all (as mentioned under point 2 above).

5. A TSO application cannot access IMS databases at all (as mentioned under point 3 above).

6. IMS, CICS, and TSO applications may all be running concurrently and may even be sharing the same DB2 database(s).

For the reader unfamiliar with IMS and/or CICS and/or TSO, we offer the following words of encouragement: It is not necessary to be familiar with these subsystems in order to understand the capabilities of DB2. It is sufficient to understand that a program that uses the facilities of DB2 must operate under exactly one of IMS, CICS, and TSO, and not a mixture. Note, however, that a TSO application can be executed as a TSO batch application on one occasion and as a TSO online application on another; the I/O statements in the program can be directed to conventional data sets on one occasion and to the terminal on another, provided of course that the program has been written in such a way as to be ready for either eventuality.

## 1.3   RELATED PRODUCTS

A number of other IBM program products are more or less closely related to DB2. Of these, the principal ones are as follows:

### SQL/DS (Structured Query Language / Data System)

SQL/DS is, as already indicated, a relational DBMS for the DOS/VSE and VM/CMS operating systems. It is part of the DB2 "family" in the sense that essentially the same language, namely SQL, is used in both systems. To be more precise,

---

*For the benefit of readers who are familiar with MVS and/or TSO, a TSO batch application is nothing more than a regular MVS batch application that happens to be run under the control of the TSO terminal monitor program (TMP). See Section 14.9.

the data manipulation statements and the major data definition statements are the same in both, except for certain minor details. The stored data format is not the same, however; but utilities are provided to assist in migrating data from a SQL/DS database to a DB2 database or vice versa.*

*Note:* SQL/DS includes as part of the base product:

(a) an interactive query and report writer interface called ISQL ("Interactive SQL"); and

(b) a facility ("DL/I Extract") for copying specified data from a DOS DL/I database into a SQL/DS database so that it can be accessed via the ISQL interface. (DOS DL/I is essentially a trimmed-down version of IMS for DOS/VSE. "DL/I" is the database access language used in both DOS DL/I and IMS.)

The situation in DB2 with regard to such facilities differs somewhat from that of SQL/DS. The DB2 base product does include an interactive interface, somewhat akin to ISQL, called DB2I ("DB2 Interactive"). However, DB2I is really intended for data processing professionals—application programmers, for example—rather than for casual users. The true end-user interface for DB2 is provided by a separate front-end product called QMF (see below for details). Likewise, the "DL/I Extract" function is provided in the DB2 environment by another separate product, DXT (again, see below for details).

**QMF (Query Management Facility)**

QMF is a sophisticated query / report-writer front-end for both DB2 (under TSO) and SQL/DS (under DOS/VSE or VM/CMS). Note that it is a separate product; from DB2's point of view, in fact, it is nothing more than a particular online TSO application. QMF allows end-users to enter *ad hoc* queries in either SQL or QBE ("Query-By-Example") and to produce a variety of formatted reports from the results of such queries. It thus resembles the builtin query / report-writer interface ISQL provided in SQL/DS as part of the base product. However, the range of

---

*It is not just in the stored data format that the two systems differ, of course. There are numerous other distinctions to be drawn, most of them having to do with the fact that DB2 is specifically designed for the large-system (MVS) environment. For example, the amount of database data that can be stored online in a DB2 system is constrained only by the amount of online storage available, whereas SQL/DS is limited to a single online database of 64 billion bytes (theoretical maximum; the practical maximum is somewhat less). Likewise, the DB2 security mechanism is considerably more elaborate than that of SQL/DS, reflecting the fact that there are probably many more users, and many more categories of user, in a DB2 installation than in a SQL/DS installation. But it is not the purpose of this book to spell out all such differences in detail.

facilities provided by QMF greatly exceeds that found in ISQL; in particular, ISQL does not support the QBE language.

Chapter 15 provides more information on QMF (and DXT).

### DXT (Data Extract)

DXT is a generalized data copying program. It allows a specified subset of the data in a given IMS database or VSAM or SAM data set to be copied into a sequential file that is in a format suitable for loading (via the appropriate load utility) into either a DB2 database or a SQL/DS database. As already mentioned, Chapter 15 provides more information on DXT.

### 1.4   DB2: A RELATIONAL SYSTEM

DB2 databases are relational. *A relational database is a database that is perceived by its users as a collection of tables (and nothing but tables).* An example (the suppliers-and-parts database) is shown in Fig. 1.3.

As you can see, this database consists of three tables, namely S, P, and SP.

- Table S represents suppliers. Each supplier has a supplier number (S#), unique to that supplier; a supplier name (SNAME), not necessarily unique; a rating or status value (STATUS); and a location (CITY). For the sake of the example, we assume that each supplier is located in exactly one city.

- Table P represents parts (more accurately, kinds of part). Each kind of part has a part number (P#), which is unique; a part name (PNAME); a color

| S | S# | SNAME | STATUS | CITY | | SP | S# | P# | QTY |
|---|----|-------|--------|------|---|----|----|----|----|
|   | S1 | Smith | 20 | London | |   | S1 | P1 | 300 |
|   | S2 | Jones | 10 | Paris | |   | S1 | P2 | 200 |
|   | S3 | Blake | 30 | Paris | |   | S1 | P3 | 400 |
|   | S4 | Clark | 20 | London | |   | S1 | P4 | 200 |
|   | S5 | Adams | 30 | Athens | |   | S1 | P5 | 100 |
|   |    |       |    |        | |   | S1 | P6 | 100 |

| P | P# | PNAME | COLOR | WEIGHT | CITY | | S2 | P1 | 300 |
|---|----|-------|-------|--------|------|---|----|----|----|
|   |    |       |       |        |      | | S2 | P2 | 400 |
|   | P1 | Nut | Red | 12 | London | | S3 | P2 | 200 |
|   | P2 | Bolt | Green | 17 | Paris | | S4 | P2 | 200 |
|   | P3 | Screw | Blue | 17 | Rome | | S4 | P4 | 300 |
|   | P4 | Screw | Red | 14 | London | | S4 | P5 | 400 |
|   | P5 | Cam | Blue | 12 | Paris | |    |    |    |
|   | P6 | Cog | Red | 19 | London | |    |    |    |

**Fig. 1.3**  The suppliers-and-parts database (sample values)

(COLOR); a weight (WEIGHT); and a location where parts of that type are stored (CITY). For the sake of the example, again, we assume that each kind of part comes in exactly one color and is stored in a warehouse in exactly one city.

- Table SP represents shipments. It serves in a sense to connect the other two tables together. For example, the first row of table SP in Fig. 1.3 connects a specific supplier from table S (namely, supplier S1) with a specific part from table P (namely, part P1); in other words, it represents a shipment of parts of kind P1 by the supplier called S1 (and the shipment quantity is 300). Thus, each shipment has a supplier number (S#), a part number (P#), and a quantity (QTY). For the sake of the example, once again, we assume that there can be at most one shipment at any given time for a given supplier and a given part; thus, for a given shipment, the combination of S# value and P# value is unique with respect to the set of shipments currently appearing in the table.

This example is of course extremely simple, much more simple than any real example that you are likely to encounter in practice. Nevertheless, it is adequate to illustrate most of the points that we need to make in this book, and we will use it as the basis for most (not all) of the examples in the following chapters. You should therefore take a little time to familiarize yourself with it now.

*Note:* There is nothing wrong with using more descriptive names (such as SUPPLIERS, PARTS, and SHIPMENTS) in place of the rather terse names S, P, and SP; indeed, descriptive names are generally to be recommended in practice. But in the case of the suppliers-and-parts database specifically, the three tables are referenced so frequently in the chapters that follow that very short names seemed desirable. Long names tend to become irksome with much repetition.

A couple of points arising from the example are worth calling out explicitly:

- First, note that all data values are *atomic*. That is, at every row-and-column position in every table there is always exactly one data value, never a set of values. Thus, for example, in table SP (looking at the first two columns only, for simplicity), we have

```
S#   P#
--   --

 .    .
S2   P1
S2   P2

 .    .
S4   P2
S4   P4
S4   P5

 .    .
 .    .
```

instead of

```
S#     P#
--     ----- ---------

 .      .
S2    { P1, P2 }

 .      .
S4    { P2, P4, P5 }

 .      .
 .      .
```

A column such as P# in the second version of this table represents what is sometimes called a "repeating group." A repeating group is a column that contains *sets* of data values (different numbers of values in different rows), instead of just one value in each row. *Relational databases do not allow repeating groups.* The second version of the table above would not be permitted in a relational system.

▪ Second, note that the entire information content of the database is represented as *explicit data values*. This method of representation (as explicit values in column positions within rows of tables) is the *only* method available in a relational database. Specifically, there are no "links" or pointers connecting one table to another. For example, there is a connexion (as already pointed out) between the S1 row of table S and the P1 row of table P, because supplier S1 supplies part P1; but that connexion is represented, not by pointers, but by the existence of a row in table SP in which the S# value is S1 and the P# value is P1. In nonrelational systems (such as IMS), by contrast, such information is typically represented by some kind of physical link or pointer that is explicitly visible to the user.

At this point the reader may be wondering why a database such as that in Fig. 1.3 is called "relational." The answer is simple: "Relation" is just a mathematical term for a table (to be precise, a table of a certain specific kind—details to follow in Chapter 3). Thus, for example, we can say that the database of Fig. 1.3 consists of three *relations*. For the most part, in fact, you can take "relation" and "table" as synonymous. Relational systems have their origin in the mathematical theory of relations; of course, this does not mean that you need to be a mathematician in order to use a relational system, but it does mean that there is a respectable body of theoretical results that can be applied to practical problems of database usage, such as the problem of database design.

If it is true that a relation is just a table, then why not simply call it a table and have done with it? The answer is that we very often do (and in this book we usually will). However, it is worth taking a moment to understand why the term "relation" was introduced in the first place. Briefly, the explanation is as follows. Relational systems are based on what is called *the relational model of data*. The

relational model, in turn, is an abstract theory of data that is based in part on the
mathematical theory mentioned earlier. The principles of the relational model
were originally laid down by one man, Dr. E. F. Codd of IBM. It was late in
1968 that Codd, a mathematician by training, first realized that the discipline of
mathematics could be used to inject some solid principles and rigor into a field—
database management—that, prior to that time, was all too deficient in any such
qualities. Codd's ideas were first widely published in a now classic paper, "A
Relational Model of Data for Large Shared Data Banks" (Communications of
the ACM *13*, No. 6, June 1970). Since that time, those ideas (by now almost
universally accepted) have had a wide-ranging influence on just about every
aspect of database technology, and indeed on other fields as well, such as the
field of artificial intelligence and natural language processing.

Now, the relational model as originally formulated by Codd very deliberately
made use of certain terms—such as the term "relation" itself—that were not
familiar in data processing circles at that time, even though the concepts in some
cases were. The trouble was, many of the more familiar terms were very fuzzy.
They lacked the precision necessary to a formal theory of the kind that Codd was
proposing. For example, consider the term "record." At different times that single
term can mean either a record *instance* or a record *type*; a *COBOL-style* record
(which allows repeating groups) or a *flat* record (which does not); a *logical* record
or a *physical* record; a *stored* record or a *virtual* record; and so on. The formal
relational model therefore does not use the term "record" at all; instead, it uses
the term "tuple" (short for "n-tuple"), which was given a precise definition by
Codd when he first introduced it. We do not give that definition here; for our
purposes, it is sufficient to say that the term "tuple" corresponds approximately
to the notion of a *flat record instance* (just as the term "relation" corresponds
approximately to the notion of a table). If you wish to study some of the more
formal literature on relational database systems, you will of course have to familiarize yourself with the formal terminology, but in this book we are not trying to
be very formal, and we will stick for the most part to terms such as "record"
that are reasonably familiar. Fig. 1.4 shows the terms we will be using most
heavily (table, record, row, field, column). For interest it also gives the corresponding formal term in each case. Note that we use the terms "record" and

```
formal relational term        informal equivalents
----------------------        --------------------
    relation                      table
    tuple                         record, row
    attribute                     field, column
```

**Fig. 1.4** Some terminology

"row" interchangeably, and the terms "field" and "column" likewise. Note also, therefore, that we are definitely taking "record" to mean "record instance" and "field" to mean "field type."

## 1.5   THE SQL LANGUAGE

Fig. 1.3 (the suppliers-and-parts database) of course represents that database as it appears at some particular instant in time. It is a *snapshot* of the database. Fig. 1.5, by contrast, shows the *structure* of that database; it shows how the database is defined or described.*

As you can see, the definition includes one CREATE TABLE statement for each of the three tables. CREATE TABLE is an example of a SQL *data definition* statement. Each CREATE TABLE statement specifies the name of the table to be created, the names of its columns, and the data types of those columns (possibly some additional information also, not illustrated in the example).

It is not our purpose at this point to describe the CREATE TABLE statement in detail. That detailed description appears later, in Chapter 3. One point that

```
CREATE TABLE S
     ( S#        CHAR(5),
       SNAME     CHAR(20),
       STATUS    SMALLINT,
       CITY      CHAR(15) ) ;

CREATE TABLE P
     ( P#        CHAR(6),
       PNAME     CHAR(20),
       COLOR     CHAR(6),
       WEIGHT    SMALLINT,
       CITY      CHAR(15) ) ;

CREATE TABLE SP
     ( S#        CHAR(5),
       P#        CHAR(6),
       QTY       INTEGER ) ;
```

**Fig. 1.5** The suppliers-and-parts database (data definition)

---

*Throughout this book we show SQL statements, commands, etc., in upper case, for clarity. In practice it is usually more convenient to enter such statements and commands in lower case. DB2 will accept both.

does need to be stressed right at the outset, however, is that CREATE TABLE is an *executable statement*. (In fact, every statement in the SQL language is executable, as we shall see.) If the three CREATE TABLEs in Fig. 1.5 are entered at a terminal, exactly as shown, the system will actually build the three tables, then and there. Initially, of course, the tables will be empty—that is, they will each contain just the row of column headings, no data rows as yet. However, we can immediately go on to insert such data rows (possibly via the SQL INSERT statement, to be discussed in Chapter 6), and, in just a few minutes' work, we can have a (probably small, but still useful and usable) database at our disposal, and can start doing some useful things with it. So this simple example illustrates right away one of the advantages of relational systems in general (and DB2 in particular): They are very easy to use (ease of "getting on the air" is of course just one aspect of ease of use in general). As a result, they can make users very productive. We shall see many other advantages later.

*Note:* Although it really has nothing to do with the subject of this section (namely, the SQL language), it is worth mentioning in passing that DB2 is specifically designed to be easy to install as a *system*—by which we mean that, not only is it easy to "install" or create a new DB2 database at any time, but it is also easy to install the overall system in the first place. In other words, the process of building the necessary DB2 library data sets, specifying the required system parameters, defining certain system defaults, etc., is deliberately made as simple as possible. Sample programs are provided to verify that system installation has been performed correctly. The overall installation procedure should typically take from one to two working days.

To continue with the example: Having created our three tables, and loaded some records into them, we can now start doing useful work with them, using the *data manipulation* statements of SQL. One of the things we can do is *data retrieval* (specified in SQL by the SELECT statement). An example of data retrieval is shown in Fig. 1.6.

(a)  Interactive (DB2I):

```
        SELECT  CITY                    Result:    CITY
        FROM    S                                  ------
        WHERE   S# = 'S4' ;                        London
```

(b)  Embedded in PL/I (could be COBOL, FORTRAN, or Assembler):

```
    EXEC SQL SELECT  CITY                Result:    XCIT
             INTO    :XCIT                          ------
             FROM    S                              London
             WHERE   S# = 'S4' ;
```

**Fig. 1.6**  A retrieval example

A particularly significant feature of SQL as implemented in DB2 (and SQL/DS, incidentally) is that the same language is available at *two different interfaces*, namely an interactive interface (DB2I, in the case of DB2) and an application programming interface. Fig. 1.6(a) shows an example of the interactive interface, DB2I. Here, the user has typed the SELECT statement at a terminal, and DB2 has responded—through its DB2I component- –by displaying the result ("London") directly at that terminal. Fig. 1.6(b) shows essentially the same SELECT statement embedded in an application program (a PL/I program, in the example). In this second case the statement will be executed when the program is executed, and the result "London" will be returned, not to a terminal, but to the program variable XCIT (by virtue of the INTO clause in the SELECT; XCIT is just an input area within the program). Thus, SQL is both an *interactive query language* and a *database programming language*. This remark applies to the entire SQL language; that is, any SQL statement that can be entered at a terminal can alternatively be embedded in a program. Note in particular that the remark applies even to statements such as CREATE TABLE; you can create tables from within an application program, if it makes sense in your application to do so and if you are authorized to perform such operations. SQL statements can be embedded in programs written in any of the following languages: PL/I, COBOL, FORTRAN, and System/370 Assembler Language. (In addition, IBM has stated its intention of supporting BASIC and APL at some future date.)

*Note:* The prefix EXEC SQL is needed in Fig. 1.6(b) to distinguish the SQL statement from the PL/I statements that surround it. Likewise, an INTO clause is needed to designate the input area, as we have seen, and the variable named in that clause must have a colon prefix in order to distinguish it from a SQL column-name. So, of course, it is not one hundred percent true that the SELECT statement is the same at both interfaces. But it is broadly true, if we overlook the minor differences of detail.

We are now in a position to understand how DB2 looks to the user. By "user" here we mean either an end-user at an online terminal or an application programmer writing in PL/I, COBOL, FORTRAN, or Assembler Language. (We remark in passing that we will use the term "user" consistently throughout this book with either or both of these two meanings.) As already explained, each such user will be using SQL to operate on tables. See Fig. 1.7.

The first point to be made concerning Fig. 1.7 is that there will normally be many users, of both kinds, all operating on the same data at the same time. DB2 will automatically apply the necessary controls (basically locking; see Chapter 11) to ensure that those users are all protected from one another—that is, to guarantee that one user's updates cannot cause another user's operations to produce an incorrect result.

Next, note that the tables in the figure are also of two kinds, namely *base tables* and *views*. A base table is a "real" table—i.e., a table that physically

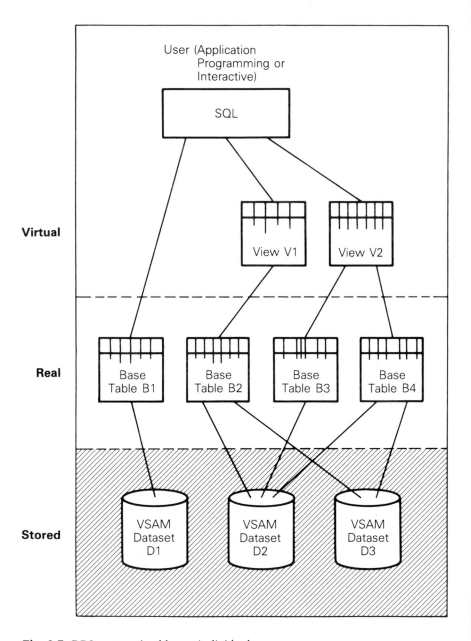

**Fig. 1.7**  DB2 as perceived by an individual user

exists, in the sense that there exist physically stored records, and possibly physical indexes, in one or more VSAM data sets, that directly represent that table in storage. By contrast, a view is a "virtual" table—i.e., a table that does not directly exist in physical storage, but looks to the user as if it did. Views can be thought of as different ways of looking at the "real" tables. As a trivial example, a given user might have a view of the suppliers base table S in which only those suppliers in London were visible. Views are defined, in a manner to be explained in Chapter 8, in terms of one or more of the underlying base tables.

*Note:* The foregoing paragraph should not be interpreted as saying that a base table is physically stored as a table—i.e., as a set of physically adjacent stored records, with each stored record consisting simply of a direct copy of a row of the base table. There are numerous differences, some to be discussed later, between a base table and its storage representation. The point is that users can always think of base tables as "physically existing," without having to concern themselves with how those tables are actually implemented in storage. In fact, the whole point of a relational database is to allow users to deal with data in the form of tables *per se*, instead of in terms of the storage representation of such tables. To repeat from Section 1.4, a relational database is a database that is *perceived by its users* as a collection of tables. It is *not* just a database in which data is physically stored as tables.

Like base tables, views can be created at any time. The same is true of indexes. (The CREATE TABLE statement already discussed is for creating "real" or base tables. There is an analogous CREATE VIEW statement for creating views or "virtual" tables, and an analogous CREATE INDEX statement for creating indexes.) Similarly, base tables (and views and indexes) can be "dropped" (that is to say, destroyed) at any time, using DROP TABLE or DROP VIEW or DROP INDEX. With regard to indexes, however, note carefully that although the user (that is, *some* user, probably a database administrator—see Chapter 9) is responsible for creating and destroying them, the user is *not* responsible for saying when those indexes should be used. Indexes are never mentioned in SQL data manipulation statements such as SELECT. The decision as to whether or not to use a particular index in responding to, say, a particular SELECT operation is made by the system, not by the user. We shall have more to say on this topic in Chapter 2.

The user interface to DB2 is the SQL language. We have already indicated (a) that SQL can be used in both interactive and embedded environments, and (b) that it provides both data definition and data manipulation functions (in fact, as we shall see later, it provides certain "data control" functions as well). The major data definition functions:

```
CREATE TABLE
CREATE VIEW
CREATE INDEX
```

```
DROP TABLE
DROP VIEW
DROP INDEX
```

have already been touched on. The major data manipulation functions (in fact, the only ones, if we temporarily disregard some embedded-SQL-only functions) are

```
SELECT
UPDATE
DELETE
INSERT
```

We give examples (Fig. 1.8) of SELECT and UPDATE to illustrate an additional point, namely the fact that SQL data manipulation statements typically operate on entire sets of records, instead of just on one record at a time. Given the sample data of Fig. 1.3, the SELECT statement (Fig. 1.8(a)) returns a set of four values, not just a single value; and the UPDATE statement (Fig. 1.8(b)) changes two records, not just one. In other words, SQL is a *set-level language*.

Set-level languages such as SQL are sometimes described as "nonprocedural," on the grounds that users specify *what*, not *how* (i.e., they say what data they want without specifying a procedure for getting it). In other words, the process of "navigating" around the physical database to locate the desired data is performed automatically by the system, not manually by the user. However, "nonprocedural" is not really a very satisfactory term, because procedurality and nonprocedurality are not absolutes. The best that can be said is that some language A is either more or less procedural than some other language B. Perhaps a better way of putting matters is to say that a language such as SQL is at *a higher level of abstraction* than a language such as COBOL (or a language such as DL/I, come to that). With a language like SQL, in other words, the system handles

```
(a) SELECT  S#                          Result:  S#
    FROM    SP                                   --
    WHERE   P# = 'P2' ;                          S1
                                                 S2
                                                 S3
                                                 S4

(b) UPDATE  S                           Result:  Status doubled for S1
    SET     STATUS = 2 * STATUS                  and S4
    WHERE   CITY = 'London' ;
```

**Fig. 1.8** SQL data manipulation examples

more of the details than it does with a language like COBOL (or DL/I). Fundamentally, it is this raising of the level of abstraction that is responsible for the increased productivity that relational systems such as DB2 can provide.

## 1.6  SUMMARY

This brings us to the end of this preliminary chapter. We have given a brief overview of DB2, IBM's relational database management system for the MVS operating system. We have explained in outline what it means for a system to be relational; we have discussed the relational (tabular) data structure; and we have described some of the operators available in SQL for operating on data in that tabular form. In particular, we have touched on the three categories of SQL statement (data definition, data manipulation, and data control), and given examples from the first two of those categories. We remind the reader that: (a) all SQL statements are executable; (b) every SQL statement that can be entered at a terminal can also be embedded in a program in PL/I, COBOL, FORTRAN, or Assembler Language; and (c) SQL data manipulation statements (SELECT, UPDATE, etc.) are set-level. We have also sketched the different environments in which a DB2 application can run, namely IMS, CICS, and TSO. In the next chapter we will take a look at the internal structure and principal components of DB2.

## EXERCISES

**1.1** What does it mean to say that DB2 is a relational system?

**1.2** Given the sample data of Fig. 1.3, show the effect of each of the following SQL statements.

```
(a)  SELECT  SNAME
     FROM    S
     WHERE   STATUS = 30 ;

(b)  SELECT  S#, P#
     FROM    SP
     WHERE   QTY > 200 ;

(c)  UPDATE  SP
     SET     QTY = QTY + 300
     WHERE   QTY < 300 ;

(d)  DELETE
     FROM    P
     WHERE   COLOR = 'Blue'
     OR      CITY = 'Paris' ;
```

(e)  INSERT
     INTO    SP (S#, P#, QTY)
     VALUES  ('S3','P1',500) ;

**1.3** Draw a diagram illustrating the various categories of DB2 application program and the different environments in which they can run.

**1.4** What do the following acronyms stand for?

    SQL
    DB2
    DB2I
    QMF
    DXT

**1.5** What is a repeating group?

**1.6** Define the terms *relation* and *relational database*.

**1.7** Give a possible CREATE TABLE statement for the CELLAR table of Fig. 1.1. Write an *embedded* PL/I-SQL statement to retrieve the number of bottles of 1977 Zinfandel from that table.

**1.8** Define the terms *base table* and *view*.

**1.9** What do you understand by the term "automatic navigation"?

## ANSWERS TO SELECTED EXERCISES

**1.1** A relational system such as DB2 is a system in which the data is perceived as tables (and nothing but tables), and the operators available to the user are operators that generate new tables from old.

**1.2**

(a)  SNAME
     -----
     Blake
     Adams

(b)  S#   P#
     --   --
     S1   P1
     S1   P3
     S2   P1
     S2   P2
     S4   P4
     S4   P5

```
(c)  S#   P#   QTY
     --    -    ---
     S1   P2   500
     S1   P4   500
     S1   P5   400
     S1   P6   400
     S3   P2   500
     S4   P2   500
```

(Only altered rows shown.)

(d) Rows for P2, P3, and P5 deleted from table P.

(e) Row S3/P1/500 inserted into table SP.

**1.5** A repeating group is (conceptually) a column of a table that contains multiple data values per row (different numbers of values in different rows). Repeating groups are not permitted in a relational database.

**1.6** A relation is a table (without repeating groups!). A relational database is a database that is perceived by its users as a collection of relations. *Note:* More precise definitions are given in Appendix A.

**1.7**
```
CREATE TABLE CELLAR
       ( WINE      CHAR(16),
         YEAR      INTEGER,
         BOTTLES   INTEGER )  ;

EXEC SQL SELECT BOTTLES
         INTO    :XBOTT
         FROM    CELLAR
         WHERE   WINE = 'Zinfandel'
         AND     YEAR = 77  ;
```

**1.8** A base table is a "real" table; it has some direct storage representation. A view is a "virtual" table; it does not have any direct storage representation of its own. A view is like a window on to one or more underlying base tables, through which the data (or some subset of the data) in those underlying tables can be observed, possibly in some rearranged structure.

**1.9** "Automatic navigation" means that the system assumes the responsibility of searching through the physical database to locate the data the user has requested. Users specify what they want, not how to get to what they want.

# 2

# System Structure

## 2.1 MAJOR COMPONENTS

The internal structure of DB2 is quite complicated, as is only to be expected of a state-of-the-art system that provides all of the functions normally found in a modern DBMS (including, for example, recovery control, concurrency control, authorization control, and so on) and more besides. However, many of those functions, although of course crucial to the overall operation of the system, are of no direct interest to the user (in our sense of the term—i.e., an end-user or an application programmer). From the user's point of view, in fact, the system can be considered as consisting of just four major components, which we refer to as follows:*

Precompiler
Bind
Runtime Supervisor
Stored Data Manager

The functions of these four components (in outline) are as follows.

---

*The IBM manuals do not use the terms "Runtime Supervisor" or "Stored Data Manager."

## Precompiler

The *Precompiler* is a preprocessor for the application programming languages (PL/I, COBOL, FORTRAN, and Assembler Language). Its function is to analyze a source module in any one of those languages, stripping out all the SQL statements it finds and replacing them by source language CALL statements. At runtime these CALLs will pass control— indirectly—to the Runtime Supervisor. From the SQL statements it encounters, the Precompiler constructs a *Database Request Module* (DBRM), which becomes input to the Bind component (discussed in the next paragraph).

## Bind

The function of the *Bind* component is to compile one or more DBRMs to produce an *application plan*. The application plan contains the necessary machine code instructions to implement the original SQL statements from which those DBRMs were built. In particular, it includes machine code calls to the Stored Data Manager component (see below).

## Runtime Supervisor

The *Runtime Supervisor* is resident in main storage when the application program is executing. Its job is to oversee that execution. When the application program requests some database operation to be performed (loosely speaking, when it wishes to execute a SQL statement), control goes first to the Runtime Supervisor, which in turn routes control to the appropriate portion of the application plan. The application plan, in turn, passes control to the Stored Data Manager.

## Stored Data Manager

You can think of the *Stored Data Manager* as a *very sophisticated access method*. It performs all of the normal access method functions—for example, retrieval, searching, update, index maintenance, and so on. Broadly speaking, the Stored Data Manager is the component that manages the physical database(s). It invokes other, lower-level components as necessary to perform detailed functions such as locking, logging, sorting, etc., during the performance of its basic task.

Fig. 2.1 summarizes the foregoing in the form of a control flow diagram. In the next section we will take a more detailed look at the principal steps in this overall process.

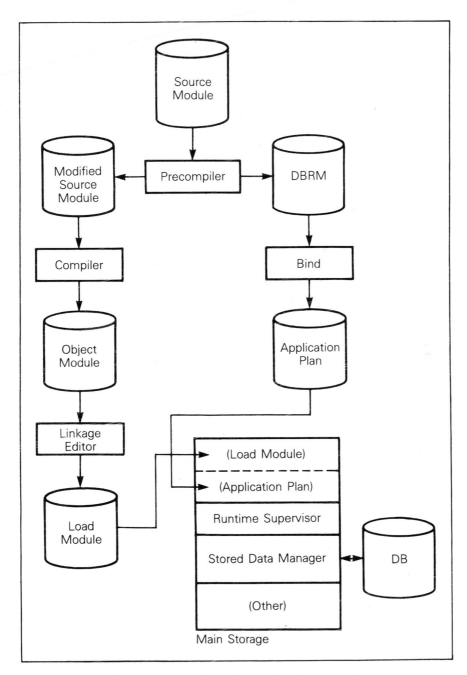

**Fig. 2.1**  DB2 application preparation and execution (overview)

## 2.2 DETAILED CONTROL FLOW

First, we consider an example of a PL/I program P (more accurately, PL/I source module P) that includes one or more SQL statements. (We take PL/I for definiteness. The overall process is of course essentially the same for the other languages.) Before P can be compiled by the PL/I compiler, it must be *precompiled* (Fig. 2.2). *Note:* If P also includes any CICS statements (of the form EXEC

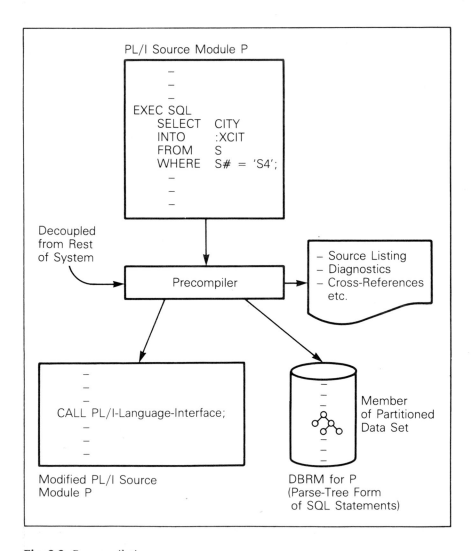

**Fig. 2.2** Precompilation

CICS ... ;), then it must also be processed by the CICS preprocessor. The DB2 Precompiler and the CICS preprocessor can be run in either order.

As explained in the previous section, the DB2 Precompiler removes all SQL statements it finds in P and replaces them by PL/I CALL statements.* (Those CALLs are directed to the PL/I Language Interface module—see below.) It uses the SQL statements to build a *Database Request Module* (DBRM) for P, which it stores away as a member of a partitioned data set. The DBRM contains a copy of the original SQL statements, together with an internal parse-tree form of those SQL statements. The Precompiler also produces a source listing, showing the original source code, diagnostics, cross-reference tables, etc.

Next, the modified PL/I source module is compiled and link-edited in the normal way (except that the PL/I Language Interface module, which is supplied with DB2, must be part of the input to the Linkage Editor). Let us agree to refer to the output of this step as "PL/I load module P."

Now we come to the Bind step (Fig. 2.3).

Bind is really an *optimizing compiler*. It converts high-level database requests (in effect, SQL statements) into optimized machine code. The input to Bind is a set of one or more DBRMs (there will be more than one if the original PL/I program consists of more than one external procedure—i.e., more than one source module). The output from Bind (i.e., the compiled code) is called an *application plan*, and is stored away in a system database called the *DB2 catalog*† (we shall have more to say about the catalog in Chapter 7). The major functions of Bind, then, are as follows.

### Syntax Checking

Bind examines the SQL statements in the input DBRM(s), parses them, and reports on any syntax errors it finds. Such checks are necessary, even though the Precompiler has already performed similar checks, because the Precompiler is decoupled from the rest of DB2: It can run even when DB2 is not available—it may even run on a different machine—and its output is not automatically protected. Thus, Bind cannot assume that its input is valid Precompiler output—the user may have constructed an invalid "DBRM" via some other mechanism.

---

*It leaves a copy of each such SQL statement in the modified source module in the form of a comment.

†More accurately, the plan is stored in the DB2 *directory*, which is effectively an extension to the catalog for the system's own use only. The difference between the two from the user's point of view is that the catalog is in a form suitable for query via ordinary SQL statements (see Chapter 7), whereas the directory is not.

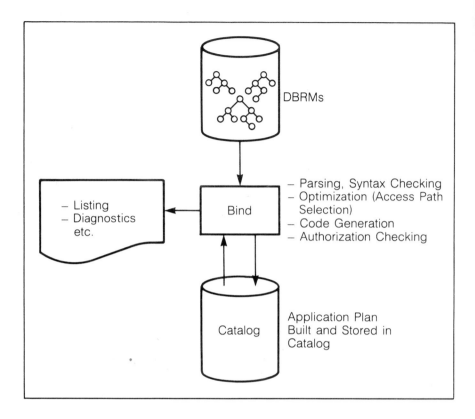

**Fig. 2.3** Bind

## Optimization

Bind includes an *optimizer* as an important subcomponent. The function of the optimizer is to choose, for each SQL manipulative statement it processes, an optimal access strategy for implementing that statement. Remember that data manipulation statements such as SELECT specify only what data the user wants, not how to get to that data; the *access path* for getting to that data will be chosen by the optimizer. Programs are thus independent of such access paths (for further discussion of this important point, see the conclusion of this section).

As an example of the foregoing, consider the SELECT statement shown in the PL/I source module P in Fig. 2.2. Even in that very simple case, there are at least two ways of performing the required retrieval: (1) by doing a physical sequential scan of (the stored version of) table S until the record for supplier S4 is found; (2) if there is an index on the S# column of that table—which there probably will be, for reasons discussed in detail in Appendices A and B—then by using that index and thus going directly to the S4 record. The optimizer will choose which of these two strategies to adopt. In general, the optimizer will make its choice on the basis of such considerations as which tables are referenced in the SQL statement (there may be more than one), how big those tables are, what indexes exist, how selective those indexes are, how the data is physically clustered on the disk, the form of the WHERE clause in the request, and so on. Bind will then generate machine code that is *tightly bound* to (i.e., highly dependent on) the optimizer's choice of strategy. For example, if the optimizer decides to make use of an index called X, then there will be machine code instructions in the application plan that refer explicitly to index X.

### Code Generation

This is the process of actually building the application plan.

### Authorization Checking

Bind will also check authorization: that is, it will check that the person doing the binding (i.e., the user who invoked Bind—see Chapter 14) is allowed to perform the operations requested in the DBRM(s) to be bound. We shall examine authorization in detail in Chapter 9.

Finally we get to execution time. Since the original program has now effectively been broken into two pieces (load module and application plan), those two pieces must somehow be brought back together again at execution time. This is how it works (see Fig. 2.4). First, the PL/I load module P is loaded into main storage; it starts to execute in the usual way. Sooner or later it reaches the first call to the PL/I Language Interface module. That module gets control and passes control in turn to the Runtime Supervisor. The Runtime Supervisor then retrieves the application plan from the system catalog, loads it into main storage, and passes control to it. The application plan in turn invokes the Stored Data Manager, which performs the necessary operations on the actual stored data and passes results back (as appropriate) to the PL/I program.

Our discussions so far have glossed over one extremely important point, which we now explain. First, as already explained, DB2 is a *compiling system*. By contrast, most other database systems— certainly all nonrelational systems, to this writer's knowledge—are *interpretive* in nature. Now, compilation is certainly advantageous from the point of view of performance; it will nearly always yield better runtime performance than will interpretation. However, it suffers

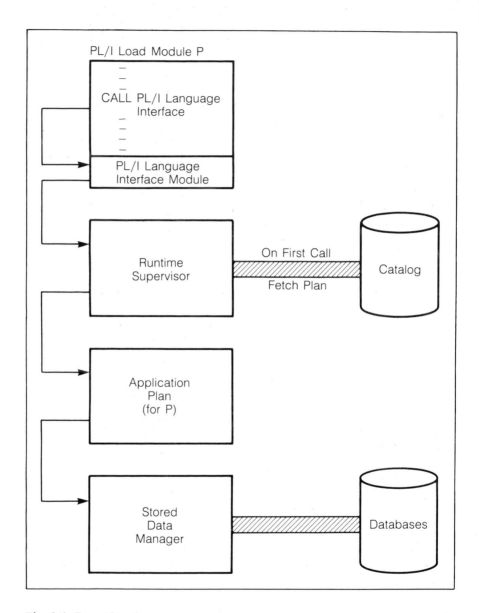

**Fig. 2.4** Execution time

from the following significant drawback: *It is possible that decisions made by the "compiler"* (actually Bind) *at compilation time are no longer valid at execution time.* The following simple example illustrates the problem:

1. Suppose program P is compiled (bound) on Monday, and Bind decides to use an index—say index X—in its strategy for P. Then the application plan for P will include explicit references to X, as explained earlier.

2. On Tuesday, some (authorized) user issues the statement

   DROP INDEX X ;

3. On Wednesday, some user tries to execute the program P. What happens?

What does happen is the following. When an index is dropped, DB2 examines all application plans in the catalog to see which of them (if any) are dependent on that index. Any such plans that it finds it marks as "invalid." When the Runtime Supervisor retrieves such a plan for execution, it sees the "invalid" marker, and therefore invokes Bind to produce a new plan—i.e., to choose some different access strategy and then to recompile the original SQL statements (which have been kept in the catalog) in accordance with that new strategy. Provided the recompilation is successful, the new plan replaces the old one in the catalog, and the Runtime Supervisor continues with the new plan. Thus the entire rebind process (or "automatic bind" as it is called) is "transparent to the user"; the only effect that might be observed is a slight delay in the execution of the first SQL statement in the program.

Note carefully that the recompilation we are talking about here is a *SQL* recompilation, not a *PL/I* recompilation. It is not the PL/I program that is invalidated by the dropping of the index, only the application plan.

We can now see how it is possible for programs to be independent of physical access paths—more specifically, how it is possible to create and drop such paths without at the same time having to change programs. As stated earlier, SQL data manipulation statements such as SELECT and UPDATE never include any explicit mention of such access paths. Instead, they simply indicate what data the user is interested in; and it is the system's responsibility (actually Bind's responsibility) to choose a path for getting to that data, and to change to another path if the old path no longer exists. We say that systems like DB2 provide a high degree of *physical data independence*: Users and user programs are not dependent on the physical structure of the stored database. The advantage of such a system—a highly significant advantage—is that it is possible to make changes in the physical database (e.g., for performance reasons) *without* having to make any corresponding changes in application programs. In a system without such independence, application programmers have to devote some significant portion of their time—a figure of 50 percent is quite typical—to making changes to existing programs that are necessitated merely by changes to the physical database. In a system like DB2, by contrast, those programmers can concentrate exclusively on the production of new applications.

One further point concerning the foregoing. Our example was in terms of a dropped *index*, and perhaps that is the commonest case in practice. However, a similar sequence of events occurs when any object (not just an index) is dropped—likewise when an authorization is revoked (see Chapter 9). Thus, for example, dropping a table will cause all plans that refer to that table to be flagged as invalid. Of course, the automatic rebind will only work in this case if another table has been created with the same name as the old one by the time the rebind is done (and maybe not even then, if there are significant differences between the old table and the new one).

We conclude this chapter by noting that SQL is *always* compiled in DB2, never interpreted, even when the statements in question are submitted through the interactive interface DB2I (or through QMF). In other words, if you enter (say) a SELECT statement at the terminal, then that statement will be compiled and an application plan generated for it; that plan will then be executed; and finally, after execution has completed, that plan will be discarded. Experience has indicated that, even in the interactive case, compilation almost always results in better overall performance than interpretation. The advantage of compilation is that the process of physically accessing the required data is done by compiled code—that is, by code that is tightly tailored to the specific request, not by generalized, interpretive code. The disadvantage is of course that there is a cost in doing the compilation, i.e., in producing that tightly tailored code. But the advantage almost always outweighs the disadvantage, sometimes dramatically so. It is only when the query is extremely simple that the cost of doing the compilation may be greater than the potential savings. An example of such a simple query might be, "Retrieve the supplier record for supplier S1"—that is, a request for a single, specific record, given a value for a field that identifies that record uniquely. Notice that this query does not really exploit the set-level facilities of SQL at all.

## EXERCISES

**2.1** Name the four major components of DB2. Draw a diagram showing the overall process of program preparation and program execution in DB2.

**2.2** List the four principal functions of Bind.

**2.3** Define *physical data independence*. Explain how DB2 provides such independence. Why is physical data independence desirable?

# 3

# Data Definition

## 3.1 INTRODUCTION

In this chapter we examine the SQL data definition statements of DB2 in some detail. It is convenient to divide those statements into two broad classes, which we may very loosely characterize as logical and physical—"logical" having to do with objects that are genuinely of interest to users, such as base tables and views, and "physical" having to do with objects that are primarily of interest to the system, such as disk volumes. Needless to say, matters are not really as clearcut as this simple classification would suggest—some "logical" statements include parameters that are really "physical" in nature, and vice versa, and some statements do not fit neatly into either category. But the classification is convenient as an aid to understanding, and we will stay with it for now. The present chapter is concerned only with "logical" data definition.

The principal logical data definition statements are listed below:

```
CREATE TABLE     CREATE VIEW     CREATE INDEX
ALTER TABLE
DROP TABLE       DROP VIEW       DROP INDEX
```

(*Note:* There is also an ALTER INDEX statement, but it falls totally into the "physical" category. There is no ALTER VIEW statement.) We defer discussion of CREATE and DROP VIEW to Chapter 8; the remaining statements above are the subject of the present chapter.

31

## 3.2 BASE TABLES

A base table is an (important) special case of the more general concept "table." Let us therefore begin by making that more general concept a little more precise.

### Definition

A *table* in a relational system consists of a row of *column headings*, together with zero or more rows of *data values* (different numbers of data rows at different times). For a given table:

(a) The column heading row specifies one or more columns (giving, among other things, a data type for each);

(b) Each data row contains exactly one data value for each of the columns specified in the column heading row. Furthermore, all the values in a given column are of the same data type, namely the data type specified in the column heading row for that column.

Two points arise in connection with the foregoing definition.

1. Note that there is no mention of *row ordering*. Strictly speaking, the rows of a relational table are considered to be unordered. (A relation is a mathematical *set*—a set of rows—and sets in mathematics do not have any ordering.) It is possible, as we shall see, to *impose* an order on those rows when they are retrieved in response to a query, but such an ordering should be regarded as nothing more than a convenience for the user—it is not intrinsic to the notion of a table.

2. In contrast to the first point, the columns of a table *are* considered to be ordered, left to right. (At least, they are considered to be so ordered in most systems, including in particular DB2.) For example, in table S (see Fig. 1.3 in Chapter 1), column S# is the first column, column SNAME is the second column, and so on. In practice, however, there are very few situations in which that left-to-right ordering is significant, and even those can be avoided with a little discipline. Such avoidance is recommended, as we shall explain later.

To turn now to base tables specifically: A base table is an *autonomous, named* table. By "autonomous" we mean that the table exists in its own right—unlike a view, which does not exist in its own right but is derived from one or more base tables (it is merely an alternative way of looking at those base tables). By "named" we mean that the table is explicitly given a name via an appropriate CREATE statement—unlike a table that is merely constructed as the result of a query, which does not have any explicit name of its own and has only ephemeral existence (for examples of such unnamed tables, see the two result tables in Fig. 1.1 in Chapter 1).

## CREATE TABLE

We are now in a position to discuss the CREATE TABLE statement in detail. The general format of that statement is as follows:

```
CREATE TABLE base-table-name
    ( column-definition [, column-definition ] ... )
    [ other parameters ] ;
```

where a "column-definition", in turn, takes the form:

```
column-name data-type [ NOT NULL ]
```

The optional "other parameters" are primarily to do with physical storage matters and are discussed (briefly) in Chapter 13. *Note:* Square brackets are used in syntactic definitions throughout this book to indicate that the material enclosed in those brackets is optional (i.e., may be omitted). An ellipsis (...) indicates that the immediately preceding syntactic unit may optionally be repeated one or more times. Material in capitals must be written exactly as shown; material in lower case must be replaced by specific values chosen by the user.

Here is an example (the CREATE TABLE statement for table S, now shown complete):

```
CREATE TABLE S
    ( S#      CHAR(5)   NOT NULL,
      SNAME   CHAR(20),
      STATUS  SMALLINT,
      CITY    CHAR(15) )  ;
```

The effect of this statement is to create a new, empty base table called *xyz*.S, where *xyz* is the name by which the user issuing the CREATE TABLE statement is known to the system (see Chapter 9). An entry describing the table is made in the system catalog. User *xyz* can refer to the table by its full name *xyz*.S or by the abbreviated name S; other users must refer to it by its full name. The table has four columns, called *xyz*.S.S#, *xyz*.S.SNAME, *xyz*.S.STATUS, and *xyz*.S.CITY, and having the indicated data types. (Data types are discussed below.) User *xyz* can refer to those columns by their full names or by the abbreviated names S.S#, S.SNAME, S.STATUS, and S.CITY; other users must use the full names. Note, however, that (regardless of whether the "*xyz*" portion is included) the "S." portion can be omitted if no ambiguity results, but it is never wrong to include it. In general, the rules concerning names are as follows: User names, such as *xyz*, are unique across the entire system; (unqualified) table names are

unique within user; and (unqualified) column names are unique within table.*
"Table" here refers to both base tables and views; that is, a view cannot have the
same name as a base table.

Once the table has been created, data can be entered into it via the INSERT
statement of SQL (discussed in Chapter 6) or via the DB2 load utility (discussed
in Chapter 14).

## Data Types

DB2 supports the following data types.

| | |
|---|---|
| INTEGER | fullword binary integer, 31 bits and sign |
| SMALLINT | halfword binary integer, 15 bits and sign |
| DECIMAL(p,q) | packed decimal number, p digits and sign ($0 < p < 16$), with assumed decimal point q digits from the right (q < p; if q = 0 it can be omitted) |
| FLOAT | doubleword floating point number n, represented by a hexadecimal fraction f of 15 digits precision ($-1 < f < +1$) and a binary integer exponent e ($-65 < e < +64$), such that n = f * (16 ** e) (approx. range of magnitudes for n = 5.4E−79 to 7.2E+75; see the explanation of FLOAT constants, later) |
| CHAR(n) | fixed length character string of n characters ($0 < n < 255$) |
| VARCHAR(n) | varying length character string of n characters maximum ($0 < n$; maximum value of n depends on a number of factors, but in general must be less than the "pagesize" [either 4K or 32K] for the tablespace containing the table— see Chapter 13)† |

---

*In addition, SQL keywords (CREATE, TABLE, SELECT, etc.) cannot be used as names.
The first character of any name must be "alphabetic" (A-Z or one of the special characters
#, $, @), the remainder if any must be alphabetic, numeric (0-9), or the underscore
character. Table and column names are limited to a maximum of 18 characters, user names
to a maximum of 8 characters.

†If n > 254 then the field is a "long field" and is subject to severe restrictions. Long
fields are intended for the handling of free-format data such as long text strings, rather
than for simple formatted data such as a supplier number or a shipment quantity. Fundamentally, the only operation in which such a field may be used as an operand is *assignment*,
either to the database (INSERT or UPDATE) or from the database (SELECT). Any operation that implies a comparison on a long field is not permitted. Thus, for example, long
fields cannot be indexed, nor can they be referenced in a WHERE clause or GROUP BY
clause or ORDER BY clause, and so on. (See Chapters 4 and 5 for an explanation of these
two last clauses.)

## Constants

Although it is a slight digression from the main topic of this chapter, this is a convenient point at which to summarize the various kinds of *constant* supported in DB2:

integer
: written as a signed or unsigned decimal integer, with no decimal point
: examples:   4   $-95$   +364   0

decimal
: written as a signed or unsigned decimal number, with a decimal point
: examples:   4.0   $-95.7$   +364.05   0.007

float
: written as a decimal constant, followed by the letter E, followed by an integer constant
: examples:   4E3   $-\text{\O}.\,)\text{E}46$   +364E-5   0.7E1
: (note: the expression $x$E$y$ represents the value $x * (10 ** y)$)

string
: Written *either* as a string of characters enclosed in single quotes *or* as a string of pairs of hexadecimal digits (representing the EBCDIC encodings of the characters concerned) enclosed in single quotes and preceded by the letter X
: examples:   '123 Main St.'
:            'PIG'
:            X'F1F2F340D481899540E2A31D'
:            X'D7C9C7'
: (the 1st and 3rd of these examples represent the same value, as do the 2nd and 4th)

## Null Values

To return to the main topic of this chapter: DB2 supports the concept of a *null data value*. In fact, any column can contain null values *unless* the definition of that column in CREATE TABLE explicitly specifies NOT NULL. Null is a special value that is used to represent "value unknown" or "value inapplicable." It is not the same as blank or zero. For example, a shipment record might contain a null QTY value (we know that the shipment exists but we do not know the quantity shipped); or a supplier record might contain a null STATUS value (perhaps STATUS does not apply to suppliers in San Jose for some reason).

Referring back to the CREATE TABLE for base table S, we have specified NOT NULL for S# (only). The effect of this specification is to guarantee that every supplier record in base table S will always contain a genuine (i.e., nonnull) supplier number value. By contrast, any or all of SNAME, STATUS, and CITY may be null in that same record. (Our reasons for insisting that supplier numbers should not be null will be made clear in Appendices A and B.)

A column that can accept null values is physically represented in the stored database by two columns, the data column itself and a hidden indicator column, one byte wide, that is stored as a prefix to the actual data column. An indicator column value of X'FF' indicates that the corresponding data column value is to be ignored (i.e., taken as null); an indicator column value of X'00' indicates that the corresponding data column value is to be taken as genuine.

We shall have more to say on null values in Chapters 4, 5, 6, and 10 and in Appendix B.

## ALTER TABLE

Just as a new base table can be created at any time, via CREATE TABLE, so an existing base table can be *altered* at any time by the addition of a new column at the right, via ALTER TABLE:

```
ALTER TABLE base-table-name
      ADD column-name data-type ;
```

For example:

```
ALTER TABLE S
      ADD DISCOUNT SMALLINT ;
```

This statement adds a DISCOUNT column to the S table. All existing S records are extended from four field values to five; the value of the new fifth field is null in every case. The specification NOT NULL is not permitted in ALTER TABLE. Note, incidentally, that the expansion of existing records just described does not mean that the records in the database are physically updated at this time; only their stored description in the catalog changes. Individual records are not physically changed until the next time they are the target of a SQL UPDATE statement (see Chapter 6).

## DROP TABLE

It is also possible to destroy an existing base table at any time:

```
DROP TABLE base-table-name ;
```

The specified base table is removed from the system (more precisely, the description of that table is removed from the catalog). All indexes and views defined on that base table are automatically destroyed also.

## 3.3  INDEXES

Like base tables, indexes are created and dropped using SQL data definition statements. However, CREATE INDEX and DROP INDEX (also ALTER INDEX and certain data control statements) are the *only* statements in the SQL language that refer to indexes at all; other statements—in particular, data manipulation statements such as SELECT —deliberately do not include any such references. The decision as to whether or not to use an index in responding to a particular SQL request is made not by the user but by DB2 (actually by the optimizer subcomponent of Bind), as explained in Chapter 2.

CREATE INDEX takes the general form:

```
CREATE [ UNIQUE ] INDEX index-name
     ON base-table-name ( column-name [ order ]
                        [, column-name [ order ] ] ... )
     [ other-parameters ] ;
```

The optional "other parameters" have to do with physical storage matters (as in CREATE TABLE). Each "order" specification is either ASC (ascending) or DESC (descending); if neither ASC nor DESC is specified, then ASC is assumed by default  The left-to right sequence of naming columns in the CRE-ATE INDEX statement corresponds to major-to-minor ordering in the usual way. For example, the statement

```
CREATE INDEX X ON B ( P, Q DESC, R ) ;
```

creates an index called X on base table B in which entries are ordered by ascending R-value within descending Q-value within ascending P-value. The columns P, Q, and R need not be contiguous, nor need they all be of the same data type, nor need they all be fixed length.

Once created, an index is automatically maintained (by the Stored Data Manager) to reflect updates on the base table, until such time as the index is dropped.

The UNIQUE option in CREATE INDEX specifies that no two records in the indexed base table will be allowed to take on the same value for the indexed field (or field combination) at the same time. In the case of the suppliers-and-parts database, for example, we would probably specify the following UNIQUE indexes:

```
CREATE UNIQUE INDEX XS  ON S ( S# ) ;
CREATE UNIQUE INDEX XP  ON P ( P# ) ;
CREATE UNIQUE INDEX XSP ON SP ( S#, P# ) ;
```

Indexes, like base tables, can be created and dropped at any time. In the example, however, we would probably want to create indexes XS, XP, and XSP at the time the underlying base tables S, P, and SP themselves are created; for if those base tables are nonempty at the time the CREATE INDEX statements are issued, the uniqueness constraints might already have been violated. An attempt to create a UNIQUE index on a table that does not currently satisfy the uniqueness constraint will fail.

*Note:* Two null values are considered to be equal to each other for UNIQUE indexing purposes. The point of this rather cryptic remark is that null values are *not* always considered to be equal to each other in all contexts. See the discussion of this subject in Chapter 4.

Any number of indexes can be built on a single base table. Here is another index for table S:

```
CREATE INDEX XSC ON S ( CITY ) ;
```

UNIQUE has not been specified in this case because multiple suppliers can be located in the same city.

The statement to drop an index is

```
DROP INDEX index-name ;
```

The index is destroyed (i.e., its description is removed from the catalog). If an existing application plan depends on that dropped index, then (as explained in Chapter 2) that plan will be marked as invalid by the Runtime Supervisor. When that plan is next retrieved for execution, the Runtime Supervisor will automatically invoke Bind to generate a replacement plan that supports the original SQL statements without using the now vanished index. This process is completely hidden from the user.

Given the fact that DB2 performs automatic rebinds if an existing index is dropped, the reader may be wondering whether it will also do automatic rebinds if a new index is created. The answer is no, it will not. The reason for this state of affairs is that there can be no guarantee in this case that rebinding will actually be profitable; automatic rebind might simply mean a lot of unnecessary work (existing application plans might already be using an optimum strategy). The situation is different with DROP—a plan will simply not work if it relies on a nonexistent index, so rebind is mandatory in this case. Hence, if you CREATE a new index, and you have some existing plan that you suspect could profitably be replaced, then it is your responsibility to request an explicit rebind for that plan. Explicit rebind is discussed in Chapter 14.

## 3.4  DISCUSSION

The fact that data definition statements can be executed at any time makes DB2 a very flexible system. In older (nonrelational) systems, the addition of a new type of object, such as a new record type or a new index or a new field, is an operation not to be undertaken lightly: Typically it involves bringing the entire system to a halt, unloading the database, revising and recompiling the database definition, and finally reloading the database in accordance with that revised definition. In such a system it becomes highly desirable to perform the data definition process once and for all before starting to load and use the data— which means that (a) the job of getting the system installed and operational can quite literally take months or even years of highly specialized people's time, and (b) once the system is running, it can be difficult and costly, perhaps prohibitively so, to remedy early design errors.

In DB2, by contrast, it is possible to create and load just a few base tables and then to start using that data immediately. Later, new base tables and new fields can be added in a piecemeal fashion, without having any effect on existing users of the database. It is also possible to experiment with the effects of having or not having particular indexes, again without affecting existing users at all (other than in performance, of course). Moreover, as we shall see in Chapter 8, it is even possible under certain circumstances to rearrange the structure of the database—e.g., to move a field from one table to another—and still not affect the logic of existing programs. In a nutshell, it is not necessary to go through the total database design process before any useful work can be done with the system, nor is it necessary to get everything right the first time. The system is *forgiving*.

*Caveat:* The foregoing should *not* be taken to mean that database design is unnecessary. Of course database design is still needed. However:

- It doesn't all have to be done at once.
- It doesn't have to be perfect first time.
- Logical and physical design can be tackled separately.
- If requirements change, then the design can change too, in a comparatively painless manner.
- Many new applications—typically small-scale applications, involving, for example, personal or departmental databases—become feasible in a system like DB2 that would simply never have been considered under an older (nonrelational) system, because those older systems were just too complicated to make such applications economically worthwhile.

## EXERCISES

**3.1** Fig. 3.1 shows some sample data values for a database containing information concerning suppliers (S), parts (P), and projects (J). Suppliers, parts, and projects are uniquely identified by supplier number (S#), part number (P#), and project number (J#), respec-

| S | S# | SNAME | STATUS | CITY |
|---|----|-------|--------|------|
|   | S1 | Smith | 20 | London |
|   | S2 | Jones | 10 | Paris |
|   | S3 | Blake | 30 | Paris |
|   | S4 | Clark | 20 | London |
|   | S5 | Adams | 30 | Athens |

| P | P# | PNAME | COLOR | WEIGHT | CITY |
|---|----|-------|-------|--------|------|
|   | P1 | Nut | Red | 12 | London |
|   | P2 | Bolt | Green | 17 | Paris |
|   | P3 | Screw | Blue | 17 | Rome |
|   | P4 | Screw | Red | 14 | London |
|   | P5 | Cam | Blue | 12 | Paris |
|   | P6 | Cog | Red | 19 | London |

| J | J# | JNAME | CITY |
|---|----|-------|------|
|   | J1 | Sorter | Paris |
|   | J2 | Punch | Rome |
|   | J3 | Reader | Athens |
|   | J4 | Console | Athens |
|   | J5 | Collator | London |
|   | J6 | Terminal | Oslo |
|   | J7 | Tape | London |

| SPJ | S# | P# | J# | QTY |
|-----|----|----|----|-----|
|   | S1 | P1 | J1 | 2C |
|   | S1 | P1 | J4 | 7C |
|   | S2 | P3 | J1 | 4C |
|   | S2 | P3 | J2 | 2C |
|   | S2 | P3 | J3 | 2C |
|   | S2 | P3 | J4 | 5C |
|   | S2 | P3 | J5 | 6C |
|   | S2 | P3 | J6 | 4C |
|   | S2 | P3 | J7 | 8C |
|   | S2 | P5 | J2 | 1C |
|   | S3 | P3 | J1 | 2C |
|   | S3 | P4 | J2 | 5C |
|   | S4 | P6 | J3 | 3C |
|   | S4 | P6 | J7 | 3C |
|   | S5 | P2 | J2 | 2C |
|   | S5 | P2 | J4 | 1C |
|   | S5 | P5 | J5 | 5C |
|   | S5 | P5 | J7 | 1C |
|   | S5 | P6 | J2 | 2C |
|   | S5 | P1 | J4 | 1C |
|   | S5 | P3 | J4 | 2C |
|   | S5 | P4 | J4 | 8C |
|   | S5 | P5 | J4 | 4C |
|   | S5 | P6 | J4 | 5C |

**Fig. 3.1**  The suppliers-parts-projects database

tively. The significance of an SPJ (shipment) record is that the specified supplier supplies the specified part to the specified project in the specified quantity (and the combination S#,P#,J# uniquely identifies such a record). Write a suitable set of CREATE TABLE statements for this database. *Note:* This database will be used in numerous exercises in subsequent chapters.

**3.2** Write a set of CREATE INDEX statements for the database of Exercise 3.1 to enforce the required uniqueness constraints.

**3.3** What are the main advantages of indexes? What are the main disadvantages?

**3.4** "Uniqueness" of a field or field combination is a logical property, but it is enforced in DB2 by means of an index, which is a physical construct. Discuss.

## ANSWERS TO SELECTED EXERCISES

**3.1** CREATE TABLE S
```
      ( S#      CHAR(5) NOT NULL,
        SNAME   CHAR(20),
        STATUS  SMALLINT,
        CITY    CHAR(15) ) ;
```

```
   CREATE TABLE P
      ( P#      CHAR(6) NOT NULL,
        PNAME   CHAR(20),
        COLOR   CHAR(6),
        WEIGHT  SMALLINT,
        CITY    CHAR(15) ) ;
```

```
   CREATE TABLE J
      ( J#      CHAR(4) NOT NULL,
        JNAME   CHAR(10),
        CITY    CHAR(15) ) ;
```

```
   CREATE TABLE SPJ
      ( S#      CHAR(5) NOT NULL,
        P#      CHAR(6) NOT NULL,
        J#      CHAR(4) NOT NULL,
        QTY     INTEGER ) ;
```

**3.2** CREATE UNIQUE INDEX SX   ON S   ( S# ) ;
```
   CREATE UNIQUE INDEX PX   ON P   ( P# ) ;
   CREATE UNIQUE INDEX JX   ON J   ( J# ) ;
   CREATE UNIQUE INDEX SPJX ON SPJ ( S#, P#, J# ) ;
```

**3.3** The advantages of indexes are as follows:

(a) They speed up direct access based on a given value for the indexed field (combination). Without the index, a sequential scan would be required.

(b) They speed up sequential access based on the indexed field (combination). Without the index, a sort would be required.

(c) In DB2 in particular, UNIQUE indexes serve to enforce uniqueness constraints.

The disadvantages are as follows:

(a) They take up space in the database. The space taken up by indexes can easily exceed that taken up by the data itself in a heavily indexed database.

(b) While an index may well speed up retrieval operations, it will at the same time slow down update operations. Any INSERT or DELETE on the indexed table or UPDATE on the indexed field (combination) will require an accompanying update on the index.

**3.4** An unfortunate state of affairs. DB2 is not quite as data independent as it ought to be.

# 4

# Data Manipulation I:
# Retrieval Operations

## 4.1 INTRODUCTION

SQL provides four data manipulation statements: SELECT, UPDATE, DELETE, and INSERT. This chapter and the next are concerned with the SELECT statement; Chapter 6 is concerned with the other three statements. The aim in all three chapters is to be reasonably comprehensive but *not* to replace the relevant IBM manuals. As usual, all examples are based on the suppliers-and-parts database. Also, we assume until further notice that all statements are entered interactively. The special considerations that apply to embedded SQL are ignored until Chapter 10.

   *Note:* Many of the examples, especially those in the next chapter, are quite complex. The reader should not infer that it is SQL itself that is complex. Rather the point is that common operations are so simple in SQL (and indeed in most relational languages) that examples of such operations tend to be rather uninteresting, and do not illustrate the full power of the language. Of course, we do show some simple examples first (Section 4.2). Section 4.3 is concerned with a slightly more complicated —but extremely important —facility known as *join*.

## 4.2   SIMPLE QUERIES

We start with a simple example—the query "Get supplier numbers and status for suppliers in Paris," which can be expressed in SQL as follows:

```
SELECT S#, STATUS
FROM    S
WHERE   CITY = 'Paris' ;
```

Result:

```
S#   STATUS
--   ------
S2    10
S3    30
```

The example illustrates the commonest form of the SQL SELECT statement—"*SELECT* specified fields *FROM* a specified table *WHERE* some specified condition is true." Notice that the result of the query is another table—a table that is derived in some way from the given tables in the database. In other words, the user in a relational system like DB2 is always operating in the simple tabular framework, a very attractive feature of such systems.*

Incidentally, we could equally well have formulated the query using *qualified field names* throughout:

```
SELECT S.S#, S.STATUS
FROM    S
WHERE   S.CITY = 'Paris' ;
```

It is never wrong to use qualified names, and sometimes it is essential, as we shall see in Section 4.3.

For reference, we show below the general form of the SELECT statement (ignoring the possibility of UNION, which is discussed in the next chapter).

---

*Because of this fact, we say that relational tables form a *closed system* under the retrieval operators of a language like SQL. In general, a closed system is a collection (possibly infinite) of all objects of a certain type, say OBJS, and a corresponding collection of operators, say OPS, such that (a) the operators in OPS apply to the objects in OBJS, and (b) the result of applying any such operator to any such object(s) is another object in OBJS. The practical significance of this point (in the case of relations specifically) is as follows: Since the result of one SELECT operation is another relation, it is possible, at least in principle, to apply another SELECT operation to that result, provided of course that that result has been saved somewhere. It also means, again in principle, that SELECT operations can be nested. See Sections 5.2, 6.4, and 8.1 for illustrations of these points.

```
SELECT [ DISTINCT ] item(s)
FROM    table(s)
[ WHERE   predicate ]
[ GROUP   BY field(s) [ HAVING predicate ] ]
[ ORDER   BY field(s) ] ;
```

We now proceed to illustrate the major features of this statement by means of a rather lengthy series of examples. *Note:* The GROUP BY and HAVING clauses are discussed in Chapter 5. All of the remaining clauses are at least introduced in this chapter, though the more complex aspects of those clauses are also deferred to Chapter 5.

### 4.2.1  Simple Retrieval

Get part numbers for all parts supplied.

```
SELECT P#
FROM    SP ;
```

Result:

```
P#
--
P1
P2
P3
P4
P5
P6
P1
P2
P2
P2
P4
P5
```

Notice the duplication of part numbers in this result. DB2 does not eliminate duplicates from the result of a SELECT statement unless the user explicitly requests it to do so via the keyword DISTINCT, as in the next example.

### 4.2.2  Retrieval with Duplicate Elimination

Get part numbers for all parts supplied, with redundant duplicates eliminated.

```
SELECT DISTINCT P#
FROM    SP ;
```

Result:

```
P#
--
P1
P2
P3
P4
P5
P6
```

### 4.2.3    Retrieval of Computed Values

For all parts, get the part number and the weight of the part in grams, assuming that weights are given in table P in pounds.

```
SELECT P#, WEIGHT * 454
FROM    P ;
```

Result:

```
P#
--  ----
P1  5448
P2  7718
P3  7718
P4  6356
P5  5448
P6  8626
```

The SELECT clause (and the WHERE clause) can include arithmetic expressions as well as simple field names. It is also possible to SELECT simple constants—for example:

```
SELECT P#, 'Weight in grams =', WEIGHT * 454
FROM    P ;
```

Result:

```
P#
--  ------------------  ----
P1  Weight in grams =   5448
P2  Weight in grams =   7718
P3  Weight in grams =   7718
P4  Weight in grams =   6356
P5  Weight in grams =   5448
P6  Weight in grams =   8626
```

Note that there are three columns in this result.

One further point arises in connection with this example: What happens if the weight of some part is null? Remember that null represents an unknown value. Suppose, for example, that the weight of part P1 is given as null in the database, instead of as 12. What then is the value of WEIGHT * 454 for part P1? The answer is that it is also null. In general, in fact, *any* arithmetic expression is considered to evaluate to null if any of the operands of that expression is itself null. In other words, if WEIGHT happens to be null, then all of the following expressions also have the value null:

```
WEIGHT + 454
WEIGHT - 454
WEIGHT * 454
WEIGHT / 454
```

Null values are displayed at the terminal as a dash or hyphen. See Example 4.2.10 below for further discussion of null values.

### 4.2.4  Simple Retrieval ("SELECT *")

Get full details of all suppliers.

```
SELECT *
FROM   S ;
```

Result: A copy of the entire S table.

The star or asterisk is shorthand for a list of all field names in the table(s) named in the FROM clause, in the order in which those fields are defined in the relevant CREATE TABLE statement(s). The SELECT statement shown is thus equivalent to:

```
SELECT S#, SNAME, STATUS, CITY
FROM   S ;
```

The star notation is convenient for interactive queries, since it saves keystrokes. However, it is potentially dangerous in embedded SQL (i.e., SQL within an application program), because the meaning of "*" may change if the program is rebound and another column has been added to the table in the interim. In this book we will use "SELECT *" only in contexts where it is safe to do so (basically interactive contexts only), and we recommend that actual users of DB2 do likewise.

Incidentally, it is possible to qualify the "*" by the name of the relevant table. For example, the following is legal:

```
SELECT S.*
FROM   S ;
```

### 4.2.5   Qualified Retrieval

Get supplier numbers for suppliers in Paris with status > 20.

```
SELECT  S#
FROM    S
WHERE   CITY = 'Paris'
AND     STATUS > 20 ;
```

Result:

```
S#
--
S3
```

The condition or *predicate* following WHERE may include the comparison operators =, ¬ = (not equal), >, ¬>, > =, <, ¬<, and < =; the Boolean operators AND, OR, and NOT; and parentheses to indicate a desired order of evaluation. Within such a predicate, numbers compare algebraically (negative numbers are considered to be smaller than positive numbers, regardless of their absolute magnitude), and character strings compare in accordance with their EBCDIC encoding. If two character strings of different lengths are to be compared, the shorter is conceptually padded at the right with blanks to make it the same length as the other before the comparison is done.

### 4.2.6   Retrieval with Ordering

Get supplier numbers and status for suppliers in Paris, in descending order of status.

```
SELECT  S#, STATUS
FROM    S
WHERE   CITY = 'Paris'
ORDER   BY STATUS DESC ;
```

Result:

```
S#  STATUS
--  ------
S3    30
S2    10
```

In general, the result table is not guaranteed to be in any particular order. Here, however, the user has specified that the result is to be arranged in a particular sequence before being displayed. Ordering may be specified in the same manner as in CREATE INDEX (see Section 3.3)—that is, as

```
column−name [ order ] [, column−name [ order ] ] ...
```

where, as before, "order" is either ASC or DESC, and ASC is the default. Each "column-name" must identify a column of the *result table*. Thus, for example, the following is illegal:

```
SELECT S#
FROM    S
ORDER   BY CITY ;
```

It is also possible to identify columns in the ORDER BY clause by "column-number" instead of "column-name", where "column-number" refers to the ordinal (left-to-right) position of the column in question within the result table. This feature makes it possible to order a result on the basis of a "computed column," which does not have a name. For example, to order the result of Example 4.2.3 by ascending part number within ascending gram weight:

```
SELECT P#, WEIGHT * 454
FROM    P
ORDER   BY 2, P# ;              [ or ORDER BY 2, 1 ; ]
```

The "2" refers to the second column of the result table. Result:

```
P#
--  ----
P1  5448
P5  5448
P4  6356
P2  7718
P3  7718
P6  8626
```

### 4.2.7  Retrieval Using BETWEEN

Get parts whose weight is in the range 16 to 19 (inclusive).

```
SELECT P#, PNAME, COLOR, WEIGHT, CITY
FROM    P
WHERE   WEIGHT BETWEEN 16 AND 19 ;
```

Result:

```
P#  PNAME  COLOR  WEIGHT  CITY
--  -----  -----  ------  ------
P2  Bolt   Green    17    Paris
P3  Screw  Blue     17    Rome
P6  Cog    Red      19    London
```

NOT BETWEEN can also be specified—for example,

```
SELECT P#, PNAME, COLOR, WEIGHT, CITY
FROM    P
WHERE   WEIGHT NOT BETWEEN 16 AND 19 ;
```

Result:

```
P#  PNAME  COLOR  WEIGHT   CITY
──  ─────  ─────  ──────   ──────
P1  Nut    Red      12     London
P4  Screw  Red      14     London
P5  Cam    Blue     12     Paris
```

### 4.2.8   Retrieval Using IN

Get parts whose weight is any one of the following: 12, 16, 17.

```
SELECT P#, PNAME, COLOR, WEIGHT, CITY
FROM    P
WHERE   WEIGHT IN ( 12, 16, 17 ) ;
```

Result:

```
P#  PNAME  COLOR  WEIGHT   CITY
──  ─────  ─────  ──────   ──────
P1  Nut    Red      12     London
P2  Bolt   Green    17     Paris
P3  Screw  Blue     17     Rome
P5  Cam    Blue     12     Paris
```

The IN predicate is really just a shorthand for a predicate involving a sequence of individual comparisons all "ORed" together. The foregoing SELECT statement is equivalent to the following:

```
SELECT P#, PNAME, COLOR, WEIGHT, CITY
FROM    P
WHERE   WEIGHT = 12
OR      WEIGHT = 16
OR      WEIGHT = 17 ;
```

NOT IN is also available:

```
SELECT P#, PNAME, COLOR, WEIGHT, CITY
FROM    P
WHERE   WEIGHT NOT IN ( 12, 16, 17 ) ;
```

Result:

```
P#   PNAME   COLOR   WEIGHT   CITY
--   -----   -----   ------   ------
P4   Screw   Red       14     London
P6   Cog     Red       19     London
```

Like the IN predicate, the NOT IN predicate can be regarded merely as a shorthand for another predicate that does not use NOT IN. Exercise: Show the "expanded form" of the foregoing example.

### 4.2.9   Retrieval Using LIKE

Get all parts whose names begin with the letter C.

```
SELECT  P#, PNAME, COLOR, WEIGHT, CITY
FROM    P
WHERE   PNAME LIKE 'C%' ;
```

Result:

```
P#   PNAME   COLOR   WEIGHT   CITY
--   -----   -----   ------   ------
P5   Cam     Blue      12     Paris
P6   Cog     Red       19     London
```

In general, a LIKE predicate takes the form

```
column-name LIKE character-string-constant
```

where "column-name" must designate a column of type CHAR or VARCHAR. For a given record, the predicate evaluates to *true* if the value within the designated column conforms to the pattern specified by "character-string-constant." Characters within that constant are interpreted as follows:

- The __ character (break or underscore) stands for *any single character*.
- The % character (percent) stands for *any sequence of n characters* (where n may be zero).
- All other characters simply stand for themselves.

In the example, therefore, the SELECT statement will retrieve records from table P for which the PNAME value begins with the letter C and has any sequence of zero or more characters following that C.

Here are some more examples of LIKE:

```
ADDRESS LIKE '%Berkeley%'
```
will evaluate to *true* if ADDRESS contains the string "Berkeley" anywhere inside it

```
S# LIKE 'S__ __'
```
will evaluate to *true* if S# is exactly 3 characters long and the 1st is an S

```
PNAME LIKE '%c__ __ __'
```
will evaluate to *true* if PNAME is 4 characters long or more and the last but three is a c

```
CITY NOT LIKE '%E%'
```
will evaluate to *true* if CITY does not contain an E

### 4.2.10  Retrieval Involving NULL

Suppose for the sake of the example that supplier S5 has a status value of null, rather than 30. Get supplier numbers for suppliers with status greater than 25.

```
SELECT  S#
FROM    S
WHERE   STATUS > 25 ;
```

Result:

```
S#
--
S3
```

Supplier S5 does not qualify. When a null value is compared with some other value in evaluating a predicate, regardless of the comparison operator involved, the result of the comparison is never considered to be *true*—even if that other value is also null. In other words, if STATUS happens to be null, then none of the following comparisons evaluates to *true*.*

```
STATUS > 25
STATUS <= 25
STATUS = 25
STATUS ¬= 25
STATUS = NULL        [This is illegal syntax. See below.]
STATUS ¬= NULL       [So is this.]
```

Thus, if we issue the query

```
SELECT  S#
FROM    S
WHERE   STATUS <= 25 ;
```

---

*Actually they all evaluate to the *unknown* truth value. In the presence of null values, it is necessary to adopt a three-valued logic, in which the truth values are *true*, *false*, and *unknown*. (Unknown is really the null truth value, as a matter of fact.) The SELECT statement retrieves records for which the WHERE predicate evaluates to *true*, i.e., not to *false* and not to *unknown*.

and compare the result with that of the previous query, supplier S5 will not appear in either of them. The result is:

```
S#
--
S1
S2
S4
```

A special predicate of the form

```
column-name IS [ NOT ] NULL
```

is provided for testing for the presence [or absence] of null values. For example:

```
SELECT S#
FROM   S
WHERE  STATUS IS NULL ;
```

Result:

```
S#
--
S5
```

The syntax "STATUS = NULL" is illegal, because *nothing*—not even null itself—is considered to be equal to null. (Despite this fact, however, two null values *are* considered to be duplicates of each other for duplicate elimination purposes. That is, SELECT DISTINCT will produce at most one null value in the result. Likewise, a UNIQUE index will permit at most one null value in the indexed column. Finally, null values are also treated as if they were all equal— and greater than all nonnull values—for the purposes of ORDER BY.)

We note in passing that the symbol NULL is not allowed in a SELECT clause. For example, the following is illegal:

```
SELECT P#, 'Weight =', NULL
FROM   P
WHERE  WEIGHT IS NULL ;
```

## 4.3   JOIN QUERIES

The ability to "join" two or more tables is one of the most powerful features of relational systems. In fact, it is the availability of the join operation, almost more than anything else, that distinguishes relational from nonrelational systems (see Appendix A). So what is a join? Loosely speaking, it is *a query in which data is retrieved from more than one table*. Here is a simple example.

### 4.3.1  Simple Equijoin

Get all combinations of supplier and part information such that the supplier and part in question are located in the same city (i.e., are "colocated," to coin an ugly but convenient term).

```
SELECT  S.*, P.*
FROM    S, P
WHERE   S.CITY = P.CITY ;
```

Notice that the field references in the WHERE clause here *must* be qualified by the names of the containing tables. Result:

| S# | SNAME | STATUS | S.CITY | P# | PNAME | COLOR | WEIGHT | P.CITY |
|----|-------|--------|--------|----|-------|-------|--------|--------|
| S1 | Smith | 20 | London | P1 | Nut | Red | 12 | London |
| S1 | Smith | 20 | London | P4 | Screw | Red | 14 | London |
| S1 | Smith | 20 | London | P6 | Cog | Red | 19 | London |
| S2 | Jones | 10 | Paris | P2 | Bolt | Green | 17 | Paris |
| S2 | Jones | 10 | Paris | P5 | Cam | Blue | 12 | Paris |
| S3 | Blake | 30 | Paris | P2 | Bolt | Green | 17 | Paris |
| S3 | Blake | 30 | Paris | P5 | Cam | Blue | 12 | Paris |
| S4 | Clark | 20 | London | P1 | Nut | Red | 12 | London |
| S4 | Clark | 20 | London | P4 | Screw | Red | 14 | London |
| S4 | Clark | 20 | London | P6 | Cog | Red | 19 | London |

(We have shown the two CITY columns in this result explicitly as S.CITY and P.CITY, to avoid ambiguity.)

Explanation: It is clear from the English language statement of the problem that the required data comes from two tables, namely S and P. In the SQL formulation of the query, therefore, we first name both those tables in the FROM clause, and we then express the connection between them (i.e., the fact that the CITY values must be equal) in the WHERE clause. To understand how this works, imagine yourself looking at two rows, one row from each of the two tables—say the two rows shown here:

| S# | SNAME | STATUS | CITY | P# | PNAME | COLOR | WEIGHT | CITY |
|----|-------|--------|------|----|-------|-------|--------|------|
| S1 | Smith | 20 | London | P1 | Nut | Red | 12 | London |

From these two rows you can see that supplier S1 and part P1 are indeed "colocated." These two rows will generate the result row

| S# | SNAME | STATUS | S.CITY | P# | PNAME | COLOR | WEIGHT | P.CITY |
|----|-------|--------|--------|----|-------|-------|--------|--------|
| S1 | Smith | 20 | London | P1 | Nut | Red | 12 | London |

because they satisfy the predicate in the WHERE clause (S.CITY = P.CITY). Similarly for all other pairs of rows having matching CITY values. Notice that supplier S5 (located in Athens) does not appear in the result, because there are no parts stored in Athens; likewise, part P3 (stored in Rome) also does not appear in the result, because there are no suppliers located in Rome.

The result of this query is said to be a *join* of tables S and P over matching CITY values. The term "join" is also used to refer to the operation of constructing such a result. The condition S.CITY = P.CITY is said to be a *join condition* or *join predicate*. A number of further points arise in connection with this example, some major, some minor.

- The fields in a join predicate must either both be numeric or both be character strings. The data types are not required to be identical. For performance reasons, however, it is generally a good idea if they are.

- There is no requirement that the fields in a join predicate be identically named, though they very often will be.

- There is no requirement that the comparison operator in a join predicate be equality, though it very often will be. Examples of where it is not are given below (Example 4.3.2 and latter part of Example 4.3.6). If it is equality, then the join is sometimes called an *equijoin*.

- The WHERE clause in a join-SELECT can include other conditions in addition to the join predicate itself. Example 4.3.3 below illustrates this possibility.

- It is of course possible to SELECT just specified fields from a join, instead of necessarily having to SELECT all of them. Examples 4.3.4 – 4.3.6 below illustrate this possibility.

- The expression

```
SELECT S.*, P.*
FROM   S, P
. . . . .      ;
```

can be further abbreviated to simply

```
SELECT *
FROM   S, P
. . . . .      ;
```

Alternatively, of course, it can be expanded to

```
SELECT S#, SNAME, STATUS, S.CITY,
       P#, PNAME, COLOR, WEIGHT, P.CITY
FROM   S, P
. . . . .      ;
```

In this formulation, S.CITY and P.CITY in the SELECT clause *must* be referred to by their qualified names, as shown, because the unqualified name CITY would be ambiguous. See the introduction to Section 4.2 if you need to refresh your memory concerning qualified field-names.

- The equijoin by definition must produce a result containing two identical columns. If one of those two columns is eliminated, what is left is called the *natural* join. To construct the natural join of S and P over cities in SQL, we could write:

```
SELECT S#, SNAME, STATUS, S.CITY,
       P#, PNAME, COLOR, WEIGHT
FROM   S, P
WHERE  S.CITY = P.CITY ;
```

Natural join is probably the single most useful form of join—so much so, that we often use the unqualified term "join" to refer to this case specifically.

- It is also possible to form a join of three, four, …, or any number of tables. Example 4.3.5 below shows a join involving three tables.

- The following is an alternative (and helpful) way to think about how joins may conceptually be constructed. First, form the *Cartesian product* of the tables listed in the FROM clause. The Cartesian product of a set of n tables is the table consisting of all possible rows r, such that r is the concatenation of a row from the first table, a row from the second table, …, and a row from the nth table. For example, the Cartesian product of table S and table P (in that order) is the following table (let us call it CP):

| CP | S# | SNAME | STATUS | S.CITY | P# | PNAME | COLOR | WEIGHT | P.CITY |
|----|----|-------|--------|--------|----|-------|-------|--------|--------|
|    | S1 | Smith | 20 | London | P1 | Nut   | Red   | 12 | London |
|    | S1 | Smith | 20 | London | P2 | Bolt  | Green | 17 | Paris  |
|    | S1 | Smith | 20 | London | P3 | Screw | Blue  | 17 | Rome   |
|    | S1 | Smith | 20 | London | P4 | Screw | Red   | 14 | London |
|    | S1 | Smith | 20 | London | P5 | Cam   | Blue  | 12 | Paris  |
|    | S1 | Smith | 20 | London | P6 | Cog   | Red   | 19 | London |
|    | S2 | Jones | 10 | Paris  | P1 | Nut   | Red   | 12 | London |
|    | .  | .     | .  | .      | .  | .     | .     | .  | .      |
|    | .  | .     | .  | .      | .  | .     | .     | .  | .      |
|    | .  | .     | .  | .      | .  | .     | .     | .  | .      |
|    | S5 | Adams | 30 | Athens | P6 | Cog   | Red   | 19 | London |

(The complete table contains 5 * 6 = 30 rows.) Now eliminate from this Cartesian product all those rows that do not satisfy the join predicate. What is left is the required join. In the case at hand, we eliminate from CP all those rows in which S.CITY is not equal to P.CITY; and what is left is exactly the join shown earlier.

By the way, it is perfectly possible (though perhaps unusual) to formulate a SQL query whose result is a Cartesian product. For example:

```
SELECT S.*, P.*
FROM   S, P ;
```

Result: Table CP as shown above.

### 4.3.2 Greater-Than Join

Get all combinations of supplier and part information such that the supplier city follows the part city in alphabetical order.

```
SELECT S.*, P.*
FROM   S, P
WHERE  S.CITY > P.CITY ;
```

Result:

| S# | SNAME | STATUS | S.CITY | P# | PNAME | COLOR | WEIGHT | P.CITY |
|----|-------|--------|--------|----|-------|-------|--------|--------|
| S2 | Jones | 10 | Paris | P1 | Nut | Red | 12 | London |
| S2 | Jones | 10 | Paris | P4 | Screw | Red | 14 | London |
| S2 | Jones | 10 | Paris | P6 | Cog | Red | 19 | London |
| S3 | Blake | 30 | Paris | P1 | Nut | Red | 12 | London |
| S3 | Blake | 30 | Paris | P4 | Screw | Red | 14 | London |
| S3 | Blake | 30 | Paris | P6 | Cog | Red | 19 | London |

### 4.3.3 Join Query with an Additional Condition

Get all combinations of supplier information and part information where the supplier and part concerned are colocated, but omitting suppliers with status 20.

```
SELECT S.*, P.*
FROM   S, P
WHERE  S.CITY = P.CITY
AND    S.STATUS ¬= 20;
```

Result:

| S# | SNAME | STATUS | S.CITY | P# | PNAME | COLOR | WEIGHT | P.CITY |
|----|-------|--------|--------|----|-------|-------|--------|--------|
| S2 | Jones | 10 | Paris | P2 | Bolt | Green | 17 | Paris |
| S2 | Jones | 10 | Paris | P5 | Cam | Blue | 12 | Paris |
| S3 | Blake | 30 | Paris | P2 | Bolt | Green | 17 | Paris |
| S3 | Blake | 30 | Paris | P5 | Cam | Blue | 12 | Paris |

### 4.3.4 Retrieving Specified Fields from a Join

Get all supplier-number/part-number combinations such that the supplier and part in question are colocated.

```
SELECT S.S#, P.P#
FROM   S, P
WHERE  S.CITY = P.CITY ;
```

Result:

```
S#   P#
--   --
S1   P1
S1   P4
S1   P6
S2   P2
S2   P5
S3   P2
S3   P5
S4   P1
S4   P4
S4   P6
```

### 4.3.5 Join of Three Tables

Get all pairs of city names such that a supplier located in the first city supplies a part stored in the second city. For example, supplier S1 supplies part P1; supplier S1 is located in London, and part P1 is stored in London; so "London,London" is a pair of cities in the result.

```
SELECT DISTINCT S.CITY, P.CITY
FROM   S, SP, P
WHERE  S.S# = SP.S#
AND    SP.P# = P.P# ;
```

Result:

```
S.CITY   P.CITY
------   ------
London   London
London   Paris
London   Rome
Paris    London
Paris    Paris
```

As an exercise, the reader should decide which particular supplier/part combinations give rise to which particular result rows in this example.

### 4.3.6 Joining a Table with Itself

Get all pairs of supplier numbers such that the two suppliers concerned are colocated.

```
SELECT FIRST.S#, SECOND.S#
FROM   S FIRST, S SECOND
WHERE  FIRST.CITY = SECOND.CITY ;
```

As can be seen, this query involves a join of table S with itself (over matching cities). Table S therefore appears twice in the FROM clause. To distinguish between the two appearances, we introduce arbitrary *aliases* FIRST and SECOND in that clause, and use those aliases as explicit qualifiers in the SELECT and WHERE clauses. Result:

```
S#  S#
--  --
S1  S1
S1  S4
S2  S2
S2  S3
S3  S2
S3  S3
S4  S1
S4  S4
S5  S5
```

We can tidy up this result by extending the WHERE clause as follows:

```
SELECT FIRST.S#, SECOND.S#
FROM   S FIRST, S SECOND
WHERE  FIRST.CITY = SECOND.CITY
AND    FIRST.S# < SECOND.S# ;
```

The effect of the condition FIRST.S# < SECOND.S# is twofold: (a) It eliminates pairs of supplier numbers of the form (x,x); (b) it guarantees that the pairs (x,y) and (y,x) will not both appear. Result:

```
S#  S#
--  --
S1  S4
S2  S3
```

This is the first example we have seen in which the use of aliases has been necessary. However, it is never wrong to introduce such aliases, even when their use is not essential, and sometimes they can help to make the statement clearer. We shall occasionally make use of them in our examples in the next chapter.

## 4.4   SUMMARY

We have now come to the end of the first of our two chapters on the SELECT statement. We have illustrated:

- the SELECT clause itself, including the use of constants, expressions, and "SELECT *"
- the use of DISTINCT to eliminate duplicates, including the use of DISTINCT with a join
- the FROM clause (with one or more tables), including the use of aliases
- the use of ORDER BY to order the result
- the WHERE clause, including:
  - comparison operators $=, \neg =, >, >=, \neg >, <, <=, \neg <$
  - join predicates
  - Boolean operators AND, OR, NOT
  - special operators [NOT] BETWEEN, [NOT] IN, [NOT] LIKE
  - special comparison "field IS [NOT] NULL"

In the next chapter we will consider some more complex features of the SELECT statement—to be specific, the "subquery" feature, the existential quantifier, the use of builtin functions, and the union operator.


## EXERCISES

All of the following exercises are based on the suppliers-parts-projects database (see the exercises in Chapter 3). In each one, you are asked to write a SELECT statement for the indicated query. For convenience we repeat the structure of the database below:

```
S    ( S#, SNAME, STATUS, CITY )
P    ( P#, PNAME, COLOR, WEIGHT, CITY )
J    ( J#, JNAME, CITY )
SPJ  ( S#, P#, J#, QTY )
```

## Simple queries

**4.1** Get full details of all projects.

**4.2** Get full details of all projects in London.

**4.3** Get supplier numbers for suppliers who supply project J1, in supplier number order.

**4.4** Get all shipments where the quantity is in the range 300 to 750 inclusive.

**4.5** Get a list of all part-color/part-city combinations, with duplicate color/city pairs eliminated.

**4.6** Get all shipments where the quantity is nonnull.

**4.7** Get project numbers and cities where the city has an "o" as the second letter of its name.

## Joins

**4.8** Get all supplier-number/part-number/project-number triples such that the indicated supplier, part, and project are all colocated.

**4.9** Get all supplier-number/part-number/project-number triples such that the indicated supplier, part, and project are not colocated.

**4.10** Get all supplier-number/part-number/project-number triples such that no two of the indicated supplier, part, and project are colocated.

**4.11** Get part numbers for parts supplied by a supplier in London.

**4.12** Get part numbers for parts supplied by a supplier in London to a project in London.

**4.13** Get all pairs of city names such that a supplier in the first city supplies a project in the second city.

**4.14** Get part numbers for parts supplied to any project by a supplier in the same city as that project.

**4.15** Get project numbers for projects supplied by at least one supplier not in the same city.

**4.16** Get all pairs of part numbers such that some supplier supplies both the indicated parts.

## ANSWERS TO SELECTED EXERCISES

The following answers are not necessarily the only ones possible.

**4.1**
```
SELECT J#, JNAME, CITY
FROM   J ;
```
Or:
```
SELECT *
FROM   J ;
```

**4.2**
```
SELECT J#, JNAME, CITY
FROM   J
WHERE  CITY = 'London' ;
```
Or:
```
SELECT *
FROM   J
WHERE  CITY = 'London' ;
```

**4.3**
```
SELECT DISTINCT S#
FROM   SPJ
```

```
         WHERE   J# = 'J1'
         ORDER   BY  S# ;
4.4      SELECT  S#, P#, J#, QTY
         FROM    SPJ
         WHERE   QTY >= 300
         AND     QTY <= 750 ;
```

Or:

```
         SELECT  S#, P#, J#, QTY
         FROM    SPJ
         WHERE   QTY BETWEEN 300 AND 750 ;
4.5      SELECT  DISTINCT COLOR, CITY
         FROM    P ;
4.6      SELECT  S#, P#, J#, QTY
         FROM    SPJ
         WHERE   QTY IS NOT NULL ;
```

The foregoing is the "official" answer. However, the following will also work:

```
         SELECT  S#, P#, J#, QTY
         FROM    SPJ
         WHERE   QTY = QTY ;
4.7      SELECT  J#, CITY
         FROM    J
         WHERE   CITY LIKE '__o%' ;
4.8      SELECT  S#, P#, J#
         FROM    S, P, J
         WHERE   S.CITY = P.CITY
         AND     P.CITY = J.CITY ;
4.9      SELECT  S#, P#, J#
         FROM    S, P, J
         WHERE   NOT
                 ( S.CITY = P.CITY AND P.CITY = J.CITY ) ;
```

Or:

```
         SELECT  S#, P#, J#
         FROM    S, P, J
         WHERE   S.CITY ¬= P.CITY
         OR      P.CITY ¬= J.CITY ;
4.10     SELECT  S#, P#, J#
         FROM    S, P, J
         WHERE   S.CITY ¬= P.CITY
         AND     P.CITY ¬= J.CITY
         AND     J.CITY ¬= S.CITY ;
```

**4.11**  SELECT DISTINCT P#
      FROM    SPJ, S
      WHERE   SPJ.S# = S.S#
      AND     CITY = 'London' ;

**4.12**  SELECT DISTINCT P#
      FROM    SPJ, S, J
      WHERE   SPJ.S# = S.S#
      AND     SPJ.J# = J.J#
      AND     S.CITY = 'London'
      AND     J.CITY = 'London' ;

**4.13**  SELECT DISTINCT S.CITY, J.CITY
      FROM    S, SPJ, J
      WHERE   S.S# = SPJ.S#
      AND     SPJ.J# = J.J# ;

**4.14**  SELECT DISTINCT P#
      FROM    SPJ, S, J
      WHERE   SPJ.S# = S.S#
      AND     SPJ.J# = J.J#
      AND     S.CITY = J.CITY ;

**4.15**  SELECT DISTINCT J.J#
      FROM    SPJ, S, J
      WHERE   SPJ.S# = S.S#
      AND     SPJ.J# = J.J#
      AND     S.CITY ¬= J.CITY ;

**4.16**  SELECT SPJX.P#, SPJY.P#
      FROM    SPJ SPJX, SPJ SPJY
      WHERE   SPJX.S# – SPJY.S#
      AND     SPJX.P# > SPJY.P# ;

# 5

# Data Manipulation II: Retrieval Operations (Continued)

## 5.1  INTRODUCTION

In this chapter we complete our treatment of the SQL SELECT statement. The plan of the chapter is as follows:

- Section 5.2 introduces the concept of *subqueries* or *nested SELECTs*. As a matter of historical interest, we remark that it was the fact that one SELECT could be nested inside another that was the original justification for the "Structured" in the name "Structured Query Language"; however, later additions to the language have made nested SELECTs *per se* very much less important than they used to be.

- Section 5.3 is concerned with the *existential quantifier* EXISTS, a feature that (in this writer's opinion) ranks with join as one of the most important and fundamental features of the entire SQL language—though perhaps not the most easy to use.

- Section 5.4 discusses the *builtin functions* COUNT, SUM, AVG, etc.; in particular, it describes the use of the GROUP BY and HAVING clauses in connection with those functions.

- Section 5.5 discusses the UNION operator.

- Finally, in an attempt to tie together a number of the ideas introduced in this and the previous chapter, Section 5.6 presents an example of a very complex SELECT and shows in principle how that SELECT might be processed by DB2.

As you can see, the chapter is rather long, and you may wish to omit some of the more complicated portions on a first reading. However, you should read at least the first part of each section on your first pass through. One of the reasons for the length of the chapter is that SQL is a highly redundant language, in the sense that it frequently provides several different ways of formulating the same query. Since we are trying to be reasonably comprehensive in our coverage of that language, the chapter necessarily contains a certain amount of redundancy also.

One final introductory remark (which may not be very intelligible until you have read the body of the chapter): Despite our general objective of comprehensiveness, we deliberately do not include any detailed description of the ANY and ALL versions of the comparison operators (>ANY, =ALL, etc.). The reader who requires such a detailed description is referred to the IBM manuals. Our reasons for excluding those operators from this book are that they are entirely superfluous—there is no query that can be formulated with them that cannot equally well (in fact, better) be formulated using EXISTS—and furthermore they are confusing and (in this writer's opinion) dangerously error-prone. For example, the (valid) SELECT statement

```
SELECT  S.S#
FROM    S
WHERE   S.CITY ¬=ANY ( SELECT P.CITY
                       FROM    P      ) ;
```

does *not* select supplier numbers for suppliers whose city is not equal to any part city (instead, it selects supplier numbers for suppliers whose city is not equal to *some* part city). The equivalent EXISTS formulation makes the correct interpretation clear:

```
SELECT  S.S#
FROM    S
WHERE   EXISTS ( SELECT P.CITY
                 FROM    P
                 WHERE   P.CITY ¬= S.CITY ) ;
```

("select supplier numbers for suppliers such that there exists some part city that is different from the supplier city"). The natural intuitive interpretation of ¬= ANY as "not equal to any" is both incorrect and very misleading. Analogous criticisms apply to all of the ANY and ALL operators.

## 5.2 SUBQUERIES

In this section we discuss *subqueries* or *nested SELECTs*. Loosely speaking, a subquery is a SELECT-FROM-WHERE expression that is nested inside another such expression.* Subqueries are typically used to represent the set of values to be searched via an IN predicate, as the following example illustrates.

### 5.2.1 Simple Subquery

Get supplier names for suppliers who supply part P2.

```
SELECT SNAME
FROM    S
WHERE   S# IN
        ( SELECT S#
          FROM    SP
          WHERE   P# = 'P2' ) ;
```

Result:

```
SNAME
-----
Smith
Jones
Blake
Clark
```

Explanation: The system evaluates the overall query by evaluating the nested subquery first. That subquery returns the set of supplier *numbers* for suppliers who supply part P2, namely the set ('S1','S2','S3','S4'). The original query is thus equivalent to the following simpler query:

```
SELECT SNAME
FROM    S
WHERE   S# IN
        ( 'S1', 'S2', 'S3', 'S4' ) ;
```

Hence the result is as shown earlier.

The implicit name qualification in this example bears additional discussion. Observe in particular that the "S#" to the left of the IN is implicitly qualified by "S", whereas the "S#" in the subquery is implicitly qualified by "SP". The general rule is as follows: An unqualified field name is assumed to be qualified by a table name (or table alias—see Examples 5.2.3–5.2.5 below) that appears

---

*A subquery may also include GROUP BY and HAVING clauses. ORDER BY and UNION are illegal, however.

in that FROM clause that is most immediately part of the same query or subquery. In the case of the S# to the left of the IN, that clause is "FROM S"; in the case of the S# in the subquery, it is the clause "FROM SP". By way of clarification, we repeat the original query with all assumed qualifications shown explicitly:

```
SELECT  S.SNAME
FROM    S
WHERE   S.S# IN
      ( SELECT  SP.S#
        FROM    SP
        WHERE   SP.P# = 'P2' ) ;
```

It is always possible to override the implicit assumptions with explicit qualifications; see Examples 5.2.3–5.2.5 below.

There is one more (important) point to make before we move on to our next subquery example: The original problem—"Get supplier names for suppliers who supply part P2"—can equally well be expressed as a *join* query, as follows:

```
SELECT  S.SNAME
FROM    S, SP
WHERE   S.S# = SP.S#
AND     SP.P# = 'P2' ;
```

Explanation: The join of S and SP over supplier numbers consists of a table of 12 rows (one for each row in SP), in which each row consists of the corresponding row from SP extended with SNAME, STATUS, and CITY values for the supplier identified by the S# value in that row. Of these twelve rows, four are for part P2; the final result is thus obtained by extracting the SNAME values from those four rows.

The two formulations of the original query—one using a subquery, one using a join—are equally correct. It is purely a matter of taste as to which formulation a given user might prefer.

### 5.2.2   Subquery with Multiple Levels of Nesting

Get supplier names for suppliers who supply at least one red part.

```
SELECT  SNAME
FROM    S
WHERE   S# IN
      ( SELECT  S#
        FROM    SP
        WHERE   P# IN
              ( SELECT  P#
                FROM    P
                WHERE   COLOR = 'Red' ) ) ;
```

Result:

```
SNAME
-----
Smith
Jones
Clark
```

Explanation: The innermost subquery evaluates to the set ('P1','P4','P6').
The next outermost subquery evaluates in turn to the set ('S1','S2','S4'). Last,
the outermost SELECT evaluates to the final result shown. In general, subqueries
can be nested to any depth.

To make sure you understand this example, try the following exercises:

(a)  Rewrite the query with all name qualifications shown explicitly.

(b)  Write an equivalent join formulation of the same query.

### 5.2.3   Correlated Subquery

Get supplier names for suppliers who supply part P2 (same as Example 5.2.1).
We show another solution to this problem in order to illustrate another point.

```
SELECT SNAME
FROM    S
WHERE   'P2' IN
        ( SELECT P#
          FROM    SP
          WHERE   S# = S.S# ) ;
```

Explanation: In the last line here, the unqualified reference to S# is implicitly
qualified by SP; the other reference is *explicitly* qualified by S. This example
differs from the preceding ones in that the inner subquery cannot be evaluated
once and for all before the outer query is evaluated, because that inner subquery
depends on a *variable*, namely S.S#, whose value changes as the system examines
different rows of table S. Conceptually, therefore, evaluation proceeds as follows:

(a)  The system examines the first row of table S; let us assume this is the row
     for S1. The variable S.S# thus currently has the value 'S1', so the system
     evaluates the inner subquery

```
        ( SELECT P#
          FROM    SP
          WHERE   S# = 'S1' )
```

to obtain the set ('P1','P2','P3','P4','P5','P6'). Now it can complete its
processing for S1; it will select the SNAME value for S1, namely Smith, if
and only if 'P2' is in this set (which of course it is).

(b) Next the system moves on to repeat this kind of processing for the next supplier, and so on, until all rows of table S have been dealt with.

A subquery such as the one in this example is said to be a *correlated* subquery. A correlated subquery is one whose value depends upon some variable that receives its value in some outer query; such a subquery therefore has to be evaluated repeatedly (once for each value of the variable in question), instead of once and for all. We show another example of a correlated subquery below (Example 5.2.5); several further examples are given in Sections 5.3 and 5.4.

Some users like to use aliases in conjunction with correlated subqueries, in order to make the correlation clearer (see Example 4.3.6 in Chapter 4 if you need to refresh your memory concerning aliases). For example:

```
SELECT  SX.SNAME
FROM    S SX
WHERE   'P2' IN
      ( SELECT P#
        FROM    SP
        WHERE   P# = SX.S# ) ;
```

The alias in this example is the name SX, introduced in the FROM clause as an alternate name for S and then used as an explicit qualifier in the WHERE clause in the subquery (and in the outer SELECT clause). The operation of the overall statement can now be more clearly (and more accurately) explained as follows:

▪ SX is a variable that "ranges over" the records of table S (i.e., a variable that, at any given time, represents some record of table S).

▪ For each possible value of SX in turn, do the following:

  • evaluate the subquery to obtain a set, p say, of part numbers;

  • add the current value of SX.SNAME to the result set, if and only if P2 is in the set p.

In the previous version of this query, the symbol "S" was really performing two different functions: It stood for the suppliers base table itself (of course), and also for a variable that "ranged over" the records of that base table. As already stated, many users find it clearer to use two different symbols to distinguish between the two different functions.

It is never wrong to introduce an alias, and sometimes it is essential (see Example 5.2.5 below).

### 5.2.4  Subquery and Outer Query Referring to Same Table

Get supplier numbers for suppliers who supply at least one part supplied by supplier S2.

```
SELECT  DISTINCT S#
FROM    SP
WHERE   P# IN
      ( SELECT P#
        FROM    SP
        WHERE   S# = 'S2' ) ;
```

Result:

```
S#
--
S1
S2
S3
S4
```

Notice here that references to SP in the subquery do not mean the same thing as references to SP in the outer query. The two SP's are really *different variables*. Aliases can be used to make this fact explicit:

```
SELECT  DISTINCT SPX.S#
FROM    SP SPX
WHERE   SPX.P# IN
      ( SELECT SPY.P#
        FROM    SP SPY
        WHERE   SPY.S# = 'S2' ) ;
```

Equivalent join query:

```
SELECT  DISTINCT SPX.S#
FROM    SP SPX, SP SPY
WHERE   SPX.P# = SPY.P#
AND     SPY.S# = 'S2' ;
```

### 5.2.5  Correlated Subquery and Outer Query Referring to Same Table

Get part numbers for all parts supplied by more than one supplier. (Another solution to this problem is given later as Example 5.4.9.)

```
SELECT  DISTINCT SPX.P#
FROM    SP SPX
WHERE   SPX.P# IN
      ( SELECT SPY.P#
        FROM    SP SPY
        WHERE   SPY.S# ¬= SPX.S# )
```

Result:

```
P#
--
P1
P2
P4
P5
```

The operation of this query can be explained as follows: "For each row in turn, say SPX, of table SP, extract the P# value, if and only if that P# value appears in some row, say SPY, of table SP whose S# value is *not* that in row SPX." Note that at least one alias *must* be used in this formulation (either SPX or SPY, but not both, could be replaced by simply SP).

### 5.2.6   Subquery with Comparison Operator Other Than IN

Get supplier numbers for suppliers who are located in the same city as supplier S1.

```
SELECT  S#
FROM    S
WHERE   CITY =
      ( SELECT CITY
        FROM    S
        WHERE   S# = 'S1' ) ;
```

Result:

```
S#
--
S1
S4
```

Sometimes the user may know that a given subquery should return exactly one value, as in this example. In such a case a simple comparison operator (such as =, >, etc.) can be used in place of the more usual IN. However, an error will occur if the subquery in fact returns more than one value and IN has not been used. An error will *not* occur if the subquery returns no values at all; instead, the comparison is treated exactly as if the subquery had returned a null value. In other words, if x is a variable, then the comparison

```
        x   simple-comparison-operator ( subquery )   ,
```

where "subquery" returns an empty set, evaluates, not to *true* or *false*, but to the *unknown* truth value. See Chapter 4, Example 4.2.10.

Incidentally, the comparison in the foregoing example must be written as shown, with the subquery following the comparison operator. In other words, the following is illegal:

```
SELECT  S#
FROM    S
WHERE   (SELECT CITY
         FROM   S
         WHERE  S# = 'S1') = CITY ;
```

Furthermore, a subquery cannot include GROUP BY or HAVING when used with a simple comparison operator such as =, >, etc.


## 5.3   THE EXISTENTIAL QUANTIFIER

### 5.3.1   Query Using EXISTS

Get supplier names for suppliers who supply part P2 (same as Examples 5.2.1 and 5.2.3).

```
SELECT  SNAME
FROM    S
WHERE   EXISTS
        ( SELECT *
          FROM   SP
          WHERE  S# = S.S#
          AND    P# = 'P2' ) ;
```

Explanation: EXISTS here represents the *existential quantifier*, a notion borrowed from formal logic. Let the symbol "x" designate some arbitrary variable. In logic, then, the *existentially quantified predicate*

EXISTS x ( predicate-involving-x )

evaluates to *true* if and only if "predicate-involving-x" is *true* for some value of the variable x. For example, suppose the variable x stands for any integer in the range 1 to 10. Then the predicate

EXISTS x ( x < 5 )

evaluates to *true*. By contrast, the predicate

EXISTS x ( x < 0 )

evaluates to *false*.

In SQL, an existentially quantified predicate is represented by an expression of the form "EXISTS (SELECT * FROM ...)". Such an expression evaluates to *true* if and only if the result of evaluating the subquery represented by the "SELECT * FROM ..." is not empty—in other words, if and only if there exists a record in the FROM table of the subquery satisfying the WHERE condition of that subquery. (In practice, that subquery will always be of the correlated variety.)

To see how this works out in the example at hand, consider each SNAME value in turn and see whether it causes the existence test to evaluate to *true*. Suppose the first SNAME value is 'Smith' (so that the corresponding S# value is S1). Is the set of SP records having S# equal to S1 and P# equal to P2 empty? If the answer is no, then there exists an SP record with S# equal to S1 and P# equal to P2, and so 'Smith' should be one of the values retrieved. Similarly for each of the other SNAME values.

Although this first example merely shows another way of formulating a query for a problem that we already know how to handle in SQL (using either join or IN), in general EXISTS is one of the most important features of the entire SQL language. In fact, any query that can be expressed using IN can alternatively be formulated using EXISTS; however, the converse is not true (see Example 5.3.3 below, for instance).

### 5.3.2   Query Using NOT EXISTS

Get supplier names for suppliers who do not supply part P2 (inverse of Example 5.3.1).

```
SELECT  SNAME
FROM    S
WHERE   NOT EXISTS
        ( SELECT *
          FROM    SP
          WHERE   S# = S.S#
          AND     P# = 'P2' ) ;
```

Result:

```
SNAME
-----
Adams
```

The query may be paraphrased: "Select supplier names for suppliers such that there does not exist a shipment relating them to part P2." Notice how easy it is to convert the solution to the previous problem (Example 5.3.1) into this solution.

Incidentally, the parenthesized subquery in an EXISTS expression does not necessarily have to involve the "SELECT *" form of SELECT; it may, for example, be of the form "SELECT field-name FROM ...". In practice, however, it almost always will be of the "SELECT *" form, as our examples have already suggested.

### 5.3.3 Query Using NOT EXISTS

Get supplier names for suppliers who supply all parts.

There are two quantifiers commonly encountered in logic, EXISTS and *FOR-ALL*. FORALL is the *universal* quantifier. In logic, the universally quantified predicate

FORALL x ( predicate-involving-x )

evaluates to *true* if and only if "predicate-involving-x" is *true* for all values of the variable x. For example, if (again) the variable x stands for any integer in the range 1 to 10, then the predicate

FORALL x ( x < 100 )

evaluates to *true*, whereas the predicate

FORALL x ( x < 5 )

evaluates to *false*.

FORALL is fundamentally what is needed to express the query at hand; what we would like to say is something like "Select supplier names where, FORALL parts, there EXISTS an SP record saying that the supplier supplies the part." Unfortunately SQL does not directly support FORALL. However, any predicate involving FORALL can always be converted into an equivalent predicate involving EXISTS instead, by virtue of the following identity:

FORALL x ( p ) ≡ NOT ( EXISTS x ( NOT ( p ) ) )

Here "p" is any predicate involving the variable x. For example, suppose once again that x stands for any integer in the range 1 to 10. Then the predicate

FORALL x ( x < 100 )

(which of course evaluates to *true*) is equivalent to the predicate

NOT ( EXISTS x ( NOT ( x < 100 ) ) )

("there does not exist an x such that it is not the case that x is less than 100"—
i.e., "there is no x such that x $>=$ 100"). Likewise, the predicate

FORALL x ( x $<$ 5 )

(which is *false*) is equivalent to the predicate

NOT ( EXISTS x ( NOT ( x $<$ 5 ) ) )

("there does not exist an x such that it is not the case that x is less than 5"—
i.e., "there is no x such that x $>=$ 5").

As another example, suppose the variables x and y represent real numbers.
Then the predicate

FORALL x ( EXISTS y ( y $>$ x ) )

(which is *true*) is equivalent to

NOT ( EXISTS x ( NOT ( EXISTS y ( y $>$ x ) ) ) )

("there is no real number x such that there is no real number y such that y is
greater than x").*

Turning now to the problem at hand, we can convert the expression "Suppliers where FORALL parts there EXISTS an SP record saying that the supplier
supplies the part" into the equivalent expression "Suppliers where NOT EXISTS
a part such that NOT EXISTS an SP record saying that the supplier supplies the
part." Hence the SQL formulation is:

```
SELECT SNAME
FROM   S
WHERE  NOT EXISTS
     ( SELECT *
       FROM   P
       WHERE  NOT EXISTS
            ( SELECT *
              FROM   SP
              WHERE  S# = S.S#
              AND    P# = P.P# ) ) ;
```

---

*Incidentally, this example illustrates the important point that the order of quantifiers
matters in expressions involving both types. The expression FORALL x (EXISTS y (y $>$
x)) is *true*. However, the expression EXISTS y (FORALL x (y $>$ x)) ("there is a real
number y such that, for all real numbers x, y is greater than x"—i.e., "there exists a
number greater than all other numbers"), which is obtained from the first expression by
simply inverting the order of the quantifiers, is *false*.

Result:

```
SNAME
-----
Smith
```

The query may be paraphrased: "Select supplier names for suppliers such that there does not exist a part that they do not supply." In general, the easiest way to tackle complicated queries such as this one is probably to write them in a "pseudoSQL" form with FORALL quantifiers first, and then convert them, more or less mechanically, into real SQL involving NOT EXISTS instead.

### 5.3.4 Query Using NOT EXISTS

Get supplier numbers for suppliers who supply at least all those parts supplied by supplier S2.

One way to tackle this (complex) problem is to break it down into a set of simpler queries and deal with them one at a time. Thus we can first discover the set of part numbers for parts supplied by supplier S2:

```
SELECT  P#
FROM    SP
WHERE   S# = 'S2' ;
```

Result:

```
P#
--
P1
P2
```

Using CREATE TABLE and INSERT (to be discussed in Chapter 6), it is possible to save this result in a table in the database, say table TEMP. Then we can go on to discover the set of supplier numbers for suppliers who supply all parts listed in TEMP (very much as in Example 5.3.3):

```
SELECT DISTINCT S#
FROM    SP SPX
WHERE   NOT EXISTS
      ( SELECT *
        FROM    TEMP
        WHERE   NOT EXISTS
            ( SELECT *
              FROM    SP SPY
              WHERE   SPY.S# = SPX.S#
              AND     SPY.P# = TEMP.P# ) ) ;
```

Result:

```
S#
--
S1
S2
```

(Note, however, that this query differs from that of Example 5.3.3 in that it is necessary to use at least one alias, since we are extracting S# values from table SP—instead of SNAME values from table S—and so need to be able to make two simultaneous but distinct references to table SP.)

Table TEMP can now be dropped.

It is often a good idea to handle complex queries in this step-at-a-time manner, for ease of understanding. However, it is also possible to express the entire query as a single SELECT, eliminating the need for TEMP entirely:

```
SELECT DISTINCT S#
FROM     SP SPX
WHERE    NOT EXISTS
       ( SELECT *
         FROM    SP SPY
         WHERE   S# = 'S2'
         AND     NOT EXISTS
               ( SELECT *
                 FROM    SP SPZ
                 WHERE   SPZ.S# = SPX.S#
                 AND     SPZ.P# = SPY.P# ) ) ;
```

### 5.3.5   Query Using Implication

Get supplier numbers for suppliers who supply at least all those parts supplied by supplier S2 (same as previous example).

This example illustrates yet another very useful concept, that of *logical implication*. The original problem can be rephrased as follows: "Get supplier numbers for suppliers (Sx say) such that, FORALL parts Py, *IF* supplier S2 supplies part Py, *THEN* supplier Sx supplies part Py." The expression

IF p THEN q

(where p and q are predicates) is a *logical implication predicate*. It is defined to be equivalent to the predicate

NOT ( p ) OR q

In other words, the implication "IF p THEN q" (also read as "p IMPLIES q") is *false* if and only if q is *false* and p is *true*, as the truth table below indicates:

| p | q | IF p THEN q |
|---|---|---|
| T | T | T |
| T | F | F |
| F | T | T |
| F | F | T |

Many English language problem statements are very naturally expressed in terms of logical implication (see the exercises at the end of this chapter for several examples). SQL does not support implication directly; but the foregoing definition shows how any predicate involving implication can be converted into another that does not. For example, let p be the predicate "Supplier S2 supplies part Py," and let q be the predicate "Supplier Sx supplies part Py." Then the predicate

IF p THEN q

is equivalent to the predicate

NOT ( supplier S2 supplies part Py )
OR   ( supplier Sx supplies part Py ) ;

or, in SQL terms,

```
NOT EXISTS
   ( SELECT *
     FROM    SP SPY
     WHERE   SPY.S# = 'S2' )
OR  EXISTS
   ( SELECT *
     FROM    SP SPZ
     WHERE   SPZ.S# = Sx
     AND     SPZ.P# = SPY.P# )
```

Hence the predicate

FORALL Py ( IF p THEN q ) ,

which is equivalent to

NOT EXISTS Py ( NOT ( IF p THEN q ) ) ,

that is, to

NOT EXISTS Py ( NOT ( NOT ( p ) OR q ) ) ,

becomes

NOT EXISTS Py ( p AND NOT ( q ) ) ,

or, in SQL terms,

```
NOT EXISTS
   ( SELECT *
     FROM    SP SPY
     WHERE   SPY.S# = 'S2'
     AND     NOT EXISTS
          ( SELECT *
            FROM    SP SPZ
            WHERE   SPZ.S# = Sx
            AND     SPZ.P# = SPY.P# ) )
```

Hence the overall query becomes

```
SELECT DISTINCT S#
FROM    SP SPX
WHERE   NOT EXISTS
     ( SELECT *
       FROM    SP SPY
               WHERE   SPY.S# = 'S2'
               AND     NOT EXISTS
                    ( SELECT *
                      FROM    SP SPZ
                      WHERE   SPZ.S# = SPX.S#
                      AND     SPZ.P# = SPY.P# ) ) ;
```

which is as shown before, under Example 5.3.4. Thus the notion of implication provides the basis for a systematic approach to a certain class of (rather complicated) queries and their conversion into an equivalent SQL form. Exercises 5.12 – 5.18 at the end of the chapter provide practice in that approach.


## 5.4  BUILTIN FUNCTIONS

Although quite powerful in many ways, the SELECT statement as so far described is still inadequate for many practical problems. For example, even a query as simple as "How many suppliers are there?" cannot be expressed using only the constructs introduced up till now. SQL therefore provides a number of special *builtin functions* to enhance its basic retrieval power. The functions currently available are COUNT, SUM, AVG, MAX, and MIN.* Apart from the special case of "COUNT(*)" (see below), each of these functions operates on the collection of values in one column of some table—possibly a *derived* table, i.e., a table constructed in some way from the given base tables —and produces a single value (defined as follows) as its result:

COUNT     number of values in the column
SUM     sum of the values in the column
AVG     average of the values in the column
MAX     largest value in the column
MIN     smallest value in the column

For SUM and AVG the column concerned must contain numeric values. In general, the argument of the function may optionally be preceded by the keyword DISTINCT, to indicate that redundant duplicate values are to be eliminated before the function is applied. For MAX and MIN, however, DISTINCT is irrelevant and should be omitted. For COUNT, DISTINCT *must* be specified; the special function COUNT(*)—DISTINCT not allowed—is provided to count all rows in a table without any duplicate elimination. If DISTINCT is specified, then the argument must consist of just a column name (such as WEIGHT); if DISTINCT is not specified, the argument may consist of an arithmetic expression (such as WEIGHT * 454).

Any null values in the argument column are always eliminated before the function is applied, regardless of whether DISTINCT is specified, *except* for the case of COUNT(*), where nulls are handled just like nonnull values. If the argument happens to be an empty set, COUNT returns a value of zero; the other functions all return null.

### 5.4.1   Function in the SELECT Clause

Get the total number of suppliers.

```
SELECT COUNT(*)
FROM   S ;
```

Result:

```
—
5
```

---

*EXISTS is also considered as a builtin function, but it differs from the functions discussed in the present section in that it returns a truth value, not a numeric or string value—i.e., it is not a *computational* function.

### 5.4.2   Function in the SELECT Clause, with DISTINCT

Get the total number of suppliers currently supplying parts.

```
SELECT  COUNT (DISTINCT S#)
FROM    SP ;
```

Result:

```
—
4
```

### 5.4.3   Function in the SELECT Clause, with a Predicate

Get the number of shipments for part P2.

```
SELECT  COUNT(*)
FROM    SP
WHERE   P# = 'P2' ;
```

Result:

```
—
4
```

### 5.4.4   Function in the SELECT Clause, with a Predicate

Get the total quantity of part P2 supplied.

```
SELECT  SUM (QTY)
FROM    SP
WHERE   P# = 'P2' ;
```

Result:

```
—+——
1000
```

### 5.4.5   Function in a Subquery

Get supplier numbers for suppliers with status value less than the current maximum status value in the S table.

```
SELECT S#
FROM    S
WHERE   STATUS <
        ( SELECT MAX(STATUS)
          FROM    S ) ;
```

Result:

```
S#
--
S1
S2
S4
```

## 5.4.6    Function in Correlated Subquery

Get supplier number, status, and city for all suppliers whose status is greater than or equal to the average for their particular city.

```
SELECT S#, STATUS, CITY
FROM   S SX
WHERE  STATUS >=
       ( SELECT AVG(STATUS)
         FROM   S SY
         WHERE  SY.CITY = SX.CITY ) ;
```

Result:

```
S#    STATUS    CITY
--    ------    ------
S1    20        London
S3    30        Paris
S4    20        London
S5    30        Athens
```

It is not possible to include the average status for each city in this result (why not?).

## 5.4.7    Use of GROUP BY

Example 5.4.4 showed how it is possible to compute the total quantity supplied for some specific part. Suppose, by contrast, that it is desired to compute the total quantity supplied for *each* part: i.e., for each part supplied, get the part number and the total shipment quantity for that part.

```
SELECT P#, SUM(QTY)
FROM   SP
GROUP  BY P# ;
```

Result:

```
P#
--   ----
P1    600
P2   1000
P3    400
P4    500
P5    500
P6    100
```

Explanation: The GROUP BY operator conceptually rearranges the table represented by the FROM clause into partitions or *groups*, such that within any one group all rows have the same value for the GROUP BY field. (Of course, this does not mean that the table is physically rearranged in the database.) In the example, table SP is grouped so that one group contains all the rows for part P1, another contains all the rows for part P2, and so on. The SELECT clause is then applied to each group of the partitioned table (rather than to each row of the original table). Each expression in the SELECT clause must be *single-valued per group*: i.e., it can be the GROUP BY field itself (or an arithmetic expression involving that field), or a constant, or a function such as SUM that operates on all values of a given field within a group and reduces those values to a single value.

A table can be grouped by any combination of its fields. See Section 5.6 for an illustration of grouping over more than one field. Note that GROUP BY does not imply ORDER BY; to guarantee that the result in this example appears in P# order, the clause ORDER BY P# must be specified (after the GROUP BY clause). If the grouping field contains any null values, then each of those nulls will give rise to a separate group.

### 5.4.8   Use of WHERE with GROUP BY

For each part supplied, get the part number and the total quantity supplied of that part, excluding shipments from supplier S1.

```
SELECT  P#, SUM(QTY)
FROM    SP
WHERE   S# ¬= 'S1'
GROUP   BY P# ;
```

Result:

```
P#
--   ---
P1   300
P2   800
P4   300
P5   400
```

Rows that do not satisfy the WHERE clause are eliminated before any grouping is done.

### 5.4.9  Use of HAVING

Get part numbers for all parts supplied by more than one supplier (same as Example 5.2.5).

```
SELECT  P#
FROM    SP
GROUP   BY P#
HAVING COUNT(*) > 1 ;
```

Result:

```
P#
--
P1
P2
P4
P5
```

HAVING is to groups what WHERE is to rows. (If HAVING is specified, GROUP BY should also have been specified.) In other words, HAVING is used to eliminate groups just as WHERE is used to eliminate rows. Expressions in a HAVING clause must be single-valued per group.

We have already shown in Example 5.2.5 that this query can be formulated without GROUP BY (and without HAVING), using a correlated subquery. However, Example 5.2.5 is really based on a somewhat different perception of the logic involved in answering the question. It is also possible to formulate a query using essentially the *same* logic as in the GROUP BY/HAVING version, but without making explicit use of GROUP BY and HAVING at all:

```
SELECT  DISTINCT P#
FROM    SP SPX
WHERE   1 <
        ( SELECT  COUNT(*)
          FROM    SP SPY
          WHERE   SPY.P# = SPX.P# ) ;
```

The following version (using table P in place of SPX) may perhaps be clearer:

```
SELECT  P#
FROM    P
WHERE   1 <
        ( SELECT  COUNT (S#)
          FROM    SP
          WHERE   P# = P.P# ) ;
```

Yet another formulation uses EXISTS, as follows:

```
SELECT  P#
FROM    P
WHERE   EXISTS
      ( SELECT *
        FROM    SP SPX
        WHERE   SPX.P# = P.P#
        AND     EXISTS
              ( SELECT *
                FROM    SP SPY
                WHERE   SPY.P# = P.P#
                AND     SPY.S# ¬= SPX.S# ) ) ;
```

All of these alternative versions are in some respects preferable to the GROUP-BY/HAVING version, in that they are at least logically cleaner, and they specifically do not require those additional language constructs. It is certainly not clear from the original English statement of the problem—"Get part numbers for all parts supplied by more than one supplier"—that grouping as such is what is needed to answer the question (and indeed it is not needed). Nor is it immediately obvious that a HAVING condition is required rather than a WHERE condition. The GROUP-BY/HAVING version begins to look more like a procedural prescription for *solving* the problem, instead of just a straightforward logical statement of what the problem *is*. On the other hand, there is no denying that the GROUP-BY/HAVING version is the most succinct. Then again, there are some problems of this same general nature for which GROUP BY and HAVING are simply inadequate, so that one of the alternative approaches *must* be used; see Exercise 5.24 for an example of such a problem.

Finally, GROUP BY suffers from the severe restriction that it works only to one level; it is not possible to break a table into groups, then to break each of those groups into lower-level groups, and so on, and then to apply some builtin function, say SUM or AVG, at each level of grouping.*

## 5.5   UNION

The union of two sets is the set of all elements belonging to either or both of the original sets. Since a relation is a set (a set of rows), it is possible to construct the union of two relations; the result will be a set consisting of all rows appearing in either or both of the original relations. However, if that result is itself to be another relation and not just a heterogeneous mixture of rows, the two original

---

*This effect ("groups within groups," etc.) can be achieved through QMF, however. See Chapter 15.

relations must be *union-compatible*; loosely speaking, the rows in the two relations must be the same "shape." As far as SQL is concerned, two tables are union-compatible (and the UNION operator may be applied to them) if and only if:

(a)   they have the same number of columns, m say;

(b)   for all $i$ ($i$ = 1,2,...,$m$), the $i$th column of the first table and the $i$th column of the second table must have *exactly* the same data type:

- If the data type is DECIMAL($p,q$), then $p$ must be the same for both columns and $q$ must be the same for both columns.
- If the data type is CHAR($n$), then $n$ must be the same for both columns.
- If the data type is VARCHAR($n$), then $n$ must be the same for both columns.
- If NOT NULL applies to either column, then it must apply to both.

### 5.5.1   Query Involving UNION

Get part numbers for parts that either weigh more than 16 pounds or are supplied by supplier S2 (or both).

```
SELECT P#
FROM   P
WHERE  WEIGHT > 16

UNION

SELECT P#
FROM   SP
WHERE  S# = 'S2' ;
```

Result:

```
--
P1
P2
P3
P6
```

Several points arise from this simple example.

- Redundant duplicates are always eliminated from the result of a UNION. Thus, in the example, part P2 is selected by both of the two constituent SELECTs, but it appears only once in the final result.
- Any number of SELECTs can be UNIONed together. We might extend the example to include part numbers for red parts by inserting

```
UNION

SELECT P#
FROM   P
WHERE  COLOR = 'Red'
```

before the final semicolon (though the same effect could also be achieved by adding the clause OR COLOR = 'Red' to the first of the original SELECTs).

- Any ORDER BY clause in the query must appear as part of the final SELECT only, and must identify ordering columns by their ordinal position (i.e., by number).

- The ability to include constants in a SELECT clause is frequently useful in connection with UNION. For example, to indicate which of the two WHERE conditions each individual part in the result happens to satisfy:

```
SELECT P#, 'weight > 16 lb'
FROM   P
WHERE  WEIGHT > 16

UNION

SELECT P#, 'supplied by S2'
FROM   SP
WHERE  S# = 'S2'

ORDER  BY 2, 1 ;
```

Result:

```
--  --------------
P1  supplied by S2
P2  supplied by S2
P2  weight > 16 lb
P3  weight > 16 lb
P6  weight > 16 lb
```

When a string constant appears as an item to be SELECTed, it is considered to be of type VARCHAR, with length as indicated by the number of characters in the constant *and with nulls allowed.*

- The reader may be wondering whether SQL also supports any analogs of the INTERSECTION and DIFFERENCE operators (since union, intersection, and difference are commonly treated together in discussions of set theory). The intersection of two sets is the set of all elements belonging to both of the original sets; the difference of two sets is the set of all elements belonging to the first of the original sets and not to the second. SQL does not support these two operators directly, but each of them can be simulated by means of the EXISTS function. For example, let A and B each be a table consisting of a single column, namely a column of supplier numbers, and let A represent "suppliers in London" and let B represent "suppliers who supply part P1." Then:

```
SELECT  S#
FROM    A
WHERE   EXISTS
        ( SELECT  S#
          FROM    B
          WHERE   B.S# = A.S# ) ;
```

represents the intersection of A and B—i.e., suppliers in London who supply part P1—and

```
SELECT  S#
FROM    A
WHERE   NOT EXISTS
        ( SELECT  S#
          FROM    B
          WHERE   B.S# = A.S# ) ;
```

represents the difference between A and B (in that order)—i.e., suppliers in London who do not supply part P1. Exercise: What is the difference between B and A (in that order)?

## 5.6  CONCLUSION

We have now covered all of the features of the SQL SELECT statement that we intend to illustrate in this book. To conclude the chapter, we present a very contrived example that shows how many (by no means all) of those features can be used together in a single query. We also give a conceptual algorithm for the evaluation of SQL queries in general.

### 5.6.1  A Comprehensive Example

For all red and blue parts such that the total quantity supplied is greater than 350 (excluding from the total all shipments for which the quantity is less than or equal to 200), get the part number, the weight in grams, the color, and the maximum quantity supplied of that part; and order the result by descending part number within ascending values of that maximum quantity.

```
SELECT P.P#, 'Weight in grams =', P.WEIGHT * 454, P.COLOR,
            'Max shipped quantity =', MAX (SP.QTY)
FROM   P, SP
WHERE  P.P# = SP.P#
AND    P.COLOR IN ('Red','Blue')
AND    SP.QTY > 200
GROUP  BY P.P#, P.WEIGHT, P.COLOR
HAVING SUM (QTY) > 350
ORDER  BY 6, P.P# DESC ;
```

Result:

```
P#                                COLOR
--  -------------------  ----  -----  ------------------------  ---
P1  Weight in grams =    5448  Red    Max shipped quantity =    300
P5  Weight in grams =    5448  Blue   Max shipped quantity =    400
P3  Weight in grams =    7718  Blue   Max shipped quantity =    400
```

Explanation: The clauses of a SELECT statement are applied in the order suggested by that in which they are written—with the exception of the SELECT clause itself, which is applied between the HAVING clause (if any) and the ORDER BY clause (if any). In the example, therefore, we can imagine the result being constructed as follows.

1. *FROM.* The FROM clause is evaluated to yield a new table that is the Cartesian product of tables P and SP.

2. *WHERE.* The result of Step 1 is reduced by the elimination of all rows that do not satisfy the WHERE clause. In the example, rows not satisfying the predicate

```
P.P# = SP.P# AND P.COLOR IN ('Red','Blue') AND SP.QTY > 200
```

are eliminated.

3. *GROUP BY.* The result of Step 2 is grouped by values of the field(s) named in the GROUP BY clause. In the example, those fields are P.P#, P.WEIGHT, and P.COLOR. (*Note:* In theory P.P# alone would be sufficient as the grouping field, since P.WEIGHT and P.COLOR are themselves single-valued per part number. However, DB2 is not aware of this latter fact, and will raise an error condition if P.WEIGHT and P.COLOR are omitted from the GROUP BY clause, because they are *included* in the SELECT clause. The basic problem here is that DB2 does not support primary keys. See Appendix A.)

4. *HAVING.* Groups not satisfying the condition

```
SUM (QTY) > 350
```

are eliminated from the result of Step 3.

5. *SELECT.* Each group in the result of Step 4 generates a single result row, as follows. First, the part number, weight, color, and maximum quantity are extracted from the group. Second, the weight is converted to grams. Third, the two string constants 'Weight in grams =' and 'Max shipped quantity =' are inserted at the appropriate points in the row.

6. *ORDER BY.* The result of Step 5 is ordered in accordance with the specifi cations of the ORDER BY clause to yield the final result.

It is of course true that the query shown above is quite complex—but think how much work it is doing. A conventional program to do the same job in a language such as COBOL could easily be nine pages long, instead of just nine lines as above, and the work involved in getting that program operational would be significantly greater than that needed to construct the SQL version shown. In practice, of course, most queries will be much simpler than this one anyway.

## EXERCISES

As in the previous chapter, all of the following exercises are based on the suppliers-parts-projects database (see the exercises in Chapter 3). In each one, you are asked to write a SELECT statement for the indicated query (except for numbers 15–18 and 26, q.v.). For convenience we repeat the structure of the database below:

```
S     ( S#, SNAME, STATUS, CITY )
P     ( P#, PNAME, COLOR, WEIGHT, CITY )
J     ( J#, JNAME, CITY )
SPJ   ( S#, P#, J#, QTY )
```

Within each section, the exercises are arranged in approximate order of increasing difficulty. You should try at least some of the easy ones in each group. Numbers 12–18 are quite difficult.

## Subqueries

**5.1** Get project names for projects supplied by supplier S1.

**5.2** Get colors of parts supplied by supplier S1.

**5.3** Get part numbers for parts supplied to any project in London.

**5.4** Get project numbers for projects using at least one part available from supplier S1.

**5.5** Get supplier numbers for suppliers supplying at least one part supplied by at least one supplier who supplies at least one red part.

**5.6** Get supplier numbers for suppliers with a status lower than that of supplier S1.

**5.7** Get supplier numbers for suppliers supplying some project with part P1 in a quantity greater than the average shipment quantity of part P1 for that project. (*Note:* This exercise requires the AVG builtin function.)

## EXISTS

**5.8** Repeat Exercise 5.3 to use EXISTS in your solution.

**5.9** Repeat Exercise 5.4 to use EXISTS in your solution.

**5.10** Get project numbers for projects not supplied with any red part by any London supplier.

**5.11** Get project numbers for projects supplied entirely by supplier S1.

**5.12** Get part numbers for parts supplied to all projects in London.

**5.13** Get supplier numbers for suppliers who supply the same part to all projects.

**5.14** Get project numbers for projects supplied with at least all parts available from supplier S1.

For the next four exercises (5.15-5.18), convert the SQL SELECT statement shown back into an English equivalent.

```
5.15 SELECT DISTINCT J#
     FROM    SPJ SPJX
     WHERE   NOT EXISTS
           ( SELECT *
             FROM    SPJ SPJY
             WHERE   SPJY.J# = SPJX.J#
             AND     NOT EXISTS
                   ( SELECT *
                     FROM    SPJ SPJZ
                     WHERE   SPJZ.P# = SPJY.P#
                     AND     SPJZ.S# = 'S1' ) ) ;
```

```
5.16 SELECT DISTINCT J#
     FROM    SPJ SPJX
     WHERE   NOT EXISTS
           ( SELECT *
             FROM    SPJ SPJY
             WHERE   EXISTS
                   ( SELECT *
                     FROM    SPJ SPJA
                     WHERE   SPJA.S# = 'S1'
                     AND     SPJA.P# = SPJY.P# )
             AND     NOT EXISTS
                   ( SELECT *
                     FROM    SPJ SPJB
                     WHERE   SPJB.S# = 'S1'
                     AND     SPJB.P# = SPJY.P#
                     AND     SPJB.J# = SPJX.J# ) ) ;
```

**5.17**  SELECT  DISTINCT J#

```
5.17  SELECT  DISTINCT  J#
      FROM    SPJ SPJX
      WHERE   NOT EXISTS
            ( SELECT *
              FROM    SPJ SPJY
              WHERE   EXISTS
                    ( SELECT *
                      FROM    SPJ SPJA
                      WHERE   SPJA.P# = SPJY.P#
                      AND     SPJA.J# = SPJX.J# )
              AND     NOT EXISTS
                    ( SELECT *
                      FROM    SPJ SPJB
                      WHERE   SPJB.S# = 'S1'
                      AND     SPJB.P# = SPJY.P#
                      AND     SPJB.J# = SPJX.J# ) ) ;

5.18  SELECT  DISTINCT  J#
      FROM    SPJ SPJX
      WHERE   NOT EXISTS
            ( SELECT *
              FROM    SPJ SPJY
              WHERE   EXISTS
                    ( SELECT *
                      FROM    SPJ SPJA
                      WHERE   SPJA.S# = SPJY.S#
                      AND     SPJA.P# IN
                            ( SELECT P#
                              FROM    P
                              WHERE   COLOR = 'Red' )
                      AND     NOT EXISTS
                            ( SELECT *
                              FROM    SPJ SPJB
                              WHERE   SPJB.S# = SPJY.S#
                              AND     SPJB.J# = SPJX.J# ) ) ) ;
```

## Builtin functions

**5.19** Get the total number of projects supplied by supplier S1.

**5.20** Get the total quantity of part P1 supplied by supplier S1.

**5.21** For each part being supplied to a project, get the part number, the project number, and the corresponding total quantity.

**5.22** Get project numbers for projects whose city is first in the alphabetic list of such cities.

**5.23** Get project numbers for projects supplied with part P1 in an average quantity greater than the greatest quantity in which any part is supplied to project J1.

## Union

**5.24** Construct an ordered list of all cities in which at least one supplier, part, or project is located.

**5.25** Show the result of the following SELECT:

```
SELECT  P.COLOR
FROM    P
UNION
SELECT  P.COLOR
FROM    P ;
```

## ANSWERS TO SELECTED EXERCISES

The following answers are not necessarily the only ones possible.

```
5.1   SELECT  JNAME
      FROM    J
      WHERE   J# IN
              ( SELECT  J#
                FROM    SPJ
                WHERE   S# = 'S1' ) ;


5.2   SELECT  DISTINCT COLOR
      FROM    P
      WHERE   P# IN
              ( SELECT  P#
                FROM    SPJ
                WHERE   S# = 'S1' ) ;


5.3   SELECT  DISTINCT P#
      FROM    SPJ
      WHERE   J# IN
              ( SELECT  J#
                FROM    J
                WHERE   CITY = 'London' ) ;
```

**5.4**  SELECT  DISTINCT  J#
     FROM     SPJ
     WHERE   P# IN
              ( SELECT P#
                FROM     SPJ
                WHERE   S# = 'S1' ) ;

**5.5**  SELECT  DISTINCT  S#
     FROM     SPJ
     WHERE   P# IN
              ( SELECT P#
                FROM     SPJ
                WHERE   S# IN
                        ( SELECT S#
                          FROM     SPJ
                          WHERE   P# IN
                                  ( SELECT P#
                                    FROM     P
                                    WHERE   COLOR = 'Red' ) ) ) ;

**5.6**  SELECT  S#
     FROM     S
     WHERE   STATUS <
              ( SELECT STATUS
                FROM     S
                WHERE   S# = 'S1' ) ;

**5.7**  SELECT  DISTINCT  S#
     FROM     SPJ SPJX
     WHERE   P# = 'P1'
     AND      QTY >
              ( SELECT AVG(QTY)
                FROM     SPJ SPJY
                WHERE   P# = 'P1'
                AND      SPJY.J# = SPJX.J# ) ;

**5.8**  SELECT  DISTINCT  P#
     FROM     SPJ
     WHERE   EXISTS
              ( SELECT *
                FROM     J
                WHERE   J# = SPJ.J#
                AND      CITY = 'London' ) ;

```
5.9   SELECT DISTINCT SPJX.J#
      FROM    SPJ SPJX
      WHERE   EXISTS
            ( SELECT *
              FROM    SPJ SPJY
              WHERE   SPJY.P# = SPJX.P#
              AND     SPJY.S# = 'S1' ) ;


5.10  SELECT J#
      FROM    J
      WHERE   NOT EXISTS
            ( SELECT *
              FROM    SPJ
              WHERE   J# = J.J#
              AND     P# IN
                    ( SELECT P#
                      FROM    P
                      WHERE   COLOR = 'Red' )
              AND     S# IN
                    ( SELECT S#
                      FROM    S
                      WHERE   CITY = 'London' ) ) ;


5.11  SELECT DISTINCT J#
      FROM    SPJ SPJX
      WHERE   NOT EXISTS
            ( SELECT *
              FROM    SPJ SPJY
              WHERE   SPJY.J# = SPJX.J#
              AND     SPJY.S# ¬= 'S1' ) ;


5.12  SELECT DISTINCT P#
      FROM    SPJ SPJX
      WHERE   NOT EXISTS
            ( SELECT *
              FROM    J
              WHERE   CITY = 'London'
              AND     NOT EXISTS
                    ( SELECT *
                      FROM    SPJ SPJY
                      WHERE   SPJY.P# = SPJX.P#
                      AND     SPJY.J# = J.J# ) ) ;
```

**5.13** SELECT DISTINCT S#
    FROM    SPJ SPJX
    WHERE  EXISTS
        ( SELECT P#
        FROM    P
        WHERE  NOT EXISTS
            ( SELECT J#
            FROM    J
            WHERE  NOT EXISTS
                ( SELECT *
                FROM    SPJ SPJZ
                WHERE  SPJZ.S# = SPJX.S#
                AND    SPJZ.P# = P.P#
                AND    SPJZ.J# = J.J# ) ) ) ;

This rather complex SELECT statement may be paraphrased: "Get all suppliers (SPJX.S#) such that there exists a part (P.P#) such that there does not exist any project (J.J#) such that the supplier does not supply the part to the project"—in other words, suppliers such that there exists some part that they supply to all projects. Note the use of "SELECT P# FROM ..." and "SELECT J# FROM ..." in two of the EXISTS references; "SELECT *" would not be incorrect, but "SELECT P#" (for instance) seems a a fraction closer to the intuitive formulation—there must exist a *part* (identified by a part number), not just a row in the parts table.

**5.14** SELECT DISTINCT J#
    FROM    SPJ SPJX
    WHERE  NOT EXISTS
        ( SELECT P#
        FROM    SPJ SPJY
        WHERE  SPJY.S# = 'S1'
        AND    NOT EXISTS
            ( SELECT *
            FROM    SPJ SPJZ
            WHERE  SPJZ.P# = SPJY.P#
            AND    SPJZ.J# = SPJX.J# ) ) ;

**5.15** Get project numbers for projects that use only parts that are available from supplier S1.

**5.16** Get project numbers for projects that are supplied by supplier S1 with some of every part that supplier S1 supplies.

**5.17** Get project numbers for projects such that at least some of every part they use is supplied to them by supplier S1.

**5.18** Get project numbers for projects that are supplied by every supplier who supplies some red part.

```
5.19 SELECT COUNT (DISTINCT J#)
     FROM    SPJ
     WHERE   S# = 'S1' ;

5.20 SELECT SUM (QTY)
     FROM    SPJ
     WHERE   P# = 'P1'
     AND     S# = 'S1' ;

5.21 SELECT P#, J#, SUM(QTY)
     FROM    SPJ
     GROUP   BY P#, J# ;

5.22 SELECT J#
     FROM    J
     WHERE   CITY =
          ( SELECT MIN(CITY)
            FROM    J ) ;

5.23 SELECT J#
     FROM    SPJ
     WHERE   P# = 'P1'
     GROUP   BY J#
     HAVING  AVG(QTY) >
          ( SELECT MAX(QTY)
            FROM    SPJ
            WHERE   J# = 'J1' ) ;

5.24 SELECT CITY FROM S
     UNION
     SELECT CITY FROM P
     UNION
     SELECT CITY FROM J
     ORDER   BY 1 ;

5.25 -----
     Red
     Green
     Blue
```

# 6

# Data Manipulation III: Update Operations

## 6.1 INTRODUCTION

In the last two chapters we considered the SQL retrieval statement (SELECT) in considerable detail. Now we turn our attention to the update statements UPDATE, DELETE, and INSERT. *Note:* The term "update" unfortunately has two distinct meanings in DB2. It is used generically to refer to all three operations as a class, and also specifically to refer to the UPDATE operation *per se*. We will distinguish between the two meanings in this book by always using lower case when the generic meaning is intended and upper case when the specific meaning is intended.

Like the SELECT statement, the three update statements operate on both base tables and views. However, for reasons that are beyond the scope of this chapter, *not all views are updatable*. If the user attempts to perform an update operation on a nonupdatable view, DB2 will simply reject the operation (with some appropriate message to the user). For the purposes of the present chapter, therefore, let us assume that all tables to be updated are base tables, and defer the question of views (and of updating views, in particular) to Chapter 8.

The next three sections discuss the three update operations in detail. The syntax of those operations follows the same general pattern as that already shown for the SELECT operation; for convenience, an outline of that general syntax for the operation in question is given at the beginning of the relevant section.

## 6.2   UPDATE

The UPDATE statement has the general form

```
UPDATE table
SET    field = expression
     [, field = expression ] ...
[ WHERE  predicate ] ;
```

    All records in "table" that satisfy "predicate" are UPDATEd in accordance with the assignments ("field = expression") in the SET clause.

### 6.2.1   Single-Record UPDATE

Change the color of part P2 to yellow, increase its weight by 5, and set its city to "unknown" (NULL).

```
UPDATE P
SET    COLOR = 'Yellow',
       WEIGHT = WEIGHT + 5,
       CITY = NULL
WHERE  P# = 'P2' ;
```

    For each record to be UPDATEd (i.e., each record that satisfies the WHERE predicate, or all records if the WHERE clause is omitted), references in the SET clause to fields within that record stand for the values of those fields before any of the assignments in that SET clause have been executed.

### 6.2.2   Multiple-Record UPDATE

Double the status of all suppliers in London.

```
UPDATE S
SET    STATUS = 2 * STATUS
WHERE  CITY = 'London' ;
```

### 6.2.3   UPDATE with a Subquery

Set the shipment quantity to zero for all suppliers in London.

```
UPDATE SP
SET    QTY = 0
WHERE  'London' =
     ( SELECT CITY
       FROM   S
       WHERE  S.S# = SP.S# ) ;
```

### 6.2.4  Multiple-Table UPDATE

Change the supplier number for supplier S2 to S9.

```
UPDATE  S
SET     S# = 'S9'
WHERE   S# = 'S2' ;

UPDATE  SP
SET     S# = 'S9'
WHERE   S# = 'S2' ;
```

It is not possible to UPDATE more than one table in a single statement. To put this another way, the UPDATE clause must specify *exactly one table*. In the example, therefore, we have a problem of *integrity* (more specifically, a problem of *referential* integrity), as follows: The database becomes inconsistent after the first UPDATE—it now includes some shipments for which there is no corresponding supplier record—and it remains in that state until after the second UPDATE. (Reversing the order of the UPDATEs does not solve the problem, of course.) It is therefore important to ensure that *both* UPDATEs get executed, not just one. This question (of maintaining integrity when multiple updates are involved) is discussed at some length in Chapter 11; in addition, the problem of referential integrity specifically is described in detail in Appendix A, and an approach to handling it in DB2 is presented in Appendix B.

### 6.3  DELETE

The DELETE statement has the general form

```
DELETE
FROM    table
[ WHERE  predicate ] ;
```

All records in "table" that satisfy "predicate" are DELETEd.

### 6.3.1  Single-Record DELETE

Delete supplier S1.

```
DELETE
FROM    S
WHERE   S# = 'S1' ;
```

If table SP currently has any shipments for supplier S1, this DELETE will violate the consistency of the database (compare Example 6.2.4; as with UPDATE, there are no multiple-table DELETE operations). See Chapter 11 and Appendices A and B.

### 6.3.2   Multiple-Record DELETE

Delete all suppliers in Madrid.

```
DELETE
FROM    S
WHERE   CITY = 'Madrid' ;
```

### 6.3.3   Multiple-Record DELETE

Delete all shipments.

```
DELETE
FROM    SP ;
```

SP is still a known table ("DELETE all records" is not a DROP), but it is now empty.

### 6.3.4   DELETE with a Subquery

Delete all shipments for suppliers in London.

```
DELETE
FROM    SP
WHERE   'London' =
        ( SELECT CITY
          FROM    S
          WHERE   S.S# = SP.S# ) ;
```

### 6.4   INSERT

The INSERT statement has the general form

```
INSERT
INTO    table [ ( field [, field ] ... ) ]
VALUES ( constant [, constant ] ... ) ;
```

or

```
INSERT
INTO    table [ ( field [, field ] ... ) ]
subquery ;
```

In the first format, a row is INSERTed into "table" having the specified values for the specified fields (the *i*th constant in the list of constants corresponds to the *i*th field in the list of fields). In the second format, "subquery" is evaluated and a copy of the result (multiple rows, in general) is INSERTed into "table";

the *i*th column of that result corresponds to the *i*th field in the list of fields. In both cases, omitting the list of fields is equivalent to specifying a list of all fields in the table (see Example 6.4.2 below).

### 6.4.1 Single-Record INSERT

Add part P7 (city 'Athens', weight 2, name and color at present unknown) to table P.

```
INSERT
INTO    P ( P#, CITY, WEIGHT )
VALUES ( 'P7', 'Athens', 2 ) ;
```

A new part record is created with the specified part number, city, and weight, and with null values for name and color. (Of course, these last two fields must not have been defined as NOT NULL in the CREATE TABLE statement for table P.) The left-to-right order in which fields are named in the INSERT statement does not have to be the same as the left-to-right order in which they were specified in the CREATE (or ALTER) statement.

### 6.4.2 Single-Record INSERT, with Field Names Omitted

Add part P8 (name 'Sprocket', color 'Pink', weight 14, city 'Nice') to table P.

```
INSERT
INTO    P
VALUES ('P8', 'Sprocket', 'Pink', 14, 'Nice' ) ;
```

Omitting the list of fields is equivalent to specifying a list of all fields in the table, in the left-to-right order in which they were defined in the CREATE (or ALTER) statement. As with "SELECT *", this shorthand may be convenient for interactive SQL; however, it is potentially dangerous in embedded SQL (i.e., SQL within an application program), because the assumed list of fields may change if the program is rebound and the definition of the table has changed in the interim.

### 6.4.3 Single-Record INSERT

Insert a new shipment with supplier number S20, part number P20, and quantity 1000.

```
INSERT
INTO    SP ( S#, P#, QTY )
VALUES ('S20', 'P20', 1000 ) ;
```

Like UPDATE and DELETE, INSERT can cause referential integrity problems (in the absence of suitable controls—see Chapter 11 and Appendices A and B). In the case at hand, DB2 does not check that supplier S20 exists in table S or that part P20 exists in table P.

### 6.4.4  Multiple-Record INSERT

For each part supplied, get the part number and the total quantity supplied of that part, and save the result in the database (see Example 5.4.7).

```
CREATE TABLE TEMP
       ( P#      CHAR(6),
         TOTQTY  INTEGER ) ;

INSERT
INTO    TEMP ( P#, TOTQTY )
        SELECT P#, SUM(QTY)
        FROM   SP
        GROUP  BY P# ;
```

The SELECT is executed, just like an ordinary SELECT, but the result, instead of being returned to the user, is copied into table TEMP. Now the user can do anything he or she pleases with that copy—query it further, print it, even update it; none of those operations will have any effect whatsoever on the original data. Eventually, when it is no longer required, table TEMP can be dropped:

```
DROP TABLE TEMP ;
```

The foregoing example illustrates very nicely why the closure property of relational systems (discussed in the introduction to Section 4.2) is so important: The overall procedure works precisely because the result of a SELECT is another table. It would *not* work if the result was something other than a table.

It is not necessary for the target table to be initially empty for a multiple-record INSERT, incidentally, though for the foregoing example it is. If it is not, the new records are simply added to those already present.

One important use for INSERT … SELECT is in the construction of what is called an *outer join*. As explained in Chapter 4, the ordinary (natural) join of two tables does not include a result row for any row in either of the two original tables that has no matching row in the other. For example, the ordinary join of tables S and P over cities does not include any result row for supplier S5 or for part P3, because no parts are stored in Athens and no suppliers are located in Rome (see Example 4.3.1). In a sense, therefore, the ordinary join may be considered to *lose information* for such unmatched rows. Sometimes, however, it may be desirable to be able to preserve that information. Consider the following example.

### 6.4.5 Using INSERT ... SELECT to Construct an Outer Join

For each supplier, get the supplier number, name, status, and city, together with part numbers for all parts supplied by that supplier. If a given supplier supplies no parts at all, then show the information for that supplier in the result concatenated with a blank part number.

```
CREATE TABLE OJEX
      ( S#       CHAR(5),
        SNAME    CHAR(20),
        STATUS   SMALLINT,
        CITY     CHAR(15),
        P#       CHAR(6) ) ;

INSERT
INTO    OJEX
        SELECT S.*, SP.P#
        FROM   S, SP
        WHERE  S.S# = SP.S# ;

INSERT
INTO    OJEX
        SELECT S.*, 'bb'
        FROM   S
        WHERE  NOT EXISTS
               ( SELECT *
                 FROM   SP
                 WHERE  SP.S# = S.S# ) ;
```

Now table OJEX looks like this:

| OJEX | S# | SNAME | STATUS | CITY | P# |
|------|----|-------|--------|------|-----|
| | S1 | Smith | 20 | London | P1 |
| | S1 | Smith | 20 | London | P2 |
| | S1 | Smith | 20 | London | P3 |
| | S1 | Smith | 20 | London | P4 |
| | S1 | Smith | 20 | London | P5 |
| | S1 | Smith | 20 | London | P6 |
| | S2 | Jones | 10 | Paris | P1 |
| | S2 | Jones | 10 | Paris | P2 |
| | S3 | Blake | 30 | Paris | P2 |
| | S4 | Clark | 20 | London | P2 |
| | S4 | Clark | 20 | London | P4 |
| | S4 | Clark | 20 | London | P5 |
| | S5 | Adams | 30 | Athens | bb |

(We are using bb to represent a string of blanks.)

Explanation: The first twelve result rows as shown correspond to the first of the two INSERT ... SELECTs, and represent the ordinary natural join of S and SP over supplier numbers (except that the QTY column is not included). The final result row corresponds to the second of the two INSERT ... SELECTs, and preserves information for supplier S5, who does not supply any parts. The overall result is the *outer* natural join of S and SP over S#—again, ignoring QTY. (The ordinary join, by contrast, is sometimes referred to as an *inner* join.)

Note that two separate INSERT ... SELECTs are needed, because a subquery cannot contain a UNION.

## 6.5   CONCLUSION

This brings us to the end of our detailed discussion of the four data manipulation statements of SQL, namely SELECT, UPDATE, DELETE, and INSERT. Most of the complexity of those statements (what complexity there is) resides in the SELECT statement; once you have a reasonable understanding of SELECT, the other statements are fairly straightforward, as you can see. In practice, of course, the SELECT statement is usually pretty straightforward as well.

Despite the foregoing, however, the update operations do suffer from a couple of problems that are worth calling out explicitly.

- The first, and more important, is the referential integrity problem touched on several times already. As already mentioned, Appendices A and B between them contain a thorough discussion of this problem.

- Second, the more complex forms of the three statements suffer from a minor restriction, as follows. If the WHERE clause in UPDATE or DELETE includes a subquery, then the FROM clause in that subquery must not refer to the table that is the target of that UPDATE or DELETE. Likewise, in the subquery form of INSERT, the FROM clause in the subquery must not refer to the table that is the target of that INSERT. So, for example, to delete all suppliers whose status is lower than the average, the following will *not* work:

```
DELETE
FROM    S
WHERE   STATUS <
        ( SELECT AVG(STATUS)
          FROM    S ) ;
```

Instead, it is necessary to proceed one step at a time, as follows:

```
SELECT  AVG(STATUS)
FROM    S ;
```

Result:

```
------
  22
```

Hence:

```
DELETE
FROM    S
WHERE   STATUS < 22 ;
```

The reasons for the foregoing restrictions are not inherent but are merely a consequence of the way the operators are implemented in DB2.

In conclusion, we point out that the fact that there are only four data manipulation operations in SQL is one of the reasons for the ease of use of that language. And the fact that there *are* only four such operations is a consequence of the simplicity of the relational data structure. As we pointed out in Chapter 1, all data in a relational database is represented in exactly the same way, namely as values in column positions within rows of tables. Since there is only one way to represent anything, we need only one operator for each of the four basic functions (retrieve, change, insert, delete). By contrast, systems based on a more complex data structure fundamentally require 4n operations, where n is the number of ways that data can be represented in that system. In CODASYL-based systems, for example, where data can be represented either as records or as links between records, we typically find a STORE operation to create a record and a CONNECT operation to create a link; an ERASE operation to destroy a record and a DISCONNECT operation to destroy a link; a MODIFY operation to change a record and a RECONNECT operation to change a link; and so on. (Actually, CODASYL systems usually provide more than two ways of representing data, but records and links are the two most important.)

## EXERCISES

As usual, all of the following exercises are based on the suppliers-parts-projects database:

```
S    ( S#, SNAME, STATUS, CITY )
P    ( P#, PNAME, COLOR, WEIGHT, CITY )
J    ( J#, JNAME, CITY )
SPJ  ( S#, P#, J#, QTY )
```

Write INSERT, DELETE, or UPDATE statements (as appropriate) for each of the following problems.

**6.1** Change the color of all red parts to orange.

**6.2** Delete all projects for which there are no shipments.

**6.3** Increase the shipment quantity by 10 percent for all shipments by suppliers that supply a red part.

**6.4** Delete all projects in Rome and all corresponding shipments.

**6.5** Insert a new supplier (S10) into table S. The name and city are 'White' and 'New York', respectively; the status is not yet known.

**6.6** Construct a table containing a list of part numbers for parts that are supplied either by a London supplier or to a London project.

**6.7** Construct a table containing a list of project numbers for projects that are either located in London or are supplied by a London supplier.

**6.8** Add 10 to the status of all suppliers whose status is currently less than that of supplier S4.

**6.9** Construct the outer natural join of projects and shipments over project numbers.

**6.10** Construct the outer natural join of parts and projects over cities.

**6.11** Construct a table showing complete supplier, part, and project information (together with shipment quantity) for each shipment, together with "preserved" information for every supplier, part, and project that does not appear in the shipment table (see Example 6.4.5 for the meaning of "preserved" in this context).

## ANSWERS TO SELECTED EXERCISES

As usual the following solutions are not necessarily unique.

**6.1**
```
UPDATE  P
SET     COLOR = 'Orange'
WHERE   COLOR = 'Red' ;
```

**6.2**
```
DELETE
FROM    J
WHERE   J# NOT IN
        ( SELECT J#
          FROM   SPJ ) ;
```

**6.3**
```
CREATE TABLE REDS
       ( S#  CHAR(5) ) ;

INSERT INTO REDS ( S# )
       SELECT DISTINCT S#
       FROM   SPJ, P
       WHERE  SPJ.P# = P.P#
       AND    COLOR = 'Red' ;

UPDATE SPJ
SET    QTY = QTY * 1.1
WHERE  S# IN
```

```
        ( SELECT  S#
          FROM    REDS )  ;

    DROP TABLE REDS  ;
```

Note that the following single-statement "solution" is illegal (why?).

```
    UPDATE  SPJ
    SET     QTY = QTY * 1.1
    WHERE   S# IN
            ( SELECT DISTINCT S#
              FROM    SPJ, P
              WHERE   SPJ.P# = P.P#
              AND     P.COLOR = 'Red' )  ;
```

**6.4**  DELETE
```
    FROM    SPJ
    WHERE   'Rome'  =
            ( SELECT CITY
              FROM    J
              WHERE   J.J# = SPJ.J# )  ;

    DELETE
    FROM    J
    WHERE   CITY = 'Rome'  ;
```

**6.5**  INSERT
```
    INTO    S ( S#, SNAME, CITY )
    VALUES ('S10', 'White', 'New York' )  ;
```

Or:

```
    INSERT
    INTO    S ( S#, SNAME, STATUS, CITY )
    VALUES ('S10', 'White', NULL, 'New York' )  ;
```

**6.6**  CREATE TABLE LP
```
          ( P# CHAR(6) )  ;

    INSERT INTO LP ( P# )
            SELECT DISTINCT P#
            FROM    SPJ
            WHERE   S# IN
                    ( SELECT S#
                      FROM    S
                      WHERE   CITY = 'London' )
            OR      J# IN
                    ( SELECT J#
                      FROM    J
                      WHERE   CITY = 'London' )  ;
```

**6.7**   CREATE TABLE LJ
      ( J#   CHAR(4) )  ;

```
INSERT INTO LJ ( J# )
        SELECT J#
        FROM   J
        WHERE  CITY = 'London'
        OR     J# IN
            ( SELECT DISTINCT J#
              FROM   SPJ
              WHERE  S# IN
                  ( SELECT S#
                    FROM   S
                    WHERE  CITY = 'London' ) )  ;
```

*Note:* The following is illegal:

```
INSERT INTO LJ ( J# )
        SELECT J#
        FROM   J
        WHERE  CITY = 'London'
        UNION
        SELECT DISTINCT J#
        FROM   SPJ
        WHERE  'London' =
              ( SELECT CITY
                FROM   S
                WHERE  S.S# = SPJ.S# )  ;
```

UNION is never allowed in a subquery (in any context).

**6.8**   SELECT STATUS
     FROM   S
     WHERE  S# = 'S4'  ;

Result:

```
        STATUS
        ------
          20
```

Hence:

```
UPDATE S
SET    STATUS = STATUS + 10
WHERE  STATUS < 20 ;
```

**6.9**  ```
CREATE TABLE RES9
       ( J#    CHAR(4),
         JNAME CHAR(10),
         CITY  CHAR(15),
         S#    CHAR(5),
         P#    CHAR(6),
         QTY   INTEGER ) ;

INSERT
INTO   RES9
       SELECT J.*, SPJ.S#, SPJ.P#, SPJ.QTY
       FROM   J, SPJ
       WHERE  J.J# = SPJ.J# ;

INSERT
INTO   RES9
       SELECT J.*, 'bb', 'bb', 0
       FROM   J
       WHERE  NOT EXISTS
            ( SELECT *
              FROM   SPJ
              WHERE  SPJ.J# = J.J# ) ;
```

**6.10**  ```
CREATE TABLE RES10
       ( P#    CHAR(6),
         PNAME CHAR(20),
         COLOR CHAR(6),
         WEIGHT SMALLINT,
         CITY  CHAR(15),
         J#    CHAR(4),
         JNAME CHAR(10) ) ;

INSERT
INTO   RES10
       SELECT P.*, J#, JNAME
       FROM   P, J
       WHERE  P.CITY = J.CITY ;

INSERT
INTO   RES10
       SELECT P.*, 'bb', 'bb'
       FROM   P
       WHERE  NOT EXISTS
            ( SELECT *
              FROM   J
              WHERE  J.CITY = P.CITY ) ;
```

```
INSERT
INTO    RES10
        SELECT 'bb', 'bb', 'bb', 0, J.CITY, J.J#, J.JNAME
        FROM    J
        WHERE   NOT EXISTS
            ( SELECT *
              FROM    P
              WHERE   P.CITY = J.CITY ) ;
```

**6.11**  CREATE TABLE RES11
```
        ( S# ..., SNAME ..., STATUS ..., SCITY ...,
          P# ..., PNAME ..., COLOR ..., WEIGHT ..., PCITY ...
          J# ..., JNAME ..., JCITY ..., QTY ... ) ;
```

```
INSERT INTO RES11
SELECT S.*, P.*, J.*, SPJ.QTY
FROM    S, P, J, SPJ
WHERE   S.S# = SPJ.S#
AND     P.P# = SPJ.P#
AND     J.J# = SPJ.J# ;
```

```
INSERT INTO RES11
SELECT S.*,'bb','bb','bb', 0,'bb','bb','bb','bb', 0
FROM    S
WHERE   NOT EXISTS
    ( SELECT *
      FROM    SPJ
      WHERE   SPJ.S# = S.S# ) ;
```

```
INSERT INTO RES11
SELECT 'bb','bb', 0,'bb', P.*,'bb','bb','bb', 0
FROM    P
WHERE   NOT EXISTS
    ( SELECT *
      FROM    SPJ
      WHERE   P.P# = SPJ.P# ) ;
```

```
INSERT INTO RES11
SELECT 'bb','bb', 0,'bb','bb','bb','bb', 0,'bb', J.*, 0
FROM    J
WHERE   NOT EXISTS
    ( SELECT *
      FROM    SPJ
      WHERE   SPJ.J# = J.J# ) ;
```

# 7

# The Catalog

## 7.1 INTRODUCTION

The catalog is a system database that contains information (*descriptors*) concerning various objects that are of interest to the system itself. Examples of such objects are base tables, views, indexes, databases, application plans, access rights, and so on. Descriptor information is essential if the system is to be able to do its job properly. For example, the optimizer component of Bind uses catalog information about indexes (as well as other information) to choose an optimal access strategy, as explained in Chapter 2. Likewise, the authorization subsystem (see Chapter 9) uses catalog information about access rights to grant or deny specific user requests.

In a relational system such as DB2, the catalog itself consists of relations or tables, just like the ordinary user data tables. In DB2 specifically, the catalog consists of some 20 or 25 such tables.* It is not our purpose here to give an exhaustive description of the catalog; rather, we wish merely to give a basic introduction to its structure and content, and to give some idea as to how the

---

*The catalog is *not* the same across different SQL implementations, because the catalog for a particular system necessarily contains a great deal of information that is specific to that system. In particular, the DB2 and SQL/DS catalogs are different.

information in the catalog can be helpful to the user as well as to the system. The only catalog tables we mention at this point are the following:

- SYSTABLES

  This catalog table contains a row for every table (base table or view) in the entire system. For each such table, it gives the table name (NAME), the name of the user that created the table (CREATOR), the number of columns in the table (COLCOUNT), and many other items of information.

- SYSCOLUMNS

  This catalog table contains a row for every column of every table in the entire system. For each such column, it gives the column name (NAME), the name of the table of which that column is a part (TBNAME), the data type of the column (COLTYPE), and many other things besides.

- SYSINDEXES

  This catalog table contains a row for every index in the system. For each such index, it gives the index name (NAME), the name of the indexed table (TBNAME), the name of the user that created the index (CREATOR), and so on.

For example, the catalog structure for the suppliers-and-parts database might be as indicated in Fig. 7.1 (in outline; of course, almost all the details have been omitted).

## 7.2   QUERYING THE CATALOG

Since the catalog consists of tables, just like ordinary user tables, it can be queried by means of SQL SELECT statements just as ordinary tables can. For example, to find out what tables contain an S# column:

```
SELECT TBNAME
FROM   SYSIBM.SYSCOLUMNS
WHERE  NAME = 'S#' ;
```

Result:

```
TBNAME
------
S
SP
```

The "creator" for the catalog tables is considered to be SYSIBM. Thus, to refer to a catalog table such as SYSCOLUMNS, you will need to use SYSIBM as a prefix for the table name (as in the FROM clause in this example); otherwise, DB2 will assume that you are referring to a table of your own (i.e., the default prefix is your own system-known name, as explained in Chapter 3).

```
SYSTABLES    NAME      CREATOR   COLCOUNT       . . .
             -------   -------   --------   - - - -
             S         CJDATE           4      . . .
             P         CJDATE           5      . . .
             SP        CJDATE           3      . . .

SYSCOLUMNS   NAME      TBNAME    COLTYPE        . . .
             -------   -------   --------   - - - -
             S#        S         CHAR           . . .
             SNAME     S         CHAR           . . .
             STATUS    S         SMALLINT       . . .
             CITY      S         CHAR           . . .
             P#        P         CHAR           . . .
             PNAME     P         CHAR           . . .
             COLOR     P         CHAR           . . .
             WEIGHT    P         SMALLINT       . . .
             CITY      P         CHAR           . . .
             S#        SP        CHAR           . . .
             P#        SP        CHAR           . . .
             QTY       SP        INTEGER        . . .

SYSINDEXES   NAME      TBNAME    CREATOR        . . .
             -------   -------   --------   - - - -
             XS        S         CJDATE         . . .
             XP        P         CJDATE         . . .
             XSP       SP        CJDATE         . . .
             XSC       S         CJDATE         . . .
```

**Fig. 7.1**  Catalog structure for the suppliers-and-parts database (outline)

Another example: What columns does table S have?

```
SELECT NAME
FROM   SYSIBM.SYSCOLUMNS
WHERE  TBNAME = 'S' ;
```

Result:

```
NAME
------
S#
SNAME
STATUS
CITY
```

And one more example: How many tables has user CJDATE created?

```
SELECT  COUNT(*)
FROM    SYSIBM.SYSTABLES
WHERE   CREATOR = 'CJDATE' ;
```

A user who is not familiar with the structure of the database can use queries such as these to discover that structure. For example, a user who wishes to query the suppliers-and-parts database (say) but does not have any detailed knowledge as to exactly what tables exist in that database and exactly what columns they contain can use catalog queries to obtain that knowledge first, before going on to formulate the data queries *per se*. In a traditional (nonrelational) system, those initial queries would typically have to be directed to the system dictionary instead of to the database. Indeed, the DB2 catalog can be regarded as a rudimentary dictionary (rudimentary, in that it contains only information that is directly needed by DB2, whereas a full-scale dictionary typically contains much additional information, such as which departments receive which reports). The important difference—and a significant ease-of-use benefit for DB2—is that in DB2 the catalog and the database are queried through *the same interface*, namely SQL; by contrast, in traditional systems the dictionary and the database have always been distinct and have been accessed through different interfaces. It is interesting to speculate as to whether the DB2 catalog will ever be extended to provide a full-fledged dictionary function (such an extension should be reasonably straightforward to implement).

## 7.3  UPDATING THE CATALOG

We have seen how the catalog can be queried by means of the SQL SELECT statement. However, the catalog *cannot* be updated using the SQL UPDATE, DELETE, and INSERT statements (and DB2 will reject any attempt to do so). The reason is, of course, that allowing such operations would potentially be very dangerous: It would be far too easy to destroy information (inadvertently or otherwise) in the catalog so that DB2 would no longer be able to function correctly. Suppose, for example, that the statement

```
DELETE
FROM    SYSIBM.SYSCOLUMNS
WHERE   TBNAME = 'S'
AND     NAME = 'S#' ;
```

were allowed. Its effect would be to remove the row

```
( 'S#', 'S', CHAR, ... )
```

from the SYSCOLUMNS table. *As far as DB2 is concerned, the S# column in the S table would now no longer exist*—i.e., DB2 would no longer have any knowledge of that column. Thus, attempts to access data on the basis of values of that column—e.g.,

```
SELECT CITY
FROM   S
WHERE  S# = 'S4' ;
```

—would fail (the system would produce some error message, such as "undefined column"). Perhaps worse, attempts to update supplier records could go disastrously wrong—for example, inserting a new record might cause the supplier number to be taken as the supplier name, the supplier name as the status, and so on.

For reasons such as these, UPDATE, DELETE, and INSERT operations are (as already stated) not permitted against tables in the catalog. Instead, it is the *data definition* statements (CREATE TABLE, CREATE INDEX, etc.) that perform such updates. For example, the CREATE TABLE statement for table S causes (a) an entry to be made for S in the SYSTABLES table and (b) a set of four entries, one for each of the four columns of the S table, to be made in the SYSCOLUMNS table. (It also causes a number of other things to happen too, which are however of no concern to us here.) Thus CREATE is in some ways the analog of INSERT for the catalog. Likewise, DROP is the analog of DELETE, and ALTER is the analog of UPDATE.

*Aside:* The catalog also includes entries for the catalog tables themselves, of course. However, those entries are not created by explicit CREATE TABLE operations. Instead, they are created automatically by DB2 itself as part of the system installation procedure. In effect, they are "hard-wired" into the system.

Although (as we have just seen) the regular SQL updating statements cannot be used to update the catalog, there is one SQL statement, namely COMMENT, that does perform a kind of catalog updating function. The catalog tables SYSTABLES and SYSCOLUMNS each include a column—not shown in Fig. 7.1—called REMARKS, which can be used (in any particular row) to contain a text string that describes the object identified by the rest of that row. The COMMENT statement is used to enter such descriptions into the REMARKS column in these two tables. The following examples illustrate the two basic formats of that statement.

```
COMMENT ON TABLE S IS
        'Each row represents one supplier' ;
```

The specified string is stored in the REMARKS field in the row for table S in the SYSTABLES table, replacing any value previously stored at that position. Note that the table identified by "TABLE table-name" in a COMMENT statement can be either a base table or a view.

```
COMMENT ON COLUMN P.CITY IS
          'Location of (unique) warehouse storing this part'  ;
```

The specified string is stored in the REMARKS field in the row for column P.CITY in the SYSCOLUMNS table, replacing any value previously stored at that position. In general, the specified column can be a column of either a base table or a view.

Comments can be retrieved via the regular SQL SELECT statement.


## 7.4  SYNONYMS

It is convenient to close this chapter with a brief discussion of *synonyms*, although the topic does not really have much to do with the catalog as such (except inasmuch as synonyms are recorded in the catalog, like most other objects). Briefly, a synonym is an alternative name for a table (base table or view). In particular, you can define a synonym for a table that was created by some other user and for which you would otherwise have to use a fully qualified name. For example:

User ALPHA issues:

```
CREATE TABLE SAMPLE ...  ;
```

User BETA can refer to this table as ALPHA.SAMPLE—for instance,

```
SELECT *
FROM   ALPHA.SAMPLE ;
```

Alternatively, user BETA can issue:

```
CREATE SYNONYM IJK FOR ALPHA.SAMPLE ;
```

and can now refer to the table as simply IJK—for instance,

```
SELECT *
FROM   IJK ;
```

The name IJK is completely private and local to user BETA. Another user GAMMA can also have a private and local name IJK, distinct from user BETA's.

Another example:

```
CREATE SYNONYM TABLES FOR SYSIBM.SYSTABLES ;
```

There is also a DROP SYNONYM statement—syntax:

```
DROP SYNONYM synonym ;
```

For example:

```
DROP SYNONYM TABLES ;
```

## EXERCISES

**7.1** Sketch the details of the catalog for the suppliers-parts-projects database.

Now write SELECT statements for the following queries (numbers 7.2–7.8).

**7.2** Which tables include a CITY column?

**7.3** How many columns are there in the shipments table?

**7.4** List the names of all catalog tables.

**7.5** List the names of all users that have created a table with a CITY column, together with the names of the tables concerned.

**7.6** List the names of all users that have created at least one table, together with the number of tables created in each case.

**7.7** List the names of all tables that have at least one index.

**7.8** List the names of all tables that have more than one index.

**7.9** Write statements to do the following:

    (a) Create an appropriate comment on the SPJ table.
    (b) Change that comment to 'Ignore previous comment'.
    (c) Create an appropriate comment on the P# column of the SPJ table.
    (d) Create an appropriate comment on the XS index.
    (e) Create an appropriate synonym for the SYSCOLUMNS table.
    (f) Drop that synonym.

## ANSWERS TO SELECTED EXERCISES

As usual the following solutions are not necessarily unique.

**7.2**
```
SELECT  TBNAME
FROM    SYSIBM.SYSCOLUMNS
WHERE   NAME = 'CITY' ;
```

**7.3**
```
SELECT  COLCOUNT
FROM    SYSIBM.SYSTABLES
WHERE   NAME = 'SPJ' ;
```

**7.4**
```
SELECT  NAME
FROM    SYSIBM.SYSTABLES
WHERE   CREATOR = 'SYSIBM' ;
```

**7.5** SELECT CREATOR, NAME
FROM    SYSIBM.SYSTABLES
WHERE   NAME IN
        ( SELECT TBNAME
          FROM    SYSIBM.SYSCOLUMNS
          WHERE   NAME = 'CITY' ) ;

**7.6** SELECT CREATOR, COUNT(*)
FROM    SYSIBM.SYSTABLES
GROUP   BY CREATOR ;

**7.7** SELECT TBNAME
FROM    SYSIBM.SYSINDEXES ;

**7.8** SELECT TBNAME
FROM    SYSIBM.SYSINDEXES
GROUP   BY TBNAME
HAVING  COUNT(NAME) > 1 ;

**7.9** (a) COMMENT ON TABLE SPJ IS 'Appropriate comment' ;

(b) COMMENT ON TABLE SPJ IS 'Ignore previous comment' ;

(c) COMMENT ON COLUMN SPJ.P# IS 'Appropriate comment' ;

(d) Trick question! It is not possible to COMMENT ON an index.

(e) CREATE SYNONYM COLS FOR SYSIBM.SYSCOLUMNS ;

(f) DROP SYNONYM COLS ;

# 8

# Views

## 8.1 INTRODUCTION

Recall from Chapter 1 that a view is a *virtual table*—that is, a table that does not exist in its own right but looks to the user as if it did. (By contrast, a base table is a *real* table, in the sense that, for each row of such a table, there really is some stored counterpart of that row in physical storage. See Chapter 13.) Views are not supported by their own, physically separate, distinguishable stored data. Instead, their *definition* in terms of other tables is stored in the catalog (actually in a catalog table called SYSVIEWS). Here is an example:

```
CREATE VIEW GOOD_SUPPLIERS
    AS SELECT S#, STATUS, CITY
       FROM   S
       WHERE  STATUS > 15 ;
```

When this CREATE VIEW is executed, the subquery following the AS (which is in fact the definition of the view) is *not* executed; instead, it is simply saved in the catalog. But to the user it is now as if there really were a table in the database called GOOD__SUPPLIERS, with rows and columns as shown in the unshaded portions (only) of Fig. 8.1 below.

| GOOD__SUPPLIERS | S# | SNAME | STATUS | CITY |
|---|---|---|---|---|
| | S1 | Smith | 20 | London |
| | S2 | Jones | 10 | Paris |
| | S3 | Blake | 30 | Paris |
| | S4 | Clark | 20 | London |
| | S5 | Adams | 30 | Athens |

**Fig. 8.1**  GOOD__SUPPLIERS as a view of base table S (unshaded portions)

GOOD__SUPPLIERS is in effect a "window" into the real table S. Furthermore, that window is *dynamic*: Changes to S will be automatically and instantaneously visible through that window (provided, of course, that those changes lie within the unshaded portion of S); likewise, changes to GOOD__SUPPLIERS will automatically and instantaneously be applied to the real table S (see Section 8.4, later).

Now, depending on the sophistication of the user (and perhaps also on the application concerned), the user may or may not realize that GOOD__SUPPLIERS really is a view; some users may be aware of that fact (and of the fact that there is a real table S underneath), others may genuinely believe that GOOD__SUPPLIERS is a "real" table in its own right. Either way, it makes little difference: The point is, users may operate on GOOD__SUPPLIERS just as if it were a real table (with certain exceptions, to be discussed later). For instance, here is an example of a retrieval operation (SELECT statement) against GOOD__SUPPLIERS:

```
SELECT  *
FROM    GOOD_SUPPLIERS
WHERE   CITY ¬= 'London' ;
```

As you can see, this SELECT certainly looks just like a normal SELECT on a conventional base table. The system (actually Bind) handles such an operation by converting it into an equivalent operation on the underlying base table (or tables, plural—see Section 8.2). In the example, the equivalent operation is

```
SELECT S#, STATUS, CITY
FROM   S
WHERE  CITY ¬= 'London'
AND    STATUS > 15 ;
```

This new statement can now be compiled (i.e., bound) and executed in the usual way. The conversion is done by (in effect) *merging* the SELECT issued by the user with the SELECT that was saved in the catalog when the view was defined. From the catalog, the system knows that FROM GOOD_SUPPLIERS really means FROM S; it also knows that any selection from GOOD_SUPPLIERS must be further qualified by the WHERE condition STATUS > 15; and it also knows that "SELECT *" (from GOOD_SUPPLIERS) really means SELECT S#, STATUS, CITY (from S). Hence it is able to translate the original SELECT on the virtual table GOOD_SUPPLIERS into an equivalent SELECT on the real table S—equivalent, in the sense that the effect of executing that SELECT on the real table S is as if there really were a base table called GOOD_SUPPLIERS and the original SELECT were executed on that.

Update operations are treated in a similar manner. For example, the operation

```
UPDATE  GOOD_SUPPLIERS
SET     STATUS = STATUS + 10
WHERE   CITY = 'Paris' ;
```

will be converted by Bind into

```
UPDATE  S
SET     STATUS = STATUS + 10
WHERE   CITY = 'Paris'
AND     STATUS > 15 ;
```

Similarly for INSERT and DELETE operations.

## 8.2  VIEW DEFINITION

The general syntax of CREATE VIEW is

```
CREATE VIEW view-name
    [ ( column-name [ , column-name ] ... ) ]
      AS subquery
    [ WITH CHECK OPTION ] ;
```

As usual, the subquery cannot include either UNION or ORDER BY; apart from these restrictions, however, any table that can be retrieved via a SELECT statement can alternatively be defined as a view. Here are some examples.

```
1.  CREATE VIEW REDPARTS ( P#, PNAME, WT, CITY )
        AS SELECT P#, PNAME, WEIGHT, CITY
           FROM    P
           WHERE   COLOR = 'Red' ;
```

The effect of this statement is to create a new view called *xyz*.REDPARTS, where *xyz* is the system-known name for the user issuing the CREATE VIEW statement. User *xyz* can refer to the view as simply REDPARTS; other users can refer to it as *xyz*.REDPARTS (alternatively, of course, they can introduce a synonym for it, as discussed in Chapter 7). The view has four columns, called P#, PNAME, WT, and CITY, and corresponding respectively to the four columns P#, PNAME, WEIGHT, and CITY of the underlying base table P. If column names are not specified explicitly in the CREATE VIEW, then the view inherits column names from the source of the view in the obvious way (in the example, the inherited names would be P#, PNAME, WEIGHT, and CITY). Column names *must* be specified explicitly (for all columns of the view) if (a) any column of the view is derived from a builtin function, an arithmetic expression, or a constant (and so has no name that can be inherited), or (b) if two or more columns of the view would otherwise have the same name. See the next two examples for illustrations of each of these two cases.

```
2.   CREATE VIEW PQ ( P#, TOTQTY )
         AS SELECT P#, SUM(QTY)
            FROM   SP
            GROUP  BY P# ;
```

In this example, there is no name that can be inherited for the second column, since that column is derived from a builtin function; hence column names *must* be specified explicitly, as shown. Notice that this view is not just a simple row-and-column subset of the underlying base table (unlike the views REDPARTS and GOOD__SUPPLIERS shown earlier). It might be regarded instead as a kind of statistical summary or compression of that underlying table.

```
3.   CREATE VIEW CITY__PAIRS ( SCITY, PCITY )
         AS SELECT S.CITY, P.CITY
            FROM   S, SP, P
            WHERE  S.S# = SP.S#
            AND    SP.P# = P.P# ;
```

The meaning of this particular view is that a pair of city names $(x,y)$ will appear in the view if a supplier located in city $x$ supplies a part stored in city $y$. For example, supplier S1 supplies part P1; supplier S1 is located in London and part P1 is stored in London; and so the pair (London,London) appears in the view. Notice that the definition of this view involves a join, so that this is an example of a view that is derived from multiple underlying tables. (*Note:* We could have included the specification DISTINCT in the definition of this view if we had wished. Compare Example 4.3.5 in Chapter 4.)

```
4.   CREATE VIEW LONDON__REDPARTS
         AS SELECT P#, WT
            FROM   REDPARTS
            WHERE  CITY = 'London' ;
```

Since the definition of a view can be any valid subquery, and since a subquery can select data from views as well as from base tables, it is perfectly possible to define a view in terms of other views, as in this example.

```
5.  CREATE VIEW GOOD_SUPPLIERS
        AS SELECT S#, STATUS, CITY
           FROM   S
           WHERE  STATUS > 15
           WITH CHECK OPTION ;
```

The clause "WITH CHECK OPTION" indicates that UPDATE and INSERT operations against the view are to be checked to ensure that the UPDATEd or INSERTed row satisfies the view-defining predicate (STATUS > 15, in the example). The CHECK option is described in more detail in Section 8.4.

The syntax of DROP VIEW is

```
DROP VIEW view-name ;
```

The specified view is dropped (i.e., its definition is removed from the catalog). Any views defined in terms of that view are automatically dropped too. Here is an example:

```
DROP VIEW REDPARTS ;
```

If a base table is dropped, all views defined on that base table (or on views of that base table, etc.) are automatically dropped too.

There is no ALTER VIEW statement. The ALTER TABLE statement (which adds another column to a base table) has no effect on any existing views.

## 8.3  RETRIEVAL OPERATIONS

We have already explained in outline (in Section 8.1) how retrieval operations on a view are converted into equivalent operations on the underlying base table(s). Normally that conversion process is quite straightforward and works perfectly well, without any surprises for the user. Occasionally, however, such surprises may occur. To be specific, problems can arise if the user tries to treat a view field as a conventional field and that view field is derived from something other than a simple field of the underlying base table—for example, if it is derived from a builtin function. Consider the following example.

View definition:

```
CREATE VIEW PQ ( P#, TOTQTY )
     AS SELECT P#, SUM(QTY)
        FROM   SP
        GROUP  BY P# ;
```

(this is the "statistical summary" view from Section 8.2 [Example 2]).

Attempted query:

```
SELECT  *
FROM    PQ
WHERE   TOTQTY > 500 ;
```

If we apply the simple merging process described in Section 8.1 to combine this query with the view definition stored in the catalog, we obtain something like the following:

```
SELECT  P#, SUM(QTY)
FROM    SP
WHERE   SUM(QTY) > 500
GROUP   BY P# ;
```

And this is not a valid SELECT statement. Predicates in a WHERE clause are not allowed to refer to builtin functions such as SUM. What the original query should be converted to is something more along the following lines:

```
SELECT  P#, SUM(QTY)
FROM    SP
GROUP   BY P#
HAVING  SUM(QTY) > 500 ;
```

However, DB2 is not capable of performing such a conversion.

Here is another example of a situation in which the conversion does not work (again using the statistical summary view PQ). The attempted query is:

```
SELECT  AVG (TOTQTY)
FROM    PQ ;
```

"Converted" form:

```
SELECT  AVG ( SUM (QTY) )
FROM    SP
GROUP   BY P# ;
```

Again this is illegal. SQL does not allow builtin functions to be nested in this fashion.

The general principle that these two examples violate is: The converted form of the original query must always be a legal SQL SELECT statement.


## 8.4   UPDATE OPERATIONS

We have already stated (in Chapter 6) that *not all views are updatable*. We are now in a position to be able to amplify that statement. First, consider the two views GOOD—SUPPLIERS and CITY—PAIRS defined earlier in this chapter. For convenience, we repeat their definitions here:

```
CREATE VIEW GOOD_SUPPLIERS       |   CREATE VIEW CITY_PAIRS
                                 |       ( SCITY, PCITY )
    AS SELECT S#, STATUS, CITY   |       AS SELECT S.CITY, P.CITY
       FROM   S                  |          FROM   S, SP, P
       WHERE  STATUS > 15 ;      |          WHERE  S.S# = SP.S#
                                 |          AND    SP.P# = P.P# ;
```

Of these two views, GOOD—SUPPLIERS is updatable, while CITY—PAIRS is not. It is instructive to examine why this is so. In the case of GOOD—SUPPLIERS:

(a) We can INSERT a new row into the view, say the row ('S6',40,'Rome'), by actually inserting the corresponding row ('S6',NULL,40,'Rome') into the underlying base table.

(b) We can DELETE an existing row from the view, say the row ('S1',20,'London'), by actually deleting the corresponding row ('S1','Smith',20,'London') from the underlying base table.

(c) We can UPDATE an existing field in the view, say to change the city for supplier S1 from London to Rome, by actually making that same change in the corresponding field in the underlying base table.

We will refer to a view such as GOOD—SUPPLIERS, which is derived from a single base table by simply eliminating certain rows and certain columns of that base table, as a *row-and-column-subset* view. Row-and-column-subset views are inherently updatable, as the foregoing discussion shows by example.

Now consider the view CITY—PAIRS (which is certainly not a row-and-column-subset view). As explained earlier, one of the rows in that view is the row "London,London". Suppose it were possible for some user to UPDATE that row to (say) "Rome,Oslo". What would such an UPDATE signify? Presumably that some supplier— but we don't know who, because we discarded that information when we constructed the view—has moved from London to Rome; and similarly that some part—but we don't know which, because again we discarded that information when we constructed the view—has moved from London to Oslo. Since we don't know *which* supplier and *which* part are affected, there is no way we can go down to the underlying base tables and make the appropriate changes there. In other words, *the original UPDATE is an intrinsically unsupportable operation*. Similar arguments can be made to show that INSERT and DELETE are also intrinsically not supportable on this view.

Thus we see that some views are inherently updatable, whereas others are inherently not. Note the word "inherently" here. It is not just a question of some systems being able to support certain updates while others cannot. *No* system can consistently support updates on a view such as CITY_PAIRS unaided (by "unaided" we mean "without help from some human user"). As a consequence of this fact, it is possible to classify views as indicated in the following Venn diagram (Fig. 8.2).

Note carefully from the diagram that all row-and-column-subset views (such as GOOD_SUPPLIERS) are theoretically updatable, but that not all theoretically updatable views are row-and-column-subset views. In other words, there are some views that *are* theoretically updatable that are *not* row-and-column-subset views. The trouble is, although we know that such views exist, we do not know exactly which ones they are; it is a research problem to pin down exactly what it is that characterizes such views. For the purposes of this book, therefore, the important point is the following:

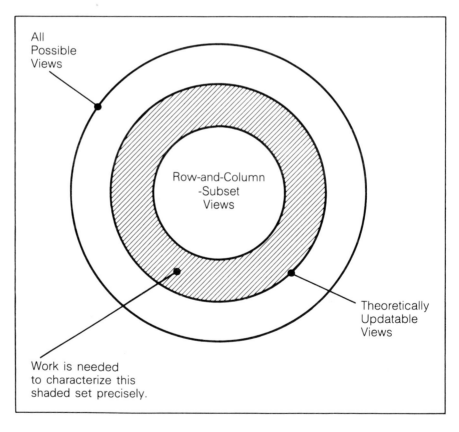

**Fig. 8.2** Classification of views

*In DB2, only row-and-column-subset views can be updated.*

(Actually this statement is a slight oversimplification; we will make it precise in a moment.) DB2 is not alone in this regard, by the way; so far as this writer is aware, no relational system currently supports update operations on views that are not row-and-column subsets.

The fact that not all views are updatable is frequently expressed as "You cannot update a join." That statement is *not* an accurate characterization of the situation, nor indeed of the problem: There are some views that are not joins that are not updatable, and there are some views that are joins that are (theoretically) updatable—although not updatable in DB2. But it is true that joins represent the "interesting case," in the sense that it would be very convenient to be able to update a view whose definition involved a join. It should be clear from the foregoing discussion that such views may indeed be updatable in some future system; but we are concerned here only with what DB2 will currently allow. Let us now make it clear exactly what that is.

In DB2, a view that is to accept updates must be derived from a single base table. Moreover:

(a)  If a field of the view is derived from an arithmetic expression or a constant, then INSERT operations are not allowed, and UPDATE operations are not allowed on that field. However, DELETE operations are allowed.

(b)  If a field of the view is derived from a builtin function, then the view is not updatable.

(c)  If the definition of the view involves GROUP BY, then the view is not updatable.

(d)  If the definition of the view involves DISTINCT, then the view is not updatable.

(e)  If the definition of the view includes a nested subquery and the FROM clause in that subquery refers to the base table on which the view is defined, then the view is not updatable.

(f)  If the FROM clause in the view definition names multiple tables, then the view is not updatable.

(In addition, of course, a view defined over a nonupdatable view is itself not updatable.)

Let us examine the reasonableness of these restrictions. We consider each of the cases (a)–(f) in turn. For each case, we begin by considering an example of a view that illustrates the restriction.

Case (a): view field derived from an arithmetic expression (or from a constant)

```
CREATE VIEW P_IN_GRAMS ( P#, GMWT )
     AS SELECT P#, WEIGHT * 454
        FROM    P ;
```

Assuming that table P is as given in Fig. 1.3 (Chapter 1), the set of rows visible through this view is as follows:

```
P_IN_GRAMS    P#    GMWT
              --    ----
              P1    5448
              P2    7718
              P3    7718
              P4    6356
              P5    5448
              P6    8626
```

It should be clear that P__IN__GRAMS cannot support INSERT operations, nor UPDATE operations on the field GMWT. (Each of those operations would require the system to be able to convert a gram weight back into pounds, without any instructions as to how to perform such a conversion.) On the other hand, DELETE operations can be supported (e.g., deleting the row for part P1 from the view can be handled by deleting the row for part P1 from the underlying base table), and so can UPDATE operations on field P# (such UPDATEs simply require a corresponding UPDATE on field P# of that base table). Similar considerations apply to a view that includes a field that is derived from a constant instead of an arithmetic expression.

Case (b): view field derived from a builtin function

```
CREATE VIEW TQ ( TOTQTY )
   AS SELECT SUM (QTY)
      FROM   SP ;
```

Sample value:

```
TQ   TOTQTY
     ------
     3100
```

It should be obvious that none of UPDATE, INSERT, DELETE makes any sense on this view.

Case (c): view defined with GROUP BY

```
CREATE VIEW PQ ( P#, TOTQTY )
   AS SELECT P#, SUM(QTY)
      FROM   SP
      GROUP  BY P# ;
```

Sample values:

```
PQ    P#    TOTQTY
      --    ------
      P1       600
      P2      1000
      P3       400
      P4       500
      P5       500
      P6       100
```

It is obvious that view PQ cannot support INSERT operations, nor UPDATE operations against field TOTQTY. DELETE operations, and UPDATE operations against field P#, theoretically *could* be defined to DELETE or UPDATE all corresponding rows in table SP—for example, the operation

```
DELETE
FROM    PQ
WHERE   P# = 'P1' ;
```

could be defined to translate into

```
DELETE
FROM    SP
WHERE   P# = 'P1' ;
```

—but such operations could equally well be expressed directly in terms of table SP anyway. And it is at least arguable that a user who is issuing such operations should probably be interested in exactly which real records are affected by those operations.

Case (d): view defined with DISTINCT

```
CREATE VIEW CC
    AS SELECT DISTINCT COLOR, CITY
        FROM    P ;
```

Sample values (with corresponding part number(s)):

```
CC    COLOR   CITY
      -----   ------
      Red     London    (from P1,P4,P6)
      Green   Paris     (from P2)
      Blue    Rome      (from P3)
      Blue    Paris     (from P5)
```

Again, it should be clear that view CC cannot support INSERT operations. (INSERTs on the underlying table P require the user to specify a P# value, because part numbers are NOT NULL.) As in case (c), DELETE and UPDATE operations *could* theoretically be defined (to DELETE or UPDATE all corresponding rows in P), but the remarks on this possibility under case (c) apply again here, with perhaps even more force.

Here is another example of case (d):

```
CREATE VIEW PC
    AS SELECT DISTINCT P#, COLOR
       FROM    P ;
```

Sample values:

```
PC    P#    COLOR
      --    -----
      P1    Red
      P2    Green
      P3    Blue
      P4    Red
      P5    Blue
      P6    Red
```

This is an example of a view that is obviously updatable in theory—all possible INSERT, DELETE, and UPDATE operations against the view are clearly well-defined. In fact, the view is really a row-and-column-subset view; but *DB2 is not aware of that fact.* To put it another way, DB2 is not aware of the fact that the DISTINCT specification is actually superfluous here; instead, it simply assumes that the presence of DISTINCT means that any given row of the view *might* be derived from multiple rows of the base table, as in the previous example, and so does not consider the view to be updatable.

Case (e): view involving subquery over same table

```
CREATE VIEW S_UNDER_AVG
    AS SELECT S#, SNAME, STATUS, CITY
       FROM    S
       WHERE   STATUS <
               ( SELECT AVG (STATUS)
                 FROM    S ) ;
```

UPDATE and DELETE operations against S_UNDER_AVG are illegal because they would violate the restriction on such operations mentioned at the end of Chapter 6 (Section 6.5). As for INSERT operations, they could in principle be supported, but they would have unpredictable effects.

Case (f): view defined from multiple tables

```
CREATE VIEW CITY_PAIRS ( SCITY, PCITY )
        AS SELECT S.CITY, P.CITY
           FROM   S, SP, P
           WHERE  S.S# = SP.S#
           AND    SP.P# = P.P# ;
```

This view is not updatable, for reasons that have already been adequately discussed. However, consider this next example:

```
CREATE VIEW P2_SUPPLIERS
    AS SELECT DISTINCT S.*
       FROM   S, SP
       WHERE  S.S# = SP.P#
       AND    SP.P# = 'P2' ;
```

This view is also not updatable in DB2, even though (once again) it is in fact a row-and-column-subset view; once again, DB2 is not capable of recognizing that fact. It is interesting to note in this example that a semantically equivalent view can be defined that *is* updatable, viz:

```
CREATE TABLE P2_SUPPLIERS
    AS SELECT S.*
       FROM   S
       WHERE  S# IN
              ( SELECT S#
                FROM   SP
                WHERE  P# = 'P2' ) ;
```

This definition does not violate the "multiple tables in the FROM clause" rule.

Finally, we return to the GOOD_SUPPLIERS view once again, in order to discuss a number of remaining issues. The definition of that view (to repeat) is:

```
CREATE VIEW GOOD_SUPPLIERS
    AS SELECT S#, STATUS, CITY
       FROM   S
       WHERE  STATUS > 15 ;
```

This view is a row-and-column-subset view and is therefore updatable. But note the following:

(a) A successful INSERT against GOOD_SUPPLIERS will have to generate a null value for the missing field SNAME (as already indicated at the start of this section). Of course, field SNAME must not have been created with the NOT NULL option if the INSERT is to succeed.

(b) With the data values given in Fig. 1.3, supplier S2 will not be visible through the GOOD__SUPPLIERS view. But that does not mean that the user can INSERT a record into that view with supplier number value S2, or UPDATE one of the other records so that its supplier number value becomes S2. Such an operation must be rejected, just as if it had been applied directly to table S.

(c) Last, consider the following UPDATE:

```
UPDATE  GOOD__SUPPLIERS
SET     STATUS = 0
WHERE   S# = 'S1' ;
```

Should this UPDATE be accepted? If it is, it will have the effect of removing supplier S1 from the view, since the S1 record will no longer satisfy the view-defining predicate. Likewise, the INSERT operation

```
INSERT
INTO    GOOD__SUPPLIERS ( S#, STATUS, CITY )
VALUES ( 'S8', 7, 'Stockholm' ) ;
```

(if accepted) will create a new supplier record, but that record will instantly vanish from the view. The CHECK option (mentioned in Section 8.2) is designed to deal with such situations. If the clause

```
WITH CHECK OPTION
```

is included in the definition of a view, then all INSERTs and UPDATEs against that view will be checked to ensure that the newly INSERTed or UPDATEd record does indeed satisfy the view- defining predicate (if it does not, then the operation will be rejected).

The CHECK option can be specified only if the view is updatable *and* its definition does not include a nested subquery. If the view is such that UPDATEs are legal on certain fields only (and INSERTs are not allowed at all), then the CHECK option applies only to those UPDATE operations.

## 8.5   LOGICAL DATA INDEPENDENCE

We have not yet really explained what views are for. One of the things they are for is the provision of what is called *logical data independence*. The notion of *physical* data independence was introduced in Chapter 2: A system like DB2 is said to provide physical data independence because users and user programs are not dependent on the physical structure of the stored database. A system provides *logical* data independence if users and user programs are also independent of the *logical* structure of the database. There are two aspects to such independence, namely *growth* and *restructuring*.

## Growth

As the database grows to incorporate new kinds of information, so the definition of the database must also grow accordingly. (Note: We discuss the question of growth in the database here only for completeness; it is important, but it has nothing to do with views as such.) There are two possible types of growth that can occur:

1. The expansion of an existing base table to include a new field (corresponding to the addition of new information concerning some existing type of object—for example, the addition of a DISCOUNT field to the supplier base table);

2. The inclusion of a new base table (corresponding to the addition of a new type of object—for example, the addition of project information to the suppliers-and-parts database).

   Neither of these two kinds of change should have any effect on existing users at all (unless those users have been using "SELECT *" or INSERT with the list of field names omitted; as mentioned earlier in this book, the meanings of such statements may change if they happen to be rebound and the table concerned has been ALTERed in the interim).

## Restructuring

Occasionally it may become necessary to restructure the database in such a way that, although the overall information content remains the same, the placement of information within that database changes—i.e., the allocation of fields to tables is altered in some way. Before proceeding further, we make the point that such restructuring is generally undesirable; however, it is sometimes unavoidable. For example, it may be necessary to split a table "vertically," so that commonly required columns can be stored on a faster device and less frequently required columns on a slower device. Let us consider this case in some detail. Suppose for the sake of the example that it becomes necessary (for some reason—the precise reason is not important here) to replace base table S by the following two base tables:

```
SX  ( S#, SNAME, CITY )
SY  ( S#, STATUS )
```

*Note:* This replacement operation is not entirely trivial, incidentally. One way it might be handled is by means of the following sequence of SQL operations:

```
CREATE TABLE SX
     ( S#       CHAR(5) NOT NULL,
       SNAME    CHAR(20),
       CITY     CHAR(15) )  ;
```

```
CREATE TABLE SY
    ( S#      CHAR(5) NOT NULL,
      STATUS  SMALLINT ) ;

CREATE UNIQUE INDEX XSX ON SX ( S# ) ;

CREATE UNIQUE INDEX XSY ON SY ( S# ) ;

INSERT INTO SX ( S#, SNAME, CITY )
       SELECT S#, SNAME, CITY
       FROM   S ;

INSERT INTO SY ( S#, STATUS )
       SELECT S#, STATUS
       FROM   S ;

DROP TABLE S ;
```

The crucial point to observe in this example is that *the old table S is the join of the two new tables SX and SY* (over supplier numbers). For example, in table S we had the row ('S1','Smith',20,'London'); in SX we now have the row ('S1','Smith','London') and in SY the row ('S1',20); join them together and we get the row ('S1','Smith',20,'London'), as before. So we create a *view* that is exactly that join, and we name it S:

```
CREATE VIEW S ( S#, SNAME, STATUS, CITY )
   AS SELECT SX.S#, SX.SNAME, SY.STATUS, SX.CITY
      FROM   SX, SY
      WHERE  SX.S# = SY.S# ;
```

Any program that previously referred to base table S will now refer to view S instead. SELECT operations will continue to work exactly as before (though they will require additional analysis during the bind process and will incur additional execution-time overhead). However, update operations will no longer work, because (as explained in Section 8.4) DB2 will not allow updates against a view that is defined as a join. In other words, a user performing update operations is not immune to this type of change, but instead must make some manual alterations to the update statements concerned (and then re-precompile and rebind them).

Thus we have shown that DB2 does *not* provide complete protection against changes in the logical structure of the database (which is why such changes are not a good idea in the first place). But things may not be as bad as they seem, even if manual alterations are necessary. First, it is easy to discover which programs have to be altered in the light of any such changes; that information can be obtained from the catalog. Second, it is easy to find the statements that need to be changed in those programs; quite apart from anything else, they all start with the prefix EXEC SQL. Third, SQL is a very high-level language. The number of statements that have to be changed is therefore usually small and the meaning of those statements is usually readily apparent; as a result, the necessary changes are usually easy to make. It is *not* like having to change statements in a comparatively low-level language such as DL/I or COBOL, where the meaning of a given statement is probably highly dependent on the dynamic flow of control through the program to the statement in question. So, even though it is true that manual corrections must be made, the amount of work involved may not be all that great in practice.

To return to the SX-SY example for a moment: Actually, the view S (defined as the join of SX and SY) is a good example of a join view that *is* theoretically updatable. If we assume that there is a one-to-one correspondence between SX and SY at all times (so that any supplier appearing in SX also appears in SY, and vice versa), then the effect of all possible update operations on view S is clearly defined in terms of SX and SY. (Exercise: Do you agree with this statement?) Thus the example illustrates, not only why the ability to update join views would be a useful system feature, but also a case where such updating appears to be a feasible proposition.

## 8.6 ADVANTAGES OF VIEWS

We conclude this chapter with a brief summary of the advantages of views.

- They provide a certain amount of logical data independence in the face of restructuring in the database, as explained in the previous section.

- They allow the same data to be seen by different users in different ways (possibly even at the same time).
  This consideration is obviously important when there are many different categories of user all interacting with a single integrated database.

- The user's perception is simplified.
  It is obvious that the view mechanism allows users to focus on just the data that is of concern to them and to ignore the rest. What is perhaps not so obvious is that, for retrieval at least, that mechanism can also considerably simplify users' data manipulation operations. In particular, because the user can be provided with a view in which all underlying tables are joined together, the need for explicit operations to step from table to table can be greatly reduced. As an example, consider the view CITY__PAIRS, and contrast the SELECT needed to find cities storing parts that are available from London using that view with the SELECT needed to obtain the same result directly from the underlying base tables. In effect, the complex selection process has been moved out of the realm of data manipulation and into that of data

definition (in fact, the distinction between the two is far from clearcut in relational languages like SQL).

- Automatic security is provided for hidden data.

  "Hidden data" refers to data not visible through some given view. Such data is clearly secure from access through that particular view. Thus, forcing users to access the database via views is a simple but effective mechanism for authorization control. We will discuss this aspect of views in greater detail in the next chapter.

## EXERCISES

**8.1** Define relation SP of the suppliers-and-parts database as a view of relation SPJ of the suppliers-parts-projects database.

**8.2** Create a view from the suppliers-parts-projects database consisting of all projects (project number and city fields only) that are supplied by supplier S1 or use part P1.

**8.3** Is your solution to Exercise 8.2 an updatable view? (a) If it is, can the CHECK option be specified for it? (b) If it is not, give an updatable version, and repeat this exercise.

**8.4** Create a view consisting of supplier numbers and part numbers for suppliers and parts that are not "colocated."

**8.5** Create a view consisting of supplier records for suppliers that are located in London (only).

**8.6** Given the view definition:

```
CREATE VIEW SUMMARY ( S#, P#, MAXQ, MINQ, AVGQ )
    AS. SELECT S#, P#, MAX(QTY), MIN(QTY), AVG(QTY)
        FROM    SPJ
        GROUP   BY S#, P#
        HAVING SUM(QTY) > 50 ;
```

state which of the following operations are legal and, for those that are, give the translated equivalents:

```
(a) SELECT *
    FROM    SUMMARY ;

(b) SELECT *
    FROM    SUMMARY
    WHERE   S# ¬= 'S1' ;

(c) SELECT *
    FROM    SUMMARY
    WHERE   MAXQ > 250 ;
```

(d)  SELECT  MAXQ - MINQ, S#, P#
     FROM    SUMMARY
     WHERE   S# = 'S1'
     AND     P# = 'P1' ;

(e)  SELECT  S#
     FROM    SUMMARY
     GROUP   BY S# ;

(f)  SELECT  S#, MAXQ
     FROM    SUMMARY
     GROUP   BY S#, MAXQ ;

(g)  SELECT  S.S#, SUMMARY.AVGQ
     FROM    S, SUMMARY
     WHERE   S.S# = SUMMARY.S# ;

(h)  UPDATE  SUMMARY
     SET     S# = 'S2'
     WHERE   S# = 'S1' ;

(i)  UPDATE  SUMMARY
     SET     MAXQ = 1000
     WHERE   S# = 'S1' ;

(j)  DELETE
     FROM    SUMMARY
     WHERE   S# = 'S1' ;

**8.7** State the rules concerning the updatability of views in DB2.

**8.8** State the rules concerning the CHECK option.

**8.9** Suppose the database is restructured in such a way that tables A and B are replaced by their natural join C. To what extent can the view mechanism conceal that restructuring from existing users?

## ANSWERS TO SELECTED EXERCISES

**8.1** The problem here is: How should the field SP.QTY be defined? The sensible answer seems to be that, for a given (S#,P#) pair, SP.QTY should be the *sum* of all SPJ.QTY values, taken over all J#'s for that (S#,P#) pair.

    CREATE VIEW SP ( S#, P#, QTY )
        AS SELECT S#, P#, SUM (QTY)
           FROM    SPJ
           GROUP   BY S#, P# ;

```
8.2 CREATE VIEW JC ( J#, CITY )
       AS SELECT DISTINCT J.J#, J.CITY
          FROM    J, SPJ
          WHERE   J.J# = SPJ.J#
          AND   ( SPJ.S# = 'S1' OR
                  SPJ.P# = 'P1' ) ;
```

**8.3** The view defined in the answer to Exercise 8.2 above is not updatable, because it names multiple tables in the FROM clause. So:
(b) Updatable version:

```
CREATE VIEW JC ( J#, CITY )
    AS SELECT J.J#, J.CITY
       FROM    J
       WHERE   J.J# IN
             ( SELECT J#
               FROM    SPJ
               WHERE   S# = 'S1' )
       AND     J.J# IN
             ( SELECT J#
               FROM    SPJ
               WHERE   P# = 'P1' ) ;
```

Now repeat the exercise: (a) No.

```
8.4 CREATE VIEW NON_COLOCATED
       AS SELECT S#, P#
          FROM    S, P
          WHERE   S.CITY ¬= P.CITY ;
```

```
8.5 CREATE VIEW LONDON_SUPPLIERS
       AS SELECT S#, SNAME, STATUS
          FROM    S
          WHERE   CITY = 'London' ;
```

We have omitted the CITY column from the view, since we know its value must be 'London' for every row visible through the view. Note, however, that this omission means that any record INSERTed through the view will vanish instantly, since its CITY field will be set to null.

**8.6** Only (a), (b), and (d) are legal. Note in particular that (g) is not legal: A view whose definition includes a GROUP BY cannot be joined to another table. We give the translated equivalent for (d) only:

```
SELECT MAX(QTY) - MIN(QTY), S#, P#
FROM    SPJ
WHERE   S# = 'S1'
AND     P# = 'P1'
GROUP   BY S#, P#
HAVING SUM(QTY) > 50 ;
```

# 9

# Security and Authorization

## 9.1 INTRODUCTION

The term "security" is used in database contexts to mean the protection of the data in the database(s) against unauthorized disclosure, alteration, or destruction. DB2 goes far beyond most systems in the degree of security it provides. The unit of data that can be individually protected ranges all the way from an entire table to a specific data value at a specific row-and-column position within such a table. (For certain operations, in fact, the unit can also be greater than one table. For example, the unit for the console operator START and STOP commands is an entire database.) A given user can have different access privileges on different objects (e.g., SELECT privileges only on one table, SELECT and UPDATE privileges on another, and so on). Also, of course, different users can have different privileges on the same object; e.g., user A could have SELECT privileges (only) on a given table, while another user B could simultaneously have both SELECT and UPDATE privileges on that same table.

There are two more or less independent features of the system that are involved in the provision of security in DB2: (1) the view mechanism, which (as mentioned at the end of the previous chapter) can be used to hide sensitive data from unauthorized users, and (2) the authorization subsystem, which allows users having specific privileges selectively and dynamically to grant those privileges to other users, and subsequently to revoke those privileges, if desired. We exam-

141

ine the view mechanism in Section 9.3 and the authorization subsystem (the GRANT and REVOKE statements) in Section 9.4.

Of course, all decisions as to which specific privileges should be granted to which specific users are policy decisions, not technical ones. As such, they are clearly outside the jurisdiction of DB2 *per se*. All that DB2 can do is *enforce* those decisions once they are made. In order that DB2 should be able to perform this function properly:

(a) The results of those decisions must be made known to the system (this is done by means of the GRANT and REVOKE statements) and must be remembered by the system (this is done by saving them in the catalog, in the form of *authorization constraints*).

(b) There must be a means of checking a given access request against the applicable authorization constraints. (By "access request" here we mean the combination of requested operation plus target object plus requesting user.) Most such checking is done by Bind at the time the original request is bound (but see Chapter 14, Section 14.4).

(c) In order that it may be able to decide which constraints are applicable to a given request, the system must be able to recognize the source of that request— that is, it must be able to recognize which particular user a particular request is coming from. Before getting into a discussion of the view mechanism and the authorization subsystem as such, then, we must first say something about user identification in DB2 (Section 9.2).

## 9.2   USER IDENTIFICATION

Users are known to DB2 by their "authorization identifier" (authorization ID for short). The authorization ID is what we have been referring to in earlier chapters as the user's "system-known name." If you are a legitimate user of the system, some responsible person in your organization (probably the system administrator—see Section 9.4 below) will have assigned an authorization ID for your particular use. It is your responsibility to identify yourself by supplying that ID when you sign on to the system. Note that you do not sign on directly to DB2 itself; instead, you sign on to the appropriate MVS subsystem (IMS, CICS, or TSO—remember from Chapter 1 that every DB2 application must run under exactly one of these three subsystems). That subsystem will then pass your ID on to DB2 when it passes control to DB2. Thus any validation or authentication of your ID is done by the relevant subsystem, not by DB2. DB2 simply assumes that any user request that purports to come from user *xyz* (say) does in fact come from user *xyz*.

Details of the sign-on procedure (and hence of precisely how the authorization ID is specified) in each of the different environments are beyond the scope of this text.

## 9.3 VIEWS AND SECURITY

To illustrate the use of views for security purposes, we present a series of examples, based once again (for the most part) on the suppliers-and-parts database.

1. For a user permitted access to complete supplier records, but only for suppliers located in Paris:

```
CREATE VIEW PARIS_SUPPLIERS
     AS SELECT S#, SNAME, STATUS, CITY
        FROM   S
        WHERE  CITY = 'Paris' ;
```

Users of this view see a "horizontal subset"—or (better) a row subset or *value-dependent* subset— of the base table S.

2. For a user permitted access to all supplier records, but not to supplier ratings (STATUS values):

```
CREATE VIEW STATUS_HIDDEN
     AS SELECT S#, SNAME, CITY
        FROM   S ;
```

Users of this view see a "vertical subset"—or (better) a column subset or *value-independent* subset—of the base table S.

3. For a user permitted access to supplier records for suppliers in Paris (only), but not to supplier ratings:

```
CREATE VIEW PARIS_NO_RATINGS
     AS SELECT S#, SNAME, CITY
        FROM   S
        WHERE  CITY = 'Paris' ;
```

Users of this view see a row-and-column subset of the base table S.

4. For a user permitted access to catalog entries (i.e., SYSTABLES entries) for tables created by that user only:

```
CREATE VIEW MY_TABLES
     AS SELECT *
        FROM   SYSIBM.SYSTABLES
        WHERE  CREATOR = USER ;
```

The keyword USER refers to a system variable whose value is an authorization ID. It can appear in a SELECT clause or a WHERE clause (or in a SET clause in an UPDATE statement or as a value to be inserted in an INSERT statement). The authorization ID in question is the authorization ID for the user executing the SELECT clause or WHERE clause (or UPDATE statement or INSERT statement) in which it appears. In the example, therefore, it does not represent the ID of the user who creates the view, but rather the ID of the user who *uses* the view. For example, if user *xyz* issues the statement

```
SELECT *
FROM   MY__TABLES ;
```

then DB2 (actually Bind) will effectively convert that statement into

```
SELECT *
FROM   SYSIBM.SYSTABLES
WHERE  CREATOR = 'xyz' ;
```

Like the view in the first example above, this view represents a "horizontal subset" of the underlying base table. In the present example, however, different users here see different subsets (in fact, no two users' subsets overlap). Such subsets are sometimes described as *context-dependent*.

5. For a user permitted access to average shipment quantities per supplier, but not to any individual quantities:

```
CREATE VIEW AVQ ( S#, AVGQTY )
    AS SELECT S#, AVG(QTY)
       FROM   SP
       GROUP  BY S# ;
```

Users of this view see a *statistical summary* of the underlying base table S.

*Note:* The creator of the foregoing views must have at least the SELECT privilege on all the tables referenced in those view definitions. See the discussion of access privileges in the next section.

As the foregoing examples illustrate, the view mechanism of DB2 provides a very important measure of security "for free" ("for free" because the view mechanism is included in the system for other purposes anyway, as explained in Chapter 8). What is more, many authorization checks—even value-dependent checks—can be applied at compile time (bind time) instead of at execution time, a significant performance benefit. However, the view-based approach to security does suffer from some slight awkwardness on occasion—in particular, if some specific user needs different privileges over different subsets of the same table at the same time. Consider the following example. Suppose a given user is allowed to SELECT ratings (i.e., status values) for all suppliers but is allowed to UPDATE them only for suppliers in Paris. Then two views will be needed:

```
CREATE VIEW ALL_RATINGS        |   CREATE VIEW PARIS_RATINGS
   AS SELECT S#, STATUS        |      AS SELECT S#, STATUS
      FROM   S ;               |         FROM   S
                               |         WHERE  CITY = 'Paris' ;
```

SELECT operations can be directed at ALL—RATINGS but UPDATE operations must be directed at PARIS—RATINGS instead. This fact can lead to rather obscure programming. Consider, for example, the structure of a program that scans and prints all supplier ratings and also updates some of them (those for suppliers in Paris) as it goes.

Another drawback has to do with the fact that, when a record is INSERTed or UPDATEd through a view, DB2 does not require that the new or updated record satisfy the view-defining predicate. It is possible to impose such a requirement via the CHECK option, but (as explained in Chapter 8) the CHECK option cannot always be used, and in any case it *is* an option—it does not *have* to be specified. Thus, for example, view PARIS—SUPPLIERS above can prevent the user from seeing suppliers who are not in Paris, but in the absence of the CHECK option it cannot prevent the user from creating such a supplier or from moving an existing Paris supplier to some other city. (Of course, such an operation will cause the new or updated record instantly to vanish from the view, but it will still appear in the underlying base table.)

## 9.4  GRANT AND REVOKE

The view mechanism discussed in Section 9.3 allows the database to be conceptually divided up into subsets in various ways so that sensitive information can be hidden from unauthorized users. However, it does not allow for the specification of the operations that *authorized* users may execute against those subsets. That function is performed by the SQL statements GRANT and REVOKE, which we now discuss.

First, in order to be able to perform any operation at all in DB2, the user must hold the appropriate *privilege* (or authority) for that operation; otherwise, the operation will be rejected with an appropriate error message or exception code. For example, to execute the statement

```
SELECT *
FROM   S ;
```

successfully, the user must hold the SELECT privilege on table S. DB2 recognizes a wide range of privileges. Broadly speaking, however, every privilege falls into one of the following classes:

(a) *table* privileges, which have to do with operations such as SELECT that apply to tables (both base tables and views);

(b) *plan* privileges, which are concerned with such things as the authority to execute a given application plan;

(c) *database* privileges, which apply to such operations as the creation of a table within a particular database;

(d) *use* privileges, which have to do with the use of certain storage objects, namely storage groups, tablespaces, and buffer pools (see Chapter 13);

and finally

(e) *system* privileges, which apply to certain system-wide operations, such as the operation of creating a new database.

There are also certain "bundled" privileges, which serve in effect as short-hand for collections of other privileges (not always from just one of the foregoing five classes). In particular, the *system administration* privilege (SYSADM) is shorthand for the collection of all other privileges in the system. Thus a user holding the SYSADM privilege can perform any operation in the entire system, providing it is legal. (An example of an operation that would not be "legal" in this sense would be an attempt to drop one of the catalog tables. Even a user with SYSADM authority cannot do that.)

Now, when DB2 is first installed, part of the installation process involves the designation of one specially privileged user as the *system administrator* for that installed system. (The system administrator is identified to DB2 by an author-ization ID, of course, just like everyone else.) That user, who is automatically given the SYSADM privilege, will be responsible for overall control of the system throughout the system's lifetime; for example, monitoring execution and collect-ing performance and accounting statistics are part of the system administrator's job. But here we are concerned only with security considerations. To return to the main thread of the discussion, therefore: Initially, then, there is one user who can do everything—in particular, he or she can grant privileges to other users— and nobody else can do anything at all.

Note, incidentally, that although the system administrator is of course a holder of the SYSADM privilege, not all holders of the SYSADM privilege are the system administrator; other users can subsequently be granted the SYSADM privilege also, *but that privilege can subsequently be revoked again.* The SYS-ADM privilege can never be revoked from the system administrator.*

---

*Of course, this paragraph should not be construed to mean that there really is a single person who is the system administrator for all time (even if, e.g., that person leaves the company). Rather, there is a single unchanging *authorization ID* that is considered by the system to identify the system administrator. Anyone who can sign on to the system under that ID (and can pass the applicable validation tests) will be treated as the system admin-istrator so long as he or she remains signed on. Those validation tests *can* of course be changed from time to time, and probably should be.

Next, a user who creates an object—say a base table—is automatically given full privileges on that object, including in particular the privilege of granting such privileges to another user. Of course, "full privileges" here does not include privileges that do not make sense. For example, if user U has the SELECT privilege (only) on base table T, and if U creates some view V that is based on T, then U certainly does not receive UPDATE privileges on V. Likewise, if U creates a view C that is a join of tables A and B, then U does not receive UPDATE privileges on C, regardless of whether U holds such privileges on A and B, because DB2 does not permit *any* update operations against a join view.

## GRANT

Granting privileges is done by means of the GRANT statement. The general format of that statement is:

```
GRANT privileges [ ON object-type objects ] TO users ;
```

where "privileges" is a list of one or more privileges, separated by commas, or the phrase ALL PRIVILEGES; "users" is either a list of one or more authorization IDs, separated by commas, or the special keyword PUBLIC; "objects" is a list of names of one or more objects (all of the same type), separated by commas; and "object-type" indicates the type of that object or those objects. The ON clause does not apply when the privileges being granted are system privileges. Here are some examples:

Table privileges:

```
GRANT SELECT ON TABLE S TO CHARLEY ;

GRANT SELECT, UPDATE(STATUS,CITY) ON TABLE S
                  TO JUDY, JACK, JOHN ;

GRANT ALL PRIVILEGES ON TABLE S, P, SP TO WALT, TED ;

GRANT SELECT ON TABLE P TO PUBLIC ;

GRANT DELETE ON S TO PHIL ;
```

*Note:* If "object-type" is TABLE, it can be omitted, as in the final example here.

Plan privileges:

```
GRANT EXECUTE ON PLAN PLANB TO JUDY ;
```

Database privileges:

```
GRANT CREATETAB ON DATABASE DBX TO SHARON ;
```

User SHARON is permitted to create tables in database DBX. See Chapter 13 for a discussion of databases.

Use privileges:

```
GRANT USE OF TABLESPACE TSE TO COLIN;
```

User COLIN is permitted to use tablespace TSE to store any tables he may create (again, see Chapter 13 for more information).

System privileges:

```
GRANT CREATEDBC TO JACQUES, MARYANN ;
```

Users JACQUES and MARYANN are permitted to create new databases. If they do so, they will automatically be given the DBCTRL privilege over those databases (see the end of this section).

It is not our purpose here to give a complete and exhaustive treatment of all of the various privileges that DB2 recognizes. We will, however, give a complete treatment of table privileges, since those are probably the ones of widest interest. The privileges that apply to tables (both base tables and views) are as follows:

```
SELECT
UPDATE (can be column-specific)
DELETE
INSERT
```

The remaining two apply to base tables only:

```
ALTER (privilege to execute ALTER TABLE on the table)
INDEX (privilege to execute CREATE INDEX on the table)
```

To *create* a table, as already mentioned, requires CREATETAB authority for the database to which the table is to belong. To create a view requires SELECT authority on every table referenced in the definition of that view. Note that SELECT authority, unlike UPDATE authority, is not column-specific. The reason for this fact is that the effect of a column-specific SELECT authority can always be obtained by granting (non-column-specific) SELECT authority on a *view* consisting of just the relevant columns.


## REVOKE

If user U1 grants some privilege to some other user U2, user U1 can subsequently *revoke* that privilege from user U2. Revoking privileges is done by means of the REVOKE statement, whose general format is very similar to that of the GRANT statement:

```
REVOKE privileges [ ON object-type objects ] FROM users ;
```

Revoking a given privilege from a given user causes all application plans bound by that user to be flagged as "invalid," and hence causes an automatic rebind on the next invocation of each such plan. (The process is essentially analogous to what happens when an object such as an index is dropped.) Here are some examples of the REVOKE statement:

```
REVOKE SELECT ON TABLE S FROM CHARLEY ;
REVOKE UPDATE ON TABLE S FROM JOHN ;
REVOKE CREATETAB ON DATABASE DBX FROM NANCY, JACK ;
REVOKE SYSADM FROM SAM ;
```

It is not possible to be column-specific when revoking an UPDATE privilege.


### The GRANT Option

If user U1 has the authority to grant a privilege P to another user U2, then user U1 also has the authority to grant that privilege P to user U2 "with the GRANT option" (by specifying WITH GRANT OPTION in the GRANT statement). Passing the GRANT option along from U1 to U2 in this way means that U2 in turn now has the authority to grant the privilege P to some third user U3. And therefore, of course, U2 also has the authority to pass the GRANT option along to U3 as well, etc., etc. For example:

User U1:

```
GRANT SELECT ON TABLE S TO U2 WITH GRANT OPTION ;
```

User U2:

```
GRANT SELECT ON TABLE S TO U3 WITH GRANT OPTION ;
```

User U3:

```
GRANT SELECT ON TABLE S TO U4 WITH GRANT OPTION ;
```

And so on. If user U1 now issues

```
REVOKE SELECT ON TABLE S FROM U2 ;
```

then the revocation will *cascade* (that is, U2's GRANT to U3 and U3's GRANT to U4 will also be revoked automatically). Note, however, that it does *not* follow that U2 and U3 and U4 no longer have SELECT authority on table S—they may additionally have obtained such authority from some other user U5. When U1 REVOKEs, it is only authorities that are derived from U1 that are in fact canceled. For example, consider the following sequence of events:

User U1 at time t1:

```
GRANT SELECT ON TABLE S TO U2 WITH GRANT OPTION ;
```

User U5 at time t2:

```
GRANT SELECT ON TABLE S TO U2 WITH GRANT OPTION ;
```

User U2 at time t3:

```
GRANT SELECT ON TABLE S TO U3 ;
```

User U1 at time t4:

```
REVOKE SELECT ON TABLE S FROM U2 ;
```

(t1 < t2 < t3 < t4). User U1's REVOKE at time t4 will not in fact remove the SELECT privilege on table S from user U2, because user U2 has also received that privilege from U5 at time t2. Furthermore, since user U2's GRANT to user U3 was at time t3 and t3 > t2, it is possible that that GRANT was of the privilege that was received from user U5 rather than from U1, so user U3 does not lose the privilege either. And if the REVOKE at time t4 is from user U5 instead of from user U1, users U2 and U3 would *still* keep the privilege; U2 keeps the privilege received from U1, and U2's GRANT *could* have been of the privilege received from U1 instead of U5, and so U3 again does not lose the privilege either. However, suppose the sequence of events had been as follows:

User U1 at time t1:

```
GRANT SELECT ON TABLE S TO U2 WITH GRANT OPTION ;
```

User U2 at time t2:

```
GRANT SELECT ON TABLE S TO U3 WITH GRANT OPTION ;
```

User U5 at time t3:

```
GRANT SELECT ON TABLE S TO U2 WITH GRANT OPTION ;
```

User U1 at time t4:

```
REVOKE SELECT ON TABLE S FROM U2 ;
```

User U1's REVOKE at time t4 will not remove the SELECT privilege on table S from user U2, because user U2 has also received that privilege from U5 at time t3. In contrast with the previous example, however, it *will* remove the privilege from user U3 at this time, because user U2's GRANT at time t2 *must* have been of the privilege received from user U1.

It is not possible to revoke the GRANT option without at the same time revoking the privilege to which that option applies.

## Bundled (Administrative) Privileges

For purposes of reference, we conclude this section with a brief sketch of the five "bundled" privileges, namely SYSADM, DBADM, DBCTRL, DBMAINT, and SYSOPR.

- SYSADM
  SYSADM ("system administrator") authority allows the holder to execute any operation that the system supports.
- DBADM
  DBADM ("database administration") authority on a specific database allows the holder to execute any operation that the system supports on that database.
- DBCTRL
  DBCTRL ("database control") authority on a specific database allows the holder to execute any operation that the system supports on that database, *except* for operations that access the data content of that database (e.g., utility operations such as "recover database" are allowed, but SQL data manipulation operations are not).
- DBMAINT
  DBMAINT ("database maintenance") authority on a specific database allows the holder to execute read-only maintenance functions (such as the utility operation "image copy") on that database.
- SYSOPR
  SYSOPR ("system operator") authority allows the holder to carry out console operator functions on the system (such as starting and stopping system trace activities).

For a particular database, DBADM subsumes DBCTRL, and DBCTRL subsumes DBMAINT. SYSADM, of course, subsumes everything.

## 9.5 CONCLUSION

By this point the reader may be feeling a little overwhelmed by the extent of the security facilities available with DB2. We therefore summarize below the authorization requirements that are most directly relevant to *users* (as we have defined that term).

1. First, an application programmer needs no particular authority at all to precompile a source application program (and hence to create a database request module or DBRM).

2. Binding one or more DBRMs to produce a new application plan requires the BINDADD privilege (which is a system privilege, incidentally, not a plan privilege).

3. Replacement of an existing application plan by an updated version (which may have to be done several times during the application development process) requires the BIND privilege (which is a plan privilege).

4. A user issuing the BIND command should normally have the appropriate privileges for all SQL statements in the DBRM(s) to be bound (but see Chapter 14, Section 14.4).

5. Execution of a program that invokes an application plan requires the EXE-CUTE privilege (a plan privilege) for that plan. Table privileges (etc.) are *not* required. *Note:* The BIND privilege implies the EXECUTE privilege.

6. Execution of a SQL statement (or indeed any other kind of operation) through the interactive interface DB2I or through QMF requires the privilege(s) appropriate to that particular statement or operation.

We conclude with the following two observations.

1. There is no point in a database management system providing an extensive set of security controls if it is possible to bypass those controls. DB2's security mechanism would be almost useless if (for example) it were possible to access DB2 data from a conventional MVS program via conventional VSAM calls (remember from Chapter 1 that DB2 databases are built on top of VSAM data sets). For this reason, DB2 works in harmony with its various companion sys-tems—MVS, TSO, VSAM, IMS, CICS—to guarantee that the *total* system is secure. In particular, DB2's VSAM data sets can be protected by any or all of the following: MVS passwords, VSAM passwords, and RACF (Resource Access Control Facility).* In addition, the security facilities of IMS and CICS can be used to provide all of the standard IMS and CICS controls—for example, to restrict the set of terminals from which specific applications or commands can be invoked.

2. Finally, the entire DB2 security mechanism is optional. It can be disabled if desired at DB2 installation time. If it is, then of course anyone can do anything (anything that makes sense, that is; for example, it is still not possible to drop a catalog table).

---

*As a matter of fact, the internal structure of those VSAM data sets is significantly different from the structure that VSAM expects anyway, because all space management within them is done by DB2, not by VSAM (see Chapter 13). Thus it would be a nontrivial task to understand their contents even if they could be processed through normal VSAM calls.

## EXERCISES

The following exercises are in terms of a base table called STATS, defined as follows:

```
CREATE TABLE STATS
     ( USERID        CHAR(8),
       SEX           CHAR(1),
       DEPENDENTS    DECIMAL(2),
       OCCUPATION    CHAR(20),
       SALARY        DECIMAL(7),
       TAX           DECIMAL(7),
       AUDITS        DECIMAL(2) ) ;
```

**9.1** Write SQL statements to give:

(a) User Ford SELECT privileges over the entire table.

(b) User Smith INSERT and DELETE privileges over the entire table.

(c) Each user SELECT privileges over that user's own record (only).

(d) User Nash SELECT privileges over the entire table and UPDATE privileges over the SALARY and TAX fields (only).

(e) User Todd SELECT privileges over the USERID, SALARY, and TAX fields (only).

(f) User Ward SELECT privileges as for Todd and UPDATE privileges over the SALARY and TAX fields (only).

(g) User Pope full privileges (SELECT, UPDATE, INSERT, DELETE) over records for preachers (only).

(h) User Jones SELECT privileges as for Todd and UPDATE privileges over the TAX and AUDITS fields (only).

(i) User King SELECT privileges for maximum and minimum salaries per occupation class, but no other privileges.

(j) User Clark DROP privileges on the table.

**9.2** For each of parts (a) through (j) under Exercise 9.1, write SQL statements to remove the indicated privilege(s) from the user concerned.

**9.3** Let $p$ represent some privilege; let U1, U2, ..., U8 be a set of authorization IDs; and let U1 and U5 initially be the only holders of $p$. Further, assume that U1 and U5 hold the GRANT option for $p$. Consider the following sequence of events (all GRANTs assumed to include the specification WITH GRANT OPTION):

```
User U1 at time t1:    GRANT p TO U2
User U1 at time t2:    GRANT p TO U3
User U1 at time t3:    GRANT p TO U4
User U2 at time t4:    GRANT p TO U6
User U5 at time t5:    GRANT p TO U2
User U5 at time t6:    GRANT p TO U3
User U5 at time t7:    GRANT p TO U6
User U4 at time t8:    GRANT p TO U7
```

```
User U1 at time t9:    REVOKE p FROM U2
User U1 at time t10:   REVOKE p FROM U4
User U3 at time t11:   GRANT p TO U1
User U1 at time t12:   REVOKE p FROM U3
User U3 at time t13:   GRANT p TO U7
User U5 at time t14:   REVOKE p FROM U6
User U1 at time t15:   GRANT p TO U5
User U5 at time t16:   GRANT p TO U8
User U8 at time t17:   GRANT p TO U5
User U1 at time t18:   GRANT p TO U8
User U5 at time t19:   REVOKE p FROM U8
User U1 at time t20:   GRANT p TO U3
```

At the end of this sequence, who still holds *p*?

## ANSWERS TO SELECTED EXERCISES

**9.1** (a)  GRANT SELECT ON TABLE STATS TO FORD ;

   (b)  GRANT INSERT, DELETE ON TABLE STATS TO SMITH ;

   (c)  CREATE VIEW MY_REC
            AS SELECT *
               FROM    STATS
               WHERE   USERID = USER ;

        GRANT SELECT ON TABLE MY_REC TO PUBLIC ;

   (d)  GRANT SELECT, UPDATE ( SALARY, TAX )
            ON TABLE STATS TO NASH ;

   (e)  CREATE VIEW UST
            AS SELECT USERID, SALARY, TAX
               FROM    STATS ;

        GRANT SELECT ON TABLE UST TO TODD ;

   (f)  CREATE VIEW UST
            AS SELECT USERID, SALARY, TAX
               FROM    STATS ;

        GRANT SELECT, UPDATE ( SALARY, TAX )
            ON TABLE UST TO WARD ;

   (g)  CREATE VIEW PREACHERS
            AS SELECT *
               FROM    STATS
               WHERE   OCCUPATION = 'Preacher' ;
```
```

```
GRANT ALL PRIVILEGES ON TABLE PREACHERS TO POPE ;
```

ALL PRIVILEGES on a table normally includes ALTER and INDEX privileges, but these operations do not apply to views.

(h)
```
CREATE VIEW UST
    AS SELECT USERID, SALARY, TAX
       FROM   STATS ;

CREATE VIEW UTA
    AS SELECT USERID, TAX, AUDITS
       FROM   STATS ;

GRANT SELECT ON TABLE UST TO JONES ;

GRANT UPDATE ( TAX, AUDITS ) ON TABLE UTA TO JONES ;
```

(i)
```
CREATE VIEW SALBOUNDS ( OCCUPATION, MAXSAL, MINSAL )
    AS SELECT OCCUPATION, MAX (SALARY), MIN (SALARY)
       FROM   STATS
       GROUP  BY OCCUPATION ;

GRANT SELECT ON SALBOUNDS TO KING ;
```

(j)
```
GRANT SYSADM TO CLARK ;
```

Dropping a table is not an explicitly grantable privilege. A table can be dropped only by its creator or by someone holding the SYSADM privilege or the DBADM privilege over the database containing the table.

**9.2** (a)
```
REVOKE SELECT ON TABLE STATS FROM FORD ;
```

(b)
```
REVOKE INSERT, DELETE ON TABLE STATS FROM SMITH ;
```

(c)
```
REVOKE SELECT ON TABLE MY_ REC FROM PUBLIC ;
```

Or perhaps simply:

```
DROP VIEW MY_REC ;
```

For (d) through (j) below we generally ignore the possibility of simply dropping the view (if applicable).

(d)
```
REVOKE SELECT, UPDATE ON TABLE STATS FROM NASH ;
```

(e)
```
REVOKE SELECT ON TABLE UST FROM TODD ;
```

(f)
```
REVOKE SELECT, UPDATE ON TABLE UST FROM WARD ;
```

(g)
```
REVOKE ALL PRIVILEGES ON PREACHERS FROM POPE ;
```

(h)  REVOKE SELECT ON TABLE UST FROM JONES ;

REVOKE UPDATE ON TABLE UTA FROM JONES ;

(i)  REVOKE SELECT ON TABLE SALBOUNDS FROM KING ;

(j)  REVOKE SYSADM FROM CLARK ;

**9.3** All users except U4 and U6 (i.e., users U1, U2, U3, U5, U7, U8) still hold *p*.

# 10

# Application Programming I: Embedded SQL

## 10.1 INTRODUCTION

In Chapter 1 we explained that SQL was used in DB2 both as an interactive query language and as a database programming language. Up to this point, however, we have more or less ignored the programming aspects of SQL and have tacitly assumed (where it made any difference) that the language was being used interactively. Now we turn our attention to those programming aspects specifically. In the present chapter we discuss the principal ideas behind "embedded SQL" (as it is usually called); in the next chapter we examine the concept of transaction processing; and in Chapter 12 we present an introduction (only) to a somewhat more complex subject, namely "dynamic SQL." But first things first.

The fundamental principle underlying embedded SQL, which we might call *the dual-mode principle*, is that *any SQL statement that can be used at the terminal can also be used in an application program*. Of course, as pointed out in Chapter 1, there are various differences of detail between a given interactive SQL statement and its corresponding embedded form, and SELECT statements in particular require significantly extended treatment in the programming environment (see Section 10.4); but the principle is nevertheless broadly true. (Its converse is not, incidentally; that is, there are many SQL statements that are programming statements only and cannot be used interactively, as we shall see.)

Note clearly that the dual-mode principle applies to the entire SQL language, not just to the data manipulation operations. It is true that the data manipulation operations are far and away the most frequently used in a programming context, but there is nothing wrong in embedding (for example) CREATE TABLE statements in a program, if it makes sense to do so for the application at hand.

The programming languages in which SQL can be embedded in DB2—the so-called "host languages"—are PL/I, COBOL, FORTRAN, and System/370 Assembler Language. In Section 10.2 we consider the mechanics of embedding SQL in these languages. Then in Sections 10.3 and 10.4 we present the major ideas behind the embedding of SQL data manipulation statements specifically. Finally, in Section 10.5, we present a comprehensive programming example. *Note:* For reasons of definiteness, all of our coding examples are given in terms of PL/I. Most of the ideas translate into the other languages with only minor changes. Differences from language to language are stated explicitly where they are important.

## 10.2   PRELIMINARIES

Before we can get into the embedded SQL statements *per se,* it is necessary to cover a number of preliminary details. Most of those details are illustrated by the program fragment shown in Fig. 10.1.

Points arising:

1. Embedded SQL statements are prefixed by EXEC SQL (so that they can easily be distinguished from statements of the host language), and are terminated as follows:

| | |
|---|---|
| PL/I | — semicolon |
| COBOL | — END-EXEC |
| FORTRAN | — absence of continuation character in column 6 |
| Assembler Language | — absence of continuation character in column 72 |

2. An *executable* SQL statement (from now on we will usually drop the "embedded") can appear wherever an executable host statement can appear. Note the qualifier "executable" here: Unlike interactive SQL, embedded SQL includes some statements that are purely declarative, not executable. For example, DECLARE TABLE is not an executable statement, and neither is DECLARE CURSOR (see Section 10.4).

3. SQL statements can include references to host variables; such references are prefixed with a colon to distinguish them from SQL field names. Host variables can appear in SQL data manipulation statements in the following positions (only):

   · INTO clause in SELECT (target for retrieved value)

```
        DCL GIVENS# CHAR(5) ;
        DCL RANK    FIXED BIN(15) ;
        DCL CITY    CHAR(15) ;
        DCL ALPHA   ... ;
        DCL BETA    ... ;

        EXEC SQL DECLARE S TABLE
                      ( S#      CHAR(5)  NOT NULL,
                        SNAME   CHAR(20),
                        STATUS  SMALLINT,
                        CITY    CHAR(15) ) ;

        EXEC SQL INCLUDE SQLCA ;

              . . . . . . . . . . .

        IF ALPHA > BETA THEN
GETSTC:
        EXEC SQL SELECT STATUS, CITY
                 INTO   :RANK, :CITY
                 FROM   S
                 WHERE  S# = :GIVENS# ;
              . . . . . . . . . . .

        PUT SKIP LIST ( RANK, CITY ) ;
```

**Fig. 10.1**  Fragment of a PL/I program with embedded SQL

- SELECT clause (value to be retrieved)
- WHERE clause in SELECT, UPDATE, DELETE (value to be compared)
- SET clause in UPDATE (source for updated value)
- VALUES clause in INSERT (source for inserted value)
- element of arithmetic expression in SELECT, WHERE, or SET (not VALUES), where that expression in turn evaluates to the value to be retrieved, compared, or updated from

They can also appear in certain embedded-only statements (details to follow). They cannot appear in any other SQL statements.

4. Any tables (base tables or views) used in the program should be declared by means of an EXEC SQL DECLARE statement, in order to make the program more self-documenting and to enable the Precompiler to perform certain syntax checks on the manipulative statements.

5. After any SQL statement has been executed, feedback information is returned to the program in an area called the SQL Communication Area (SQLCA). In particular, a numeric status indicator is returned in a field of the SQLCA called SQLCODE. A SQLCODE value of zero means that the statement executed successfully; a positive value means that the statement did execute, but constitutes a warning that some exceptional condition occurred (for example, a value of +100 indicates that no data was found to satisfy the request); and a negative value means that an error occurred and the statement did not complete successfully. In principle, therefore, every SQL statement in the program should be followed by a test on SQLCODE, and appropriate action taken if the value is not what was expected, but we do not show this step in Fig. 10.1 (in practice such explicit testing of SQLCODE values may *not* be necessary, as we show in Section 10.5). The SQL Communication Area is included in the program by means of the EXEC SQL INCLUDE SQLCA statement.

6. As already mentioned, the embedded SELECT statement requires an INTO clause, specifying the host variables to which values retrieved from the database are to be assigned. The variables in that INTO clause can be scalar (element) variables or structures; a structure is considered simply as a shorthand for the list of elements that make up that structure. Structures can also be used in the VALUES clause in INSERT.

7. Host variables must have a data type compatible with the SQL data type of fields they are to be compared with or assigned to or from. Data type compatibility is defined as follows: (a) SQL character data is compatible with host character data, regardless of length and regardless of whether either length is varying; (b) SQL numeric data is compatible with host numeric data, regardless of base (decimal or binary), scale (fixed or float), and precision (number of digits). DB2 will perform any necessary conversions. If significant digits or characters are lost on assignment (either to or from the program) because the receiving field is too small, an error indication is returned to the program.

8. Note that host variables and database fields can have the same name. A host variable can be an element of a structure. For example:

```
DCL 1 GIVEN,
    2 S#  CHAR(5),
    2 ... ;

EXEC SQL SELECT ...
         .....
         WHERE  S# = :GIVEN.S# ;
```

Note that PL/I-style name qualification is used in SQL statements, not COBOL-style (:GIVEN.S#, not :S# OF GIVEN), even when the host language is in fact COBOL.

So much for the preliminaries. In the rest of this chapter we concentrate on the SQL data manipulation operations SELECT, UPDATE, DELETE, and INSERT specifically. As already indicated, most of those operations can be handled in a fairly straightforward fashion (i.e., with only minor changes to their syntax). SELECT statements require special treatment, however. The problem is that executing a SELECT statement causes a *table* to be retrieved—a table that, in general, contains multiple records—and languages such as COBOL and PL/I are simply not well equipped to handle more than one record at a time. It is therefore necessary to provide some kind of bridge between the set-at-a-time level of SQL and the record-at-a-time level of the host; and *cursors* provide such a bridge. A cursor is a new kind of SQL object, one that applies to embedded SQL only (because of course interactive SQL has no need of it). It consists essentially of a kind of *pointer* that can be used to run through a set of records, pointing to each of the records in the set in turn and thus providing addressability to those records one at a time. However, we defer detailed discussion of cursors to Section 10.4, and consider first (in Section 10.3) those statements that have no need of them.

## 10.3  OPERATIONS NOT INVOLVING CURSORS

The data manipulation statements that do not need cursors are as follows:

- "Singleton SELECT"
- UPDATE (except the CURRENT form—see Section 10.4)
- DELETE (again, except the CURRENT form—Section 10.4)
- INSERT

We give examples of each of these statements in turn.

### 10.3.1  Singleton SELECT

Get status and city for the supplier whose supplier number is given by the host variable GIVENS#.

```
EXEC SQL SELECT STATUS, CITY
         INTO   :RANK, :CITY
         FROM   S
         WHERE  S# = :GIVENS# ;
```

We use the term "singleton SELECT" to mean a SELECT statement for which the retrieved table contains at most one row. In the example, if there exists exactly one record in table S satisfying the WHERE condition, then the STATUS and CITY values from that record will be delivered to the host variables RANK and CITY as requested, and SQLCODE will be set to zero. If no S record satisfies the WHERE condition, SQLCODE will be set to +100; and if more than one does, the program is in error, and SQLCODE will be set to a negative value. In these last two cases, the host variables RANK and CITY will remain unchanged.

The foregoing example raises another point. What if the SELECT statement does indeed select exactly one record, but the STATUS value (or CITY value) in that record happens to be null? With the SELECT statement as shown above, an error will occur (SQLCODE will be set to a negative value). If there is a chance that a field to be retrieved might be null, the user should supply an *indicator variable* for that field in the INTO clause as well as the normal target variable, as illustrated in the following example.

```
EXEC SQL SELECT STATUS, CITY
         INTO   :RANK:RANKIND, :CITY:CITYIND
         FROM   S
         WHERE  S# = :GIVENS# ;
IF RANKIND < 0 THEN /* STATUS was null */ ... ;
IF CITYIND < 0 THEN /* CITY was null */ ... ;
```

If the field to be retrieved is null and an indicator variable has been specified, then that indicator variable will be set to a negative value and the ordinary target variable will remain unchanged. Indicator variables are specified as shown—i.e., following the corresponding ordinary target variable and separated from that target variable by a colon. They should be declared as 15-bit signed binary integers.

*Note:* Indicator variables cannot be used in a WHERE clause. For example, the following is illegal:

```
RANKIND = -1 ;
EXEC SQL SELECT CITY
         INTO   :CITY
         FROM   S
         WHERE  STATUS = :RANK:RANKIND ;
```

The correct way to select cities where the status is null is:

```
EXEC SQL SELECT CITY
         INTO   :CITY
         FROM   S
         WHERE  STATUS IS NULL ;
```

## 10.3.2   UPDATE

Increase the status of all London suppliers by the amount given by the host variable RAISE.

```
EXEC SQL UPDATE S
         SET    STATUS = STATUS + :RAISE
         WHERE  CITY = 'London' ;
```

If no S records satisfy the WHERE condition, SQLCODE will be set to +100. Indicator variables can be used on the right-hand side of an assignment in the SET clause; for example, the sequence

```
RANKIND = -1 ;
EXEC SQL UPDATE S
         SET    STATUS = :RANK:RANKIND
         WHERE  CITY = 'London' ;
```

will set the status for all London suppliers to null. So also of course will the statement

```
EXEC SQL UPDATE S
         SET    STATUS = NULL
         WHERE  CITY = 'London' ;
```

### 10.3.3 DELETE

Delete all shipments for suppliers whose city is given by the host variable CITY.

```
EXEC SQL DELETE
         FROM    SP
         WHERE   :CITY =
                 ( SELECT CITY
                 FROM    S
                 WHERE   S.S# = SP.S# ) ;
```

Again SQLCODE will be set to +100 if no records satisfy the WHERE condition.

### 10.3.4 INSERT

Insert a new part (part number, name, and weight given by host variables PNO, PNAME, PWT, respectively; color and city unknown) into table P.

```
EXEC SQL INSERT
         INTO    P ( P#, PNAME, WEIGHT )
         VALUES ( :PNO, :PNAME, :PWT ) ;
```

Once again indicator variables are legal; for example, if PCOLOR and PCITY are two further host variables, and if COLORIND and CITYIND are corresponding indicator variables, then the sequence

```
COLORIND = -1 ;
CITYIND  = -1 ;
EXEC SQL INSERT
         INTO   P ( P#, PNAME, COLOR, WEIGHT, CITY )
         VALUES ( :PNO, :PNAME, :PCOLOR:COLORIND,
                         :PWT, :PCITY:CITYIND ) ;
```

has the same effect as the INSERT shown above.

For simplicity, we will ignore indicator variables and the possibility of null values in most of what follows (both in this chapter and in the next two chapters).

## 10.4 OPERATIONS INVOLVING CURSORS

Now we turn to the case of a SELECT that selects a whole set of records, not just one. As explained in Section 10.2, what is needed here is a mechanism for accessing the records in the set one by one; and *cursors* provide such a mechanism. The process is illustrated in outline in the example of Fig. 10.2, which is intended to retrieve supplier details (S#, SNAME, and STATUS) for all suppliers in the city given by the host variable Y.

Explanation: the DECLARE X CURSOR . . . statement defines a cursor called X, with an associated query as specified by the SELECT that forms part of that DECLARE. The SELECT is not executed at this point; DECLARE CURSOR is a purely declarative statement. The SELECT *is* executed when the cursor is opened, in the procedural part of the program. The FETCH ... INTO ... statement is used to retrieve records of the result set, placing retrieved values into host variables in accordance with the specifications of the INTO clause in

```
EXEC SQL DECLARE X CURSOR FOR      /* define cursor X     */
         SELECT S#, SNAME, STATUS
         FROM   S
         WHERE  CITY = :Y ;

EXEC SQL OPEN X ;                   /* execute the query   */
         DO WHILE ( more-records-to-come ) ;
             EXEC SQL FETCH X INTO :S#, :SNAME, :STATUS ;
                                    /* fetch next supplier */
             . . . . . . . . .
         END ;
EXEC SQL CLOSE X ;                  /* deactivate cursor X */
```

**Fig. 10.2** Retrieving multiple records

that statement. (For simplicity we have given the host variables the same names as the corresponding database fields. Note that the SELECT in the cursor declaration does not have an INTO clause of its own.) Since there will be multiple records in the result set, the FETCH will normally appear within a loop (DO ... END in PL/I); the loop will be repeated so long as there are more records still to come in that result set. On exit from the loop, cursor X is closed (deactivated) via an appropriate CLOSE statement.

Now let us consider cursors and cursor operations in more detail. First, a cursor is declared by means of a DECLARE CURSOR statement, which takes the general form

```
EXEC SQL DECLARE cursor-name CURSOR
         FOR subquery [ UNION subquery ] ...
       [ FOR UPDATE OF column-name [, column-name ] ...
         | order-by-clause ] ;
```

For an example, see Fig. 10.2. As previously stated, the DECLARE CURSOR statement is declarative, not executable; it declares a cursor with the specified name and having the specified subquery (or set of UNIONcd subqueries) permanently associated with it. Notice that those subqueries can include host variable references. If the cursor will be used in UPDATE CURRENT statements (see later in this section), then the declaration must include a FOR UPDATE clause, specifying all fields that will be updated via this cursor; if not, then it may optionally include an ORDER BY clause, as in a conventional SELECT statement. That ORDER BY clause will control the order in which result rows are retrieved via FETCH. Note, therefore, that it is not possible to retrieve a set of records via a cursor in some specified order *and* UPDATE some of those records via that same cursor at the same time.

A program can include any number of DECLARE CURSOR statements, each of which must (of course) be for a different cursor.

Three executable statements are provided specifically for operating on cursors: OPEN, FETCH, and CLOSE.

1. The statement

```
EXEC SQL OPEN cursor-name ;
```

opens or *activates* the specified cursor (which must not currently be open). In effect, the SELECT statement associated with that cursor is executed (using the current values for any host variables referenced within that SELECT statement); a set of records is thus identified and becomes the *active set* for the cursor. The cursor also identifies a *position* within that set, namely the position just before the first record in the set. (Active sets are always considered to have an ordering, so that the concept of position has meaning. The ordering is either that defined by the ORDER BY clause or a system-determined ordering in the absence of such a clause.)

2. The statement

```
EXEC SQL FETCH cursor-name INTO target [, target ] ... ;
```

where each "target" is of the form

```
: host-variable [ : host-variable ]
```

(as in singleton SELECT), and where the identified cursor must be open, advances that cursor to the next record in the active set and then assigns field values from that record to host variables in accordance with the INTO clause. As explained earlier, FETCH is normally executed within a program loop, as shown in Fig. 10.2. If there is no next record when FETCH is executed, then SQLCODE is set to +100 and no data is retrieved.

Note, incidentally, that "fetch next" is the *only* cursor movement operation. It is not possible to move a cursor (e.g.) "forward three positions" or "backward two positions," etc.

3. The statement

```
EXEC SQL CLOSE cursor-name ;
```

closes or *deactivates* the specified cursor (which must currently be open). The cursor now has no corresponding active set. However, it can now be opened again, in which case it will acquire another active set—probably not exactly the same set as before, especially if the values of host variables referenced in the SELECT statement have changed in the meantime. Note that changing the values of those host variables while the cursor is open has no effect on the active set.

Two further statements can include references to cursors. These are the CURRENT forms of UPDATE and DELETE. If a cursor, X say, is currently positioned on a particular record in the database, then it is possible to UPDATE or DELETE the "current of X," i.e., the record on which X is positioned. Syntax:

```
EXEC SQL UPDATE table-name
         SET    field-name = expression
              [, field-name = expression ] ...
         WHERE  CURRENT OF cursor-name ;


EXEC SQL DELETE
         FROM    table-name
         WHERE   CURRENT OF cursor-name ;
```

For example:

```
EXEC SQL UPDATE S
          SET    STATUS = STATUS + :RAISE
          WHERE  CURRENT OF X ;
```

UPDATE CURRENT and DELETE CURRENT are not permitted if the SELECT statement in the cursor declaration involves UNION or ORDER BY, or if that SELECT statement would define a nonupdatable view if it were part of a CREATE VIEW statement (see Section 8.4 in Chapter 8). In the case of UPDATE CURRENT, as explained earlier, the DECLARE statement must include a FOR UPDATE clause identifying all the fields that appear as targets of a SET clause in an UPDATE CURRENT statement for that cursor.

## 10.5 A COMPREHENSIVE EXAMPLE

We conclude this chapter with a contrived but comprehensive example (Fig. 10.3) to illustrate a number of additional points. The program accepts four input values: a part number (GIVENP#), a city name (GIVENCIT), a status increment (GIVENINC), and a status level (GIVENLVL). The program scans all suppliers of the part identified by GIVENP#. For each such supplier, if the supplier city is GIVENCIT, then the status is increased by GIVENINC; otherwise, if the status is less than GIVENLVL, the supplier is deleted, together with all shipments for that supplier. In all cases supplier information is listed on the printer, with an indication of how that particular supplier was handled by the program.

Points arising:

1. First, we have ignored throughout the possibility that some field to be retrieved may be null. This simplification was introduced purely to reduce the size of the example.

2. Next, note the two DECLAREs for tables S and SP. It is obvious that those declarations are nothing but slight textual variations on the corresponding CREATE TABLE statements of SQL. A special utility program, the declarations generator (DCLGEN), is provided to construct such declarations on the user's behalf. (*Note:* The name DCLGEN is usually pronounced "deckle gen," with a soft g.) Basically, DCLGEN uses the information in the DB2 catalog to build either or both of the following:

- a DECLARE statement for the table
- a corresponding PL/I or COBOL declaration for a structure the same shape as the table (to be used as a target for retrieval and/or a source for update)

```
SQLEX: PROC OPTIONS (MAIN) ;

        DCL GIVENP#        CHAR(6) ;
        DCL GIVENCIT       CHAR(15) ;
        DCL GIVENINC       FIXED BINARY(15) ;
        DCL GIVENLVL       FIXED BINARY(15) ;
        DCL S#             CHAR(5) ;
        DCL SNAME          CHAR(20) ;
        DCL STATUS         FIXED BINARY(15) ;
        DCL CITY           CHAR(15) ;
        DCL DISP           CHAR(7) ;
        DCL MORE_SUPPLIERS BIT(1) ;

        EXEC SQL INCLUDE SQLCA ;

        EXEC SQL DECLARE S TABLE
                    ( S#       CHAR(5)  NOT NULL,
                      SNAME    CHAR(20),
                      STATUS   SMALLINT,
                      CITY     CHAR(20) ) ;

        EXEC SQL DECLARE SP TABLE
                    ( S#       CHAR(5)  NOT NULL,
                      P#       CHAR(6)  NOT NULL,
                      QTY      INTEGER ) ;

        EXEC SQL DECLARE Z CURSOR FOR
                 SELECT S#, SNAME, STATUS, CITY
                 FROM   S
                 WHERE  EXISTS
                     ( SELECT *
                       FROM   SP
                       WHERE  SP.S# = S.S#
                       AND    SP.P# = :GIVENP# )
                 FOR UPDATE OF STATUS ;

        EXEC SQL WHENEVER NOT FOUND CONTINUE ;
        EXEC SQL WHENEVER SQLERROR CONTINUE ;
        EXEC SQL WHENEVER SQLWARNING CONTINUE ;

        ON CONDITION ( DBEXCEPTION )
        BEGIN ;
           PUT SKIP LIST ( SQLCA ) ;
           EXEC SQL ROLLBACK ;
           GO TO QUIT ;
        END ;
```

**Fig. 10.3** A comprehensive example (part 1 of 2)

```
      GET LIST ( GIVENP#, GIVENCIT, GIVENINC, GIVENLVL ) ;
      EXEC SQL OPEN Z ;
      IF SQLCODE ⌐= 0
      THEN SIGNAL CONDITION ( DBEXCEPTION ) ;
      MORE_SUPPLIERS = '1'B ;
      DO WHILE ( MORE_SUPPLIERS ) ;
         EXEC SQL FETCH Z INTO :S#, :SNAME, :STATUS, :CITY ;
         SELECT ;          /* a PL/I SELECT, not a SQL SELECT */
         WHEN ( SQLCODE = 100 )
            MORE_SUPPLIERS = '0'B ;
         WHEN ( SQLCODE ⌐= 100 & SQLCODE ⌐= 0 )
            SIGNAL CONDITION ( DBEXCEPTION ) ;
         WHEN ( SQLCODE = 0 )
            DO ;
               DISP = 'bbbbbbb' ;
               IF CITY = GIVENCIT
               THEN
                  DO ;
                     EXEC SQL UPDATE S
                              SET     STATUS = STATUS | .GIVENINC
                              WHERE   CURRENT OF Z ;
                     IF SQLCODE ⌐= 0
                     THEN SIGNAL CONDITION ( DBEXCEPTION ) ;
                     DISP = 'UPDATED' ;
                  END ;
               ELSE
                  IF STATUS < GIVENLVL
                  THEN
                     DO ;
                        EXEC SQL DELETE
                                 FROM   SP
                                 WHERE  S# = :S# ;
                        IF SQLCODE ⌐= 0 & SQLCODE ⌐= 100
                        THEN SIGNAL CONDITION ( DBEXCEPTION ) ;
                        EXEC SQL DELETE
                                 FROM   S
                                 WHERE  CURRENT OF Z ;
                        IF SQLCODE ⌐= 0
                        THEN SIGNAL CONDITION ( DBEXCEPTION ) ;
                        DISP = 'DELETED' ;
                     END ;
                  PUT SKIP LIST ( S#, SNAME, STATUS,
                                         CITY, DISP ) ;
            END ;   /* WHEN ( SQLCODE = 0 ) ... */
         END ;   /* PL/I SELECT */
      END ;   /* DO WHILE */
      EXEC SQL CLOSE Z ;
      EXEC SQL COMMIT ;
QUIT: RETURN ;
   END ;   /* SQLEX */
```

**Fig.10.3** A comprehensive example (part 2 of 2)

DCLGEN stores its output as a member of a partitioned data set under a user-specified name. That output can then be included into a host program by means of the statement

```
EXEC SQL INCLUDE member ;
```

where "member" is the name of the member concerned.

It can be seen from the foregoing that DCLGEN (like the catalog) provides some of the functions that have traditionally been considered the responsibility of a separate dictionary product in older systems.

3. As explained in Section 10.2, every SQL statement should in principle be followed by a test of the returned SQLCODE value. The WHENEVER statement is provided to simplify this process. The WHENEVER statement has the syntax:

```
EXEC SQL WHENEVER condition action ;
```

where "condition" is one of the following:

```
NOT FOUND
SQLWARNING
SQLERROR
```

and "action" is either CONTINUE or a GO TO statement. WHENEVER is not an executable statement; rather, it is a directive to the Precompiler. "WHENEVER condition GO TO label" causes the Precompiler to insert an "IF condition GO TO label" statement after each executable SQL statement it encounters. "WHENEVER condition CONTINUE" causes the Precompiler not to insert any such statements (the implication being that the programmer will insert such statements by hand). The three "conditions" are defined as follows:

```
NOT FOUND     means     SQLCODE = 100
SQLWARNING    means     SQLCODE > 0 and SQLCODE ¬= 100
SQLERROR      means     SQLCODE < 0
```

Each WHENEVER statement the Precompiler encounters on its sequential scan through the program text (for a particular condition) overrides the previous one it found (for that condition). At the start of the program text there is an implicit WHENEVER statement for each of the three possible conditions, specifying CONTINUE in each case.

In the sample program, all exception-testing is done explicitly, for tutorial reasons. If any exception occurs, control is passed to a procedure that prints diagnostic information (the SQL Communication Area, in the example), issues a ROLLBACK (see subsection 4. below), and then branches to the final RETURN.

4. When a program updates the database in some way, that update should initially be regarded as *tentative only*—tentative in the sense that, if something subse-

quently goes wrong, *the update may be undone* (by the program itself or by the system). For example, if the program hits an unexpected error, say an overflow condition, and terminates abnormally, then the system will automatically undo all such tentative updates on the program's behalf. Updates remain tentative until one of two things happens: (a) A COMMIT statement is executed, which makes all tentative updates firm ("committed"); or (b) a ROLLBACK statement is executed, which undoes all tentative updates. Once committed, an update is guaranteed never to be undone (this is the definition of "committed").

In the example, the program issues COMMIT when it reaches its normal termination, but issues ROLLBACK if any SQL exception is encountered. Actually, that explicit COMMIT is not necessary; the system will automatically issue a COMMIT on the program's behalf for any program that reaches normal termination. It will also automatically issue a ROLLBACK on the program's behalf for any program that does not reach normal termination; in the example, however, an explicit ROLLBACK *is* necessary, because the program is designed to reach its normal termination even if a SQL exception occurs.

*Note:* The foregoing discussion assumes a TSO environment. COMMIT and ROLLBACK are legal only in that environment. Under IMS and CICS, the effect of COMMIT and ROLLBACK is obtained via corresponding IMS and CICS calls. The entire question of "committed updates" and the related notion of *transaction processing* is considered in much greater depth in the next chapter.

## EXERCISES

**10.1** Using the suppliers-parts-projects database, write a program with embedded SQL statements to list all supplier records, in supplier number order. Each supplier record should be immediately followed in the listing by all project records for projects supplied by that supplier, in project number order.

**10.2** Why do you think the FOR UPDATE clause is required?

**10.3** Revise your solution to Exercise 10.1 to do the following in addition: (a) Increase the status by 50 percent for any supplier who supplies more than two projects; (b) delete any supplier who does not supply any projects at all.

**10.4** (Harder.) Given the tables

```
CREATE TABLE PARTS
      ( P# ... NOT NULL,
        DESCRIPTION ... ) ;

CREATE TABLE PART_STRUCTURE
      ( MAJOR_P# ... NOT NULL,
        MINOR_P# ... NOT NULL,
        QTY      ... ) ;
```

where PART_STRUCTURE shows which parts (MAJOR_P#) contain which other parts (MINOR_P#) as first-level components, write a SQL program to list all component parts of a given part, to all levels (the "parts explosion" problem). *Note:* The following sample values may help you visualize this problem:

| MAJOR__P# | MINOR__P# | QTY |
|-----------|-----------|-----|
| P1 | P2 | 2 |
| P1 | P4 | 4 |
| P5 | P3 | 1 |
| P3 | P6 | 3 |
| P6 | P1 | 9 |
| P5 | P6 | 8 |
| P2 | P4 | 3 |

## ANSWERS TO SELECTED EXERCISES

**10.1** There are basically two ways to write such a program. The first involves two cursors, CS and CJ say, defined along the following lines:

```
EXEC SQL DECLARE CS CURSOR FOR
         SELECT S#, SNAME, STATUS, CITY
         FROM   S
         ORDER  BY S# ;

EXEC SQL DECLARE CJ CURSOR FOR
         SELECT J#, JNAME, CITY
         FROM   J
         WHERE  J# IN
              ( SELECT J#
                FROM   SPJ
                WHERE  S# = :CS_S# )
         ORDER BY J# ;
```

where the host variable CS__S# contains a supplier number value, fetched via cursor CS. The logic in this case is essentially as follows:

```
EXEC SQL OPEN CS ;
DO for all S records accessible via CS ;
    EXEC SQL FETCH CS INTO :CS_S#, :CS_SN, :CS_ST, :CS_SC ;
    print CS_S#, CS_SN, CS_ST, CS_SC ;
    EXEC SQL OPEN CJ ;
    DO for all J records accessible via CJ ;
        EXEC SQL FETCH CJ INTO :CJ_J#, :CJ_JN, :CJ_JC ;
        print CJ_J#, CJ_JN, CJ_JC ;
    END ;
    EXEC SQL CLOSE CJ ;
END ;
EXEC SQL CLOSE CS ;
```

The trouble with this solution is that it does not exploit the set-level processing capabilities of SQL to the full. In effect, the programmer is hand-coding a join. The second approach uses a single cursor, and so does take advantage of SQL's set level nature; unfortunately, however, the join required is an *outer* join, so the program must first construct that outer join, as follows. (This second solution may therefore be less efficient than the first, because it effectively requires the same data to be scanned multiple times. Direct SQL support for an outer join operator, which is desirable anyway for usability reasons, might alleviate this problem.)

```
EXEC SQL CREATE TABLE TEMP
              ( S#       ... ,
                SNAME    ... ,
                STATUS ... ,
                SCITY    ... ,
                J#       ... ,
                JNAME    ... ,
                JCITY  ,,  ) ;

EXEC SQL INSERT INTO TEMP
         SELECT S#, SNAME, STATUS, S.CITY, J#, JNAME, J.CITY
         FROM   S, SPJ, J
         WHERE  S.S# = SPJ.S# AND SPJ.J# = J.J# ;

EXEC SQL INSERT INTO TEMP
         SELECT S#, SNAME, STATUS, CITY, 'bb', 'bb', 'bb'
         FROM   S
         WHERE  NOT EXISTS
                ( SELECT * FROM SPJ WHERE SPJ.S# = S.S# ) ;
```

Now:

```
EXEC SQL DECLARE CSJ CURSOR FOR
         SELECT S#, SNAME, STATUS, SCITY, J#, JNAME, JCITY
         FROM   TEMP
         ORDER  BY S#, J# ;

EXEC SQL OPEN CSJ ;
DO for all TEMP records accessible via CSJ ;
   EXEC SQL FETCH CSJ INTO :CS_S#, :CS_SN, :CS_ST, :CS_SC,
                           :CJ_J#, :CJ_JN, :CJ_JC ;
   IF CS_S# different from previous iteration
   THEN print CS_S#, CS_SN, CS_ST, CS_SC ;
   print CJ_J#, CJ_JN, CJ_JC ;
END ;
EXEC SQL CLOSE CSJ ;

EXEC SQL DROP TABLE TEMP ;
```

**10.2** Suppose the program includes a DECLARE CURSOR statement of the form

```
EXEC SQL DECLARE C CURSOR FOR
         SELECT ...
         FROM   T
         ...... ;
```

Bind is responsible for choosing an access path corresponding to the cursor C. Suppose it chooses an index based on field F of table T. The set of records accessible via C when C is activated will then be ordered according to values of F. If the program were allowed to UPDATE a value of F via the cursor C—i.e., via an UPDATE statement of the form

```
EXEC SQL UPDATE T
         SET    F = ...
         WHERE  CURRENT OF C ;
```

—then the updated record would probably have to be "moved" (logically speaking), because it would now belong in a different position with respect to the ordering of the set. In other words, cursor C would effectively jump to a new position, with unpredictable results. To avoid such a situation, the user must warn Bind of any fields to be updated, so that access paths based on those fields will *not* be chosen.

**10.3** The second of our two solutions to Exercise 10.1 operates on a copy of the real data. For this problem, therefore, we are forced to use the first approach. Apart from that consideration, the solution is basically straightforward. The relevant embedded statements are

```
EXEC SQL UPDATE S
         SET    STATUS = STATUS * 1.5
         WHERE  CURRENT OF CS ;

EXEC SQL DELETE
         FROM   S
         WHERE  CURRENT OF CS ;
```

**10.4** This is a good example of a problem that SQL in its current form does not handle well. The basic difficulty is as follows: We need to "explode" the given part to n levels, where the value of n is unknown at the time of writing the program. If it were possible, the most straightforward way of performing such an n-level "explosion" would be by means of a recursive program, in which each recursive invocation creates a new cursor, as follows:

```
GET LIST ( GIVENP# ) ;
CALL RECURSION ( GIVENP# ) ;
RETURN ;
```

```
RECURSION: PROC ( UPPER_P# ) RECURSIVE ;
        DCL UPPER_P# ... ;
        DCL LOWER_P# ... ;
        EXEC SQL DECLARE C "reopenable" CURSOR FOR
                   SELECT MINOR_P#
                   FROM    PART_STRUCTURE
                   WHERE   MAJOR_P# = :UPPER_P# ;

        print UPPER_P# ;
        EXEC SQL OPEN C ;
        DO WHILE ⌐ ( not found ) ;
           EXEC SQL FETCH C INTO :LOWER_P# ;
           CALL RECURSION ( LOWER_P# ) ;
        END ;
        EXEC SQL CLOSE C ;
END ; /* of RECURSION */
```

We have assumed that the (fictitious) specification "reopenable" means that it is legal to issue "OPEN C" for a cursor C that is already open, and that the effect of such an OPEN is to create a new *instance* of the cursor for the specified query (using the current values of any host variables referenced in that query). We have further assumed that references to C in FETCH (etc.) are references to the "current" instance of C, and that CLOSE destroys that instance and reinstates the previous instance as "current." In other words, we have assumed that a reopenable cursor forms a *stack*, with OPEN and CLOSE serving as the "push" and "pop" operators for that stack.

Unfortunately, those assumptions are purely hypothetical today. There is no such thing as a reopenable cursor in SQL today (indeed, an attempt to issue "OPEN C" for a cursor C that is already open will fail). The foregoing code is illegal. But the example makes it clear that "reopenable cursors" would be a very desirable extension to current SQL.

Since the foregoing procedure does not work, we give a sketch of one possible (but very inefficient) procedure that does.

```
        GET LIST ( GIVENP# ) ;
        CALL RECURSION ( GIVENP# ) ;
        RETURN ;

RECURSION: PROC ( UPPER_P# ) RECURSIVE ;
        DCL UPPER_P# ... ;
        DCL LOWER_P# ... INITIAL ( 'bbbbbb' ) ;
        EXEC SQL DECLARE C CURSOR FOR
                   SELECT MINOR P#
                   FROM    PART_STRUCTURE
                   WHERE   MAJOR_P# = :UPPER_P#
                   AND     MINOR_P# > :LOWER_P#
                   ORDER   BY MINOR_P# ;
```

```
      DO forever ;
         print UPPER_P# ;
         EXEC SQL OPEN C ;
         EXEC SQL FETCH C INTO :LOWER_P# ;
         IF not found THEN RETURN ;
         IF found THEN
         DO ;
            EXEC SQL CLOSE C ;
            CALL RECURSION ( LOWER_P# ) ;
         END ;
      END ;
END ; /* of RECURSION */
```

Note in this solution that the same cursor is used on every invocation of RECUR-
SION. (By contrast, new instances of UPPER__P# and LOWER__P# are created dynamically each time RECURSION is invoked; those instances are destroyed at completion of
that invocation.) Because of this fact, we have to use a trick—

```
      ... AND MINOR_P# > :LOWER_P# ORDER BY MINOR_P#
```

—so that, on each invocation of RECURSION, we ignore all immediate components
(LOWER__P#s) of the current UPPER__P# that have already been processed.

# 11

# Application Programming II: Transaction Processing

## 11.1 INTRODUCTION

The notion of transaction processing was touched on briefly at the end of the previous chapter. In this chapter, we explain in more detail what exactly a transaction is and what is meant by the term "transaction management." In particular, we discuss the problems of recovery and concurrency control that the transaction concept is intended to solve. Also, of course, we examine the relevant aspects of DB2 and SQL in some detail. Note, however, that much of the chapter is very general and could apply with little change to many other systems. The reader who is already familiar with the basic ideas of transaction processing may like to skip the background explanations and go directly to the SQL-specific material in Sections 11.3 and 11.6.

## 11.2   WHAT IS A TRANSACTION?

A transaction (as we use the term) is a *logical unit of work*. Consider the following example (a generalized version of Example 6.2.4 from Chapter 6, cast into embedded-SQL form): Change the supplier number of supplier S*x* from 'S*x*' to 'S*y*' (where S*x* and S*y* are parameters). For simplicity we omit a number of data validation checks that would normally be included in a real program; also we omit all declarations.

```
TRANEX: PROC OPTIONS ( MAIN ) ;
        EXEC SQL WHENEVER SQLERROR GO TO UNDO ;
        GET LIST ( SX, SY ) ;
        EXEC SQL UPDATE S
                SET     S# = :SY
                WHERE   S# = :SX ;
        EXEC SQL UPDATE SP
                SET     S# = :SY
                WHERE   S# = :SX ;
        EXEC SQL COMMIT ;
        GO TO FINISH ;
UNDO:   EXEC SQL ROLLBACK ;
FINISH: RETURN ;
END TRANEX ;
```

The point of the example is that what is presumably perceived by an end-user as a single, atomic operation—"Change a supplier number from S*x* to S*y*"—in fact involves *two* UPDATEs to the database. What is more, the database may not even be consistent between those two UPDATEs; to be specific, it may temporarily contain some shipment records that have no corresponding supplier record. (Note that this observation still applies if the sequence of the two UPDATEs is reversed.) Thus a transaction, or logical unit of work, is not necessarily just one SQL operation; rather, it is a *sequence* of several such operations (in general) that transforms a consistent state of the database into another consistent state, without necessarily preserving consistency at all intermediate points.

Now, it is clear that what must *not* be allowed to happen in the example is for one of the two UPDATEs to be executed and the other not (because that would leave the database in an inconsistent state). Ideally, of course, we would like a cast-iron guarantee that both UPDATEs will be executed. Unfortunately, it is impossible to provide any such guarantee: There is always a chance that things will go wrong, and go wrong moreover at the worst possible moment. For example, a system crash might occur between the two UPDATEs, or the program itself might abnormally terminate between the two with (say) an overflow error (not possible in the case at hand). But a system that supports *transaction processing* does provide the next best thing to such a guarantee. Specifically, it guarantees that if the transaction executes some updates and then a failure occurs (for whatever reason) before the transaction reaches its normal termination, *then those updates will be undone*. Thus the transaction *either* executes in its entirety *or* is totally canceled (i.e., made as if it never executed at all). In this way a sequence of operations that is fundamentally not atomic can be made to look as if it really were atomic from the end-user's point of view.

The *transaction manager* is the system component that provides this atomicity (or semblance of atomicity); and the COMMIT and ROLLBACK operations are the key to the way it works. The COMMIT operation signals *successful end-of-transaction*: It tells the transaction manager that a logical unit of work has been successfully completed, the database is (or should be) in a consistent state again, and all of the updates made by that unit of work can now be "committed" or made permanent. The ROLLBACK operation, by contrast, signals *unsuccessful* end-of-transaction: It tells the transaction manager that something has gone wrong, the database might be in an inconsistent state, and all of the updates made by the logical unit of work so far must be "rolled back" or undone. (By "update" here, of course, we include INSERT and DELETE operations as well as UPDATE operations *per se*.)

In the example, therefore, we issue a COMMIT if we get through the two UPDATEs successfully, which will commit the changes in the database and make them permanent. If anything goes wrong, however—i.e., if either UPDATE returns a negative SQLCODE value—then we issue a ROLLBACK instead, to undo any changes made so far. For the sake of the example, we show the COMMIT and ROLLBACK operations explicitly. However, as mentioned at the end of Chapter 10, under DB2 the system will automatically issue a COMMIT for any program that reaches its normal termination, and will automatically issue a ROLLBACK for any program that does not (regardless of the reason; in particular, if a program terminates abnormally because of a *system* failure, a ROLLBACK will be issued on its behalf when the system is restarted). In the example, therefore, we could have omitted the explicit COMMIT, but not the explicit ROLLBACK.

*Aside*: The reader may be wondering how it is possible to undo an update. The answer is, of course, that the system includes a *log*, on which details of all update operations—in particular, before and after values—are recorded. (In fact, the log entry for any given update is written to the log *before* that update is applied to the database. See the next section for an explanation of this point.) Thus, if it becomes necessary to undo some particular update, the system can use the corresponding log entry to restore the updated item to its previous value.

One final point: As explained in Chapter 1, the data manipulation statements of SQL are *set-level* and typically operate on multiple records at a time. What then if something goes wrong in the middle of such a statement? For example, is it possible that the second UPDATE in the example could update some of its target SP records and then fail before updating the rest? The answer is no, it is not; DB2 guarantees that all SQL statements are individually atomic, at least so far as their effect on the database is concerned. If an error does occur in the middle of such a statement, then the database will remain totally unchanged.

## 11.3   COMMIT AND ROLLBACK

From the previous section, it should be clear that COMMIT and ROLLBACK are not really database management operations, in the sense that SELECT, UPDATE, etc., are database management operations. The COMMIT and ROLLBACK statements are not instructions to the DBMS. Instead, they are instructions to the *transaction manager*; and the transaction manager is certainly not part of the DBMS—on the contrary, the DBMS is subordinate to the transaction manager, in the sense that the DBMS is just one of possibly several "resource managers" that provide services to transactions running under that transaction manager. In the case of DB2 in particular, there are three such transaction managers—IMS, CICS, and TSO —and a given DB2 transaction can run under exactly one of the three. As explained (in different terms) in Chapter 1:

- A transaction running under the IMS transaction manager can use the services of three resource managers—the IMS database system, the IMS data communications system, and DB2.

- A transaction running under the CICS transaction manager can also use the services of three resource managers—the IMS database system (again), the CICS data communications system, and DB2.

- A transaction running under the TSO transaction manager can use the services of two resource managers—the TSO terminal system, and DB2.

Consider a transaction that updates both an IMS database and a DB2 database. If that transaction completes successfully, then *all* of its updates, to both IMS data and DB2 data, must be committed; conversely, if it fails, then *all* of its updates must be rolled back. It must not be possible for the IMS updates to be committed and the DB2 updates rolled back (or conversely); for then the transaction would no longer be atomic (all or nothing). Thus, it obviously does not make sense for the transaction to issue, say, a COMMIT to IMS and a ROLLBACK to DB2; and even if it issued the same instruction to both, the system could still fail in between the two, with unfortunate results. Instead, therefore, the transaction issues a single *system-wide* COMMIT (or ROLLBACK) to the relevant transaction manager, and that transaction manager in turn guarantees that all resource managers will commit or will roll back the updates they are responsible for *in unison*. (What is more, it provides that guarantee even if the system fails in the middle of the process, thanks to a protocol known as *two-phase commit*. But the details of that protocol are beyond the scope of this book.) That is why the DBMS(s) is (are) subordinate to the transaction manager; COMMIT and ROLLBACK must be global (system-wide) operations, and the transaction manager acts as the necessary central control point to ensure that this is so.

The foregoing also explains why "commit" and "rollback" functions are requested differently in the three different DB2 environments. Since they are not really DB2 operations at all, but rather transaction manager operations, they must be requested in the style prescribed for the transaction manager in question. In the TSO environment, they are requested via the explicit SQL operators COMMIT and ROLLBACK (details below). In IMS and CICS, they are requested via the appropriate IMS and CICS calls, details of which can be found in the IBM manuals for those systems. In the remainder of this section, we concentrate on the TSO environment specifically.*

Before getting into details of the COMMIT and ROLLBACK statements as such, we first define the important notion of "synchronization point" (abbreviated synchpoint). A synchpoint represents a boundary point between two consecutive transactions; loosely speaking, it corresponds to the end of a logical unit of work, and thus to a point at which the database(s) is (are) in a state of consistency. Program initiation, COMMIT, and ROLLBACK each establish a synchpoint, and no other operation does. (Remember, however, that COMMIT and ROLLBACK may sometimes be implicit.)

## COMMIT

The SQL COMMIT statement takes the form

```
COMMIT [ WORK ] ;
```

A successful end-of-transaction is signaled and a synchpoint is established. All updates made by the program since the previous synchpoint are committed. All open cursors are closed. All record locks are released; locks acquired via LOCK TABLE will probably not be released (see Sections 11.5 and 11.6).

The optional operand WORK is purely a noiseword and has no effect on the execution of the statement.

## ROLLBACK

The SQL ROLLBACK statement takes the form

```
ROLLBACK [ WORK ] ;
```

---

*We also concentrate on the *application programming* environment. It is possible to enter COMMIT and ROLLBACK statements interactively, but the practice is not recommended because (as will become clear later in this chapter) it will usually mean that locks will be held for an undesirably long time.

An unsuccessful end-of-transaction is signaled and a synchpoint is established. All updates made by the program since the previous synchpoint are undone. All open cursors are closed. All record locks are released; locks acquired via LOCK TABLE will probably not be released (see Sections 11.5 and 11.6).

The optional operand WORK is purely a noiseword and has no effect on the execution of the statement.

A number of points arise from the foregoing definitions that are worth spelling out explicitly.

1. First, note that *every* operation in DB2 is executed within the context of some transaction. This includes SQL operations that are entered interactively through DB2I. The synchpoints for operations entered through DB2I are established in a manner to be explained in Chapter 14.

2. It follows from the definitions that transactions cannot be nested inside one another, because each COMMIT (or ROLLBACK) terminates one transaction and starts another.

3. As a consequence of the previous point, we can see that a single program execution consists of a *sequence* of one or more transactions (frequently but not necessarily just one). If it is just one, it will frequently be possible to code the program without any explicit COMMIT or ROLLBACK statements at all.

Finally, it follows from all of the above that transactions are not only the unit of work but also the unit of *recovery*. For if a transaction successfully COMMITs, then the transaction manager must guarantee that its updates will be permanently established in the database, even if the system crashes the very next moment. It is quite possible, for instance, that the system will crash after the COMMIT has been honored but before the updates have been physically written to the database (they may still be waiting in the main storage buffer and so be lost at the time of the crash). Even if that happens, the system's restart procedure will still install those updates in the database; it is able to discover the values to be written by examining the relevant entries in the log. (It follows that the log must be physically written before COMMIT processing can complete, incidentally. This rule is known as the *Write-Ahead Log Protocol.*) Thus the restart procedure will recover any units of work (transactions) that completed successfully but did not manage to get their updates physically written prior to the crash; hence, as stated earlier, the transaction can reasonably be defined as the unit of recovery.

## 11.4   THREE CONCURRENCY PROBLEMS

DB2 is a *shared system*; that is, it is a system that allows any number of transactions to access the same database at the same time. Any such system requires some kind of *concurrency control mechanism* to ensure that concurrent transactions do not interfere with each other's operation, and of course DB2 includes such a mechanism (basically *locking*) For the benefit of readers who may not be familiar with the problems that can occur in the absence of such a mechanism— in other words, with the problems that such a mechanism must be able to solve— this section is devoted to an outline explanation of those problems. We defer specific discussion of the DB2 facilities to Sections 11.5–11.7. Readers who are already familiar with the basic ideas of concurrency control may wish to turn straight to those sections.

There are essentially three ways in which things can go wrong—three ways, that is, in which a transaction, though correct in itself, can nevertheless produce the wrong answer because of interference on the part of some other transaction (in the absence of a suitable control mechanism, of course). Note, incidentally, that the interfering transaction may also be correct in itself. It is the *interleaving* of operations from the two correct transactions that produces the overall incorrect result. The three problems are:

1. the *lost update* problem,
2. the *uncommitted dependency* problem, and
3. the *inconsistent analysis* problem.

We consider each in turn.

## The Lost Update Problem

Consider the situation illustrated in Fig. 11.1. That figure is intended to be read as follows: Transaction A retrieves some record R at time t1; transaction B retrieves that same record R at time t2; transaction A updates the record (on the basis of

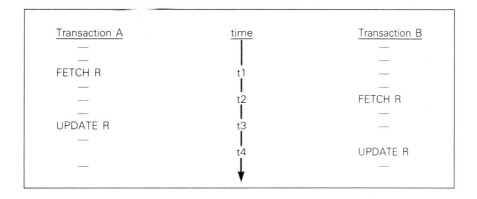

**Fig. 11.1**  Transaction A loses an update at time t4

the values seen at time t1) at time t3; and transaction B updates the same record (on the basis of the values seen at time t2, which are the same as those seen at time t1) at time t4. Transaction A's update is lost at time t4, because transaction B overwrites it without even looking at it.

## The Uncommitted Dependency Problem

The uncommitted dependency problem arises if one transaction is allowed to retrieve (or, worse, update) a record that has been updated by another transaction and has not yet been committed by that other transaction. For if it has not yet been committed, there is always a possibility that it never will be committed but will be rolled back instead—in which case the first transaction will have seen some data that now no longer exists (and in a sense "never" existed). Consider Figs. 11.2 and 11.3.

   In the first example (Fig. 11.2), transaction A sees an uncommitted update (or uncommitted change) at time t2. That update is then undone at time t3. Transaction A is therefore operating on a false assumption—namely, the assumption that record R has the value seen at time t2, whereas in fact it has whatever value it had prior to time t1. As a result, transaction A may well produce incorrect output. Note, incidentally, that the ROLLBACK of transaction B may be due to no fault of B's—it could, for example, be the result of a system crash. (And transaction A may already have terminated by that time, in which case the crash would not cause a ROLLBACK to be issued for A also.)

   The second example (Fig. 11.3) is even worse. Not only does transaction A become dependent on an uncommitted change at time t2, but it actually loses an update at time t3—because the ROLLBACK at time t3 causes record R to be

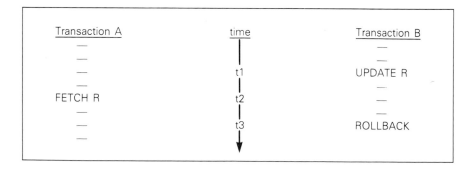

**Fig. 11.2**   Transaction A becomes dependent on an uncommitted change at
             time t2

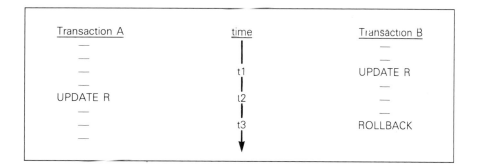

**Fig. 11.3** Transaction A updates an uncommitted change at time t2, and loses that update at time t3

restored to its value prior to time t1. This is another version of the lost update problem.

**The Inconsistent Analysis Problem**

Consider Fig. 11.4, which shows two transactions A and B operating on account (ACC) records: Transaction A is summing account balances, transaction B is transferring an amount 10 from account 3 to account 1. The result produced by A (110) is obviously incorrect; if A were to go on to write that result back into the database, it would actually leave the database in an inconsistent state. We say that A has seen an inconsistent state of the database and has therefore performed an inconsistent analysis. Note the difference between this example and the previous one: There is no question here of A being dependent on an uncommitted change, since B COMMITs all its updates before A sees ACC 3.

## 11.5 HOW DB2 SOLVES THE THREE CONCURRENCY PROBLEMS

As mentioned at the beginning of the previous section, the DB2 concurrency control mechanism—like that of most other systems currently available—is based on a technique known as *locking*. The basic idea of locking is simple: When a transaction needs an assurance that some object that it is interested in —typically a database record—will not change in some unpredictable manner while its back is turned (as it were), it *acquires a lock* on that object. The effect of the lock is to lock other transactions out of the object, and in particular to prevent them from changing it. The first transaction is thus able to carry out its processing in the certain knowledge that the object in question will remain in a stable state for as long as that transaction wishes it to.

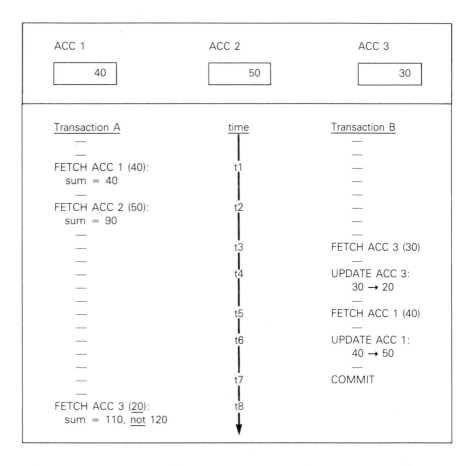

**Fig. 11.4** Transaction A performs an inconsistent analysis

We now proceed to give a more detailed explanation of the way locking works in DB2 specifically. We start by making some simplifying assumptions:

1. We assume that the only kind of object that is subject to the locking mechanism is the database record (i.e., a row of a base table). The question of locking other kinds of object is deferred to Section 11.6.

2. We discuss only two kinds of lock, namely exclusive locks (X locks) and shared locks (S locks). Other types of lock exist in some systems (in fact, DB2 itself supports additional types internally), but X and S are the only ones that are of interest to the user in DB2.

3. We consider record-level operations only (FETCH, UPDATE CURRENT, etc.). For locking purposes, set-level operations (SELECT-FROM-WHERE, etc.)

may be thought of just as shorthand for an appropriate series of record-level operations.

We now proceed with our detailed explanation.

1. First, if transaction A holds an exclusive (X) lock on record R, then a request from transaction B for a lock of either type on R will cause B to go into a wait state. B will wait until A's lock is released.

2. Next, if transaction A holds a shared (S) lock on record R, then (a) a request from transaction B for an X lock on R will cause B to go into a wait state (and B will wait until A's lock is released); (b) a request from transaction B for an S lock on R will be granted (that is, B will now also hold an S lock on R).

These first two points can conveniently be summarized by means of a *compatibility matrix* (Fig. 11.5). The matrix is interpreted as follows: Consider some record R; suppose transaction A currently has a lock on R as indicated by the entries in the column headings (dash = no lock); and suppose some distinct transaction B issues a request for a lock on R as indicated by the entries down the left-hand side (for completeness we again include the "no lock" case). An N indicates a *conflict* (B's request cannot be satisfied and B goes into a wait state), a Y indicates compatibility (B's request is satisfied). The matrix is obviously symmetric.

To continue with our explanation:

3. Transaction requests for record locks are always implicit. When a transaction successfully FETCHes a record, it automatically acquires an S lock on that record. When a transaction successfully updates a record, it automatically acquires an X lock on that record (if it already holds an S lock on the record, as it will in a FETCH ... UPDATE sequence, then the UPDATE "promotes" the S lock to X level).

|   | X | S | — |
|---|---|---|---|
| X | N | N | Y |
| S | N | Y | Y |
| — | Y | Y | Y |

**Fig. 11.5** Lock type compatibility matrix

4. X locks are held until the next synchpoint. S locks are also normally held until that time (but see the discussion of isolation level in Section 11.6).

Now we are in a position to see how DB2 solves the three problems described in the previous section. Again we consider them one at a time.

### The Lost Update Problem

Figure 11.6 is a modified version of Fig. 11.1, showing what would happen to the interleaved execution of that figure under the locking mechanism of DB2. As you can see, transaction A's UPDATE at time t3 is not accepted, because it is an implicit request for an X lock on R, and such a request conflicts with the S lock already held by transaction B; so A goes into a wait state. For analogous reasons, B goes into a wait state at time t4. Now both transactions are unable to proceed, so there is no question of any update being lost. DB2 thus solves the lost update problem by reducing it to another problem!—but at least it does solve the original problem. The new problem is called *deadlock*. To see how DB2 solves the deadlock problem, see Section 11.7.

### The Uncommitted Dependency Problem

Figs. 11.7 and 11.8 are, respectively, modified versions of Figs. 11.2 and 11.3, showing what would happen to the interleaved executions of those figures under

| Transaction A | time | Transaction B |
|---|---|---|
| — | | — |
| . | | — |
| . | | — |
| FETCH R | t1 | — |
| (acquire S lock on R) | | — |
| — | | — |
| — | t2 | FETCH R |
| — | | (acquire S lock on R) |
| — | | — |
| UPDATE R | t3 | — |
| (request X lock on R) | | — |
| wait | | — |
| wait | t4 | UPDATE R |
| wait | | (request X lock on R) |
| wait | | wait |
| wait | | wait |
| wait | | wait |

**Fig. 11.6** No update is lost, but deadlock occurs at time t4

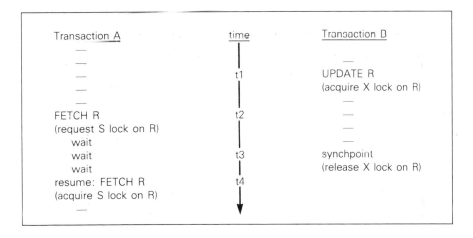

**Fig. 11.7** Transaction A is prevented from seeing an uncommitted change at time t2

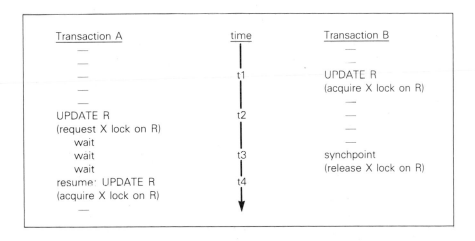

**Fig. 11.8** Transaction A is prevented from updating an uncommitted change at time t2

the locking mechanism of DB2. As you can see, transaction A's operation at time t2 (FETCH in Fig. 11.7, UPDATE in Fig. 11.8) is not accepted in either case, because it is an implicit request for a lock on R, and such a request conflicts with the X lock already held by B; so A goes into a wait state. It remains in that wait state until B reaches a synchpoint (either COMMIT or ROLLBACK), when B's lock is released and A is able to proceed; and at that point A sees a *committed* value (either the pre-B value, if B terminates with a ROLLBACK, or the post-B value otherwise). Either way, A is no longer dependent on an uncommitted update.

## The Inconsistent Analysis Problem

Fig. 11.9 is a modified version of Fig. 11.4, showing what would happen to the interleaved execution of that figure under the locking mechanism of DB2. As you can see, transaction B's UPDATE at time t6 is not accepted, because it is an implicit request for an X lock on ACC 1, and such a request conflicts with the S lock already held by A; so B goes into a wait state. Likewise, transaction A's

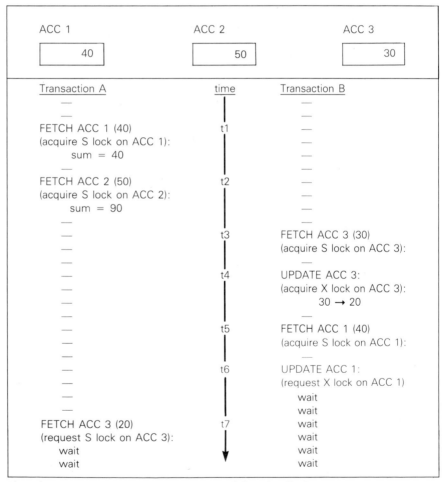

**Fig. 11.9** Inconsistent analysis is prevented, but deadlock occurs at time t6

FETCH at time t7 is also not accepted, because it is an implicit request for an S lock on ACC 3, and such a request conflicts with the X lock already held by B; so A goes into a wait state also. Thus (again) DB2 solves the original problem (the inconsistent analysis problem, in this case) by forcing a deadlock. As already mentioned, deadlock is discussed in Section 11.7.

## 11.6 EXPLICIT LOCKING FACILITIES

In addition to the implicit locking mechanism described in the previous section, DB2 provides certain explicit facilities which the programmer should at least be aware of (though the implicit facilities will be adequate in most situations). The explicit facilities—a somewhat mixed bag—consist of (1) the SQL statement LOCK TABLE, (2) the isolation level option of the BIND command, and (3) the tablespace "lockable unit" parameter.

### LOCK TABLE

The SQL LOCK TABLE statement takes the form

```
LOCK TABLE table-name IN mode MODE ;
```

where "mode" is SHARE or EXCLUSIVE, and where "table-name" must designate a base table, not a view. For example:

```
LOCK TABLE SP IN EXCLUSIVE MODE ;
```

This LOCK TABLE acquires an X lock on the *entire SP base table* on behalf of the transaction issuing the statement. (Of course, the transaction may have to wait for a while before it can acquire the lock, if some other transaction already holds a conflicting lock.) Once the lock is acquired, no other transaction will be able to acquire any lock on the table or on any part of it (in other words, no other transaction will be able to access any part of the table in any way) until the original lock is released. That lock will not be released until the *program* (not the transaction) terminates.*

If SHARE is specified instead of EXCLUSIVE, then the transaction will of course acquire an S lock instead of an X lock. Other transactions will then not be able to acquire an X lock on the table or on any part of it until the original lock is released, but they *will* be able to acquire an S lock on the table or on some part of it before that time.

---

*Under certain circumstances, not discussed in detail here, the lock will be released at the next synchpoint, rather than at program termination. In particular, this will be the case if the LOCK TABLE is entered through DB2I (in itself not particularly likely).

The purpose of the LOCK TABLE statement is as follows. If a transaction accesses a large number of individual records and locks them one at a time as described in the previous section, then the locking overhead for that transaction may be quite high, in terms of both space and time (space for holding the locks in main storage and time for acquiring them). Consider, for example, a program that scans and prints the entire shipments table. For such a program, it may well be better to acquire a single table-level lock as in the example above, and thus to dispense with the need for record-level locks (for that table) entirely. Of course, concurrency will suffer, but the performance of the individual transaction will improve, possibly to such an extent that overall system throughput will improve also.

Acquiring a table-level X lock will indeed (as just suggested) dispense with the need for record-level locks entirely for the table concerned. Acquiring a table-level S lock will dispense with the need for record-level S locks, but not for record-level X locks (again, for the table concerned); that is, if the program updates any record in the table, it will still need to acquire an X lock on that particular record, in order to prevent concurrent transactions from seeing an uncommitted change.

*Note:* Although the LOCK TABLE operation is of course defined as locking a (base) table, DB2 actually locks the *tablespace* that contains that table. See Chapter 13.


## Isolation Level

*Isolation level* is a property of an application plan. It is specified by means of a parameter on the BIND command that produces the plan. There are two possible values: RR ("repeatable read") and CS ("cursor stability"). RR is the default.

- "Cursor stability" means that if a transaction using the plan:
    - (a) obtains addressability to some particular record by setting a cursor to point to it, and thus
    - (b) acquires an S lock on that record, and then
    - (c) relinquishes its addressability to the record without updating it, and so
    - (d) does not promote its S lock to X level, then
    - (e) that S lock can be released without having to wait for the next synchpoint.
- "Repeatable read" means that record-level S locks are held until the next synchpoint, like X locks.

Isolation level CS may provide slightly more concurrency than isolation level RR, but in general it is not a good idea (that is why RR is the default). The problem with CS is that a transaction operating at that level may have a record changed "behind its back," as in Fig. 11.4, and so may produce a wrong answer. In fact, if a transaction operates under isolation level CS, then it is *always* theoretically possible to define a second transaction that can run interleaved with the first in such a way as to produce an overall incorrect result. By contrast, a transaction that operates under isolation level RR can behave completely as if it were executing in a single-user system.

Notice that although it is specified as part of the BIND command rather than as part of the program, the programmer does need to be aware of the isolation level, because the logic of the program may depend on it—that is, it may affect the way the program has to be coded.

### The Tablespace "Lockable Unit" Parameter

(We mention this topic here only for completeness. The following description may not make much sense until the reader has studied Chapter 13.)

The implicit locking mechanism of DB2 is defined in terms of record-level locks, as explained in Section 11.5. However, that definition is a *logical* definition. Physically, DB2 locks data in terms of *pages* or *tablespaces*. That is, when a given transaction logically locks some individual record, DB2 physically locks either the page or the tablespace that contains that record (depending on what was specified for the tablespace in question when that tablespace was created). For any given tablespace, the "lockable unit" can be specified as any one of the following: PAGE, TABLESPACE, or ANY.

- ANY (which is the default) means that DB2 itself will decide the appropriate physical unit of locking for the tablespace *for each plan*—that is, one plan may acquire locks at the page level, while another acquires them at the tablespace level, both on the same tablespace.

- TABLESPACE means that all locks acquired on data in the tablespace will be at the tablespace level.

- PAGE means that locks acquired on data in the tablespace will be at the page level whenever possible. Sometimes, however, DB2 will still acquire locks at the tablespace level (details beyond the scope of this text).

### 11.7   DEADLOCK

We have seen how locking can be used to solve the three basic problems of concurrency. Unfortunately, however, we have also seen that locking introduces problems of its own, principally the problem of deadlock. Section 11.5 gave two examples of deadlock. Fig. 11.10 below shows a slightly more generalized version of the problem. *Note:* The LOCK operations shown in that figure are intended

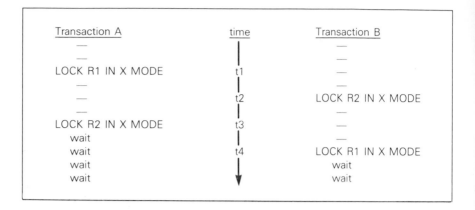

**Fig. 11.10**  An example of deadlock

to represent any operations that acquire locks, not necessarily SQL LOCK TABLE statements specifically.

Deadlock is a situation in which two or more transactions are in a simultaneous wait state, each one waiting for one of the others to release a lock before it can proceed. Fig. 11.10 shows a deadlock involving two transactions, but deadlocks involving three, four, ... transactions are also possible, at least in theory. (In practice, however, deadlocks almost never involve more than two transactions.)

If a deadlock occurs, the system will detect it and break it. Breaking a deadlock involves choosing one of the deadlocked transactions as the *victim* and (depending on the environment) either rolling it back automatically or requesting it to roll itself back (a request that cannot be refused, incidentally). Either way, the transaction will release its locks and thus allow some other transaction to proceed. In general, therefore, *any operation that requests a lock*—in particular, any SQL data manipulation operation—may be rejected with a negative SQLCODE indicating that the transaction has just been selected as the victim in a deadlock situation and has either been rolled back or is requested to do so. The problem of deadlock is thus a significant one so far as the application programmer is concerned, because application programs may need to include explicit code to deal with it if it arises. For example:

```
EXEC SQL ... ;
IF SQLCODE = value indicating "deadlock victim"
THEN DO ;
        ROLLBACK ;
        reinitialize variables from initial input data ;
        GO TO beginning of program ;
    END ;
```

Here we are assuming that the program has saved its initial input parameters somewhere (not in the database!—why not?) in preparation for just such an eventuality.

## 11.8 SUMMARY

In this rather lengthy chapter we have discussed the question of transaction management, both in general terms and as it is addressed in DB2 specifically. A transaction is a logical unit of work—also a unit of recovery and (as can be seen from the last few sections) a unit of concurrency. Transaction management is the task of supervising the execution of transactions in such a way that each transaction can be considered as an all-or-nothing proposition, even given the possibility of arbitrary failures on the part of either individual transactions or the system itself, and given also the fact that multiple independent transactions may be executing concurrently and accessing the same data. In fact, the overall function of the system might well be defined as *the reliable execution of transactions*.

In DB2 specifically, transactions are delimited by *synchpoints*, which are established by program initiation, COMMIT (successful termination), and ROLLBACK (unsuccessful termination). *Note:* COMMIT and ROLLBACK are the operations used in the TSO environment; other, analogous operations are used in the IMS and CICS environments. DB2 guarantees the atomicity of such transactions, as explained in Sections 11.2 and 11.3.

Concurrency control in DB2 is based on locking. Basically, every record a transaction accesses is locked with an S lock; if the transaction goes on to update the record, then that S lock will be promoted to X level. X locks (and S locks too, usually) are held until the next synchpoint. This simple protocol solves the three basic problems of concurrency, but also introduces the possibility of deadlock; hence application programs must be prepared to deal with that eventuality. Deadlock is signaled by a negative SQLCODE value that may potentially be returned after any SQL operation that requests a lock.

## EXERCISES

**11.1** The following list represents the sequence of events in an interleaved execution of a set of DB2 transactions T1, T2, ..., T12, all operating under isolation level RR. A, B, ... H are records, not cursors.

```
time t0         . . . . . . . . . .
time t1    (T1)    : FETCH A
time t2    (T2)    : FETCH B
    —      (T1)    : FETCH C
    —      (T4)    : FETCH D
    —      (T5)    : FETCH A
    —      (T2)    : FETCH E
```

```
—      (T2)   : UPDATE E
—      (T3)   : FETCH F
—      (T2)   : FETCH F
—      (T5)   : UPDATE A
—      (T1)   : COMMIT
—      (T6)   : FETCH A
—      (T5)   : ROLLBACK
—      (T6)   : FETCH C
—      (T6)   : UPDATE C
—      (T7)   : FETCH G
—      (T8)   : FETCH H
—      (T9)   : FETCH G
—      (T9)   : UPDATE G
—      (T8)   : FETCH E
—      (T7)   : COMMIT
—      (T9)   : FETCH H
—      (T3)   : FETCH G
—      (T10)  : FETCH A
—      (T9)   : UPDATE H
—      (T6)   : COMMIT
—      (T11)  : FETCH C
—      (T12)  : FETCH D
—      (T12)  : FETCH C
—      (T2)   : UPDATE F
—      (T11)  : UPDATE C
—      (T12)  : FETCH A
—      (T10)  : UPDATE A
—      (T12)  : UPDATE D
—      (T4)   : FETCH G
time tn        . . . . . . . . .
```

Are there any deadlocks at time t*n*?

## ANSWERS TO SELECTED EXERCISES

**11.1** At time t*n* *no* transactions are doing any useful work at all! There is one deadlock, involving transactions T2, T3, T9, and T8; in addition, T4 is waiting for T9, T12 is waiting for T4, and T10 and T11 are both waiting for T12. We can represent the situation by means of a graph (the *Wait-For Graph*), in which the nodes represent transactions and a directed edge from node T*i* to node T*j* indicates that T*i* is waiting for T*j*. Edges are labeled with the name of the record and level of lock they are waiting for.

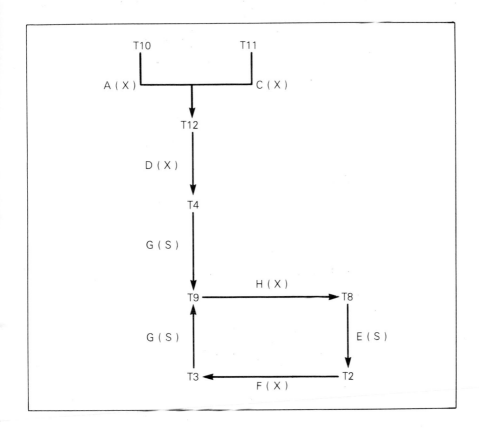

**Fig. 11.11.** The wait-for graph

# 12

# Application Programming III: Dynamic SQL

## 12.1 INTRODUCTION

"Dynamic SQL" consists of a set of embedded SQL facilities that are provided specifically to allow the construction of online applications—where by "online application" we mean a program that is written to support access to the database from an end-user at an online terminal. (The statements of dynamic SQL cannot themselves be entered interactively—they are available only in the embedded environment.) The topic of this chapter is therefore somewhat specialized; basically, the only people who need to know this material are people that are concerned with the writing of online applications. Other readers may wish to ignore the chapter altogether, at least on a first reading.

Consider what a typical online application has to do. In outline, the steps it must go through are as follows.

1. Accept a command from the terminal.
2. Analyze that command.
3. Issue appropriate SQL statements to the database.
4. Return a message and/or results to the terminal.

If the set of commands the program can accept is fairly small, as in the case of (perhaps) a program handling airline reservations, then the set of possible SQL statements to be issued may also be small and can be "hardwired" into the program. In this case, Steps 2 and 3 above will consist simply of logic to examine the input command and then branch to the part of the program that issues the predefined SQL statement(s). If, on the other hand, there can be great variability in the input, then it may not be practicable to predefine and "hardwire" SQL statements for every possible command. Instead, it is probably much more convenient to *construct* SQL statements dynamically, and then to bind and execute those constructed statements dynamically. The facilities of dynamic SQL are provided to assist in this process.

Incidentally, the process just described is exactly what happens when SQL statements themselves are entered interactively, either through DB2I or through QMF (see Section 1.3 if you need a reminder on the meaning of these two terms). In each case, an online application is executing and is ready to accept an extremely wide variety of input, namely any valid (or invalid!) SQL statement. It uses the facilities of dynamic SQL to construct suitable *embedded* SQL statements corresponding to its input, to bind and execute those constructed statements, and to return messages and results back to the terminal.

If the statement to be dynamically bound and executed is a SELECT statement, special considerations apply. (As in ordinary embedded SQL, retrieval is more complicated and involves more work on the part of the user.) Section 12.2 therefore considers the other statements first, then Section 12.3 addresses the problem of SELECT statements specifically.

## 12.2   HANDLING STATEMENTS OTHER THAN SELECT

The two principal statements of dynamic SQL are PREPARE and EXECUTE. Their use is illustrated by the following (accurate but unrealistically simple) PL/I example.

```
        DCL     SQLSOURCE CHAR(256) VARYING ;
EXEC SQL DECLARE SQLOBJ STATEMENT ;

        SQLSOURCE = 'DELETE FROM SP WHERE QTY < 100' ;
EXEC SQL PREPARE SQLOBJ FROM :SQLSOURCE ;
EXEC SQL EXECUTE SQLOBJ ;
```

Explanation: SQLSOURCE is a PL/I varying length character string variable in which the program will construct the source form (i.e., character string representation) of some SQL statement (a DELETE statement, in our particular example). SQLOBJ, by contrast, is a *SQL* variable, not a PL/I variable, that will be used to hold the object form (i.e., machine code representation) of the SQL statement whose source form is given in SQLSOURCE. (The names SQLSOURCE and SQLOBJ are arbitrary.) The assignment statement "SQLSOURCE = ... ;" assigns to SQLSOURCE the source form of a SQL DELETE statement. (As suggested in Section 12.1, the process of constructing such a source statement is likely to be somewhat more complicated in practice, involving the input and analysis of some command from the terminal.) The PREPARE statement then takes that source statement and precompiles and binds it to produce a machine code version, which it stores in SQLOBJ. Finally, the EXECUTE statement executes that machine code version and thus (in the example) causes the actual DELETE to occur. Feedback information from the DELETE will be returned in the SQLCA as usual.

Note, incidentally, that since it denotes a SQL variable, not a PL/I variable, the statement name SQLOBJ does *not* have a colon prefix in the PREPARE and EXECUTE statements.

## PREPARE

The syntax of the PREPARE statement is as follows.

```
EXEC SQL PREPARE statement-name FROM string-expression ;
```

Here "string-expression" is an expression of the host language that yields the character string representation of a SQL statement, and "statement-name" is the name of a SQL variable that will be used to contain the PREPAREd (i.e., precompiled and bound) version of that SQL statement. The statement to be PREPAREd must be one of the following (only):

```
UPDATE (including CURRENT form)
DELETE (including CURRENT form)
INSERT
SELECT

CREATE
DROP
ALTER
COMMENT

GRANT
REVOKE

COMMIT
ROLLBACK
LOCK
```

The source form of a statement to be PREPAREd must not include either EXEC SQL or a statement terminator.

## EXECUTE

The syntax of the EXECUTE statement is as follows.

```
EXEC SQL EXECUTE statement-name [ USING arguments ] ;
```

The PREPAREd SQL statement in the SQL variable identified by "statement-name" is executed. The USING clause is explained in the subsection "Arguments and Parameters" immediately following.

### Arguments and Parameters

SQL statements that are to be PREPAREd cannot include any references to host variables. However, they can contain *parameters*, denoted in the source form of the statement by question marks. Parameters can appear wherever host variables can appear. For example:

```
SQLSOURCE = 'DELETE
             FROM    SP
             WHERE   QTY > ?
             AND     QTY < ?' ;

EXEC SQL PREPARE SQLOBJ FROM :SQLSOURCE ;
```

Arguments to replace the parameters are specified when the statement is EXECUTEd, via the USING clause. For example:

```
EXEC SQL EXECUTE SQLOBJ USING :LOW, :HIGH ;
```

In the example, the statement actually executed is equivalent to the ordinary embedded statement

```
EXEC SQL DELETE FROM SP WHERE QTY > :LOW AND QTY < :HIGH ;
```

In general, the USING clause in the EXECUTE statement takes the form

```
USING argument [, argument ] ...
```

where each "argument" in turn takes the form

```
: host-variable [ : host-variable ]
```

just like a target variable reference in an INTO clause. (The optional second host variable is a null indicator variable.) The $n$th argument in the list of arguments corresponds to the $n$th parameter (i.e., $n$th question mark) in the source form of the PREPAREd statement.

## 12.3   HANDLING SELECT STATEMENTS

As indicated earlier, the procedure outlined in Section 12.2 is adequate for the dynamic preparation and execution of all SQL operations (all SQL operations that may legally be PREPAREd, that is), except SELECT. The reason that SELECT is different is that it returns data to the program; all the other statements return feedback information (in the SQLCA) only.

A program using SELECT needs to know something about the data values to be retrieved, since it has to specify a set of target variables to receive those values. In other words, it needs to know at least how many values there will be in each result row, and also what the data types and lengths of those values will be. If the SELECT is generated dynamically, it will usually not be possible for the program to know this information in advance; therefore, it must obtain the information dynamically, using another dynamic SQL statement called DESCRIBE. In outline, the procedure such a program must go through is as follows.

1.  It builds and PREPAREs the SELECT statement *without* an INTO clause. (A SELECT statement that is to be PREPAREd is not allowed to include an INTO clause.)

2.  It uses DESCRIBE to interrogate the system about the results it can expect when the SELECT is executed. The description of those results is returned in an area called the SQL Descriptor Area (SQLDA).

3.  Next, it allocates storage for a set of target variables to receive those results in accordance with what it has just learned from DESCRIBE, and places the addresses of those target variables back into the SQLDA.

4.  Finally, it retrieves the result rows one at a time by means of a cursor, using the cursor statements OPEN, FETCH, and CLOSE. It can also use UPDATE CURRENT and DELETE CURRENT on those rows, if appropriate (however, those statements will probably have to be PREPAREd and EXECUTEd versions).

In order to make these ideas a little more concrete, we present a simple example to show what such a program might look like (in outline). The example is written in PL/I. Note that it *must* be written in either PL/I or Assembler Language, because it has to be able to allocate storage dynamically; that is, an online application that is to perform data retrieval must be written in one of those two languages. By contrast, an online application that is to use only the facilities described in Section 12.2 can be written in COBOL or FORTRAN if desired.

```
        DCL SQLSOURCE CHAR(256) VARYING ;
    EXEC SQL DECLARE SQLOBJ STATEMENT ;
    EXEC SQL DECLARE X CURSOR FOR SQLOBJ ;
```

```
EXEC SQL INCLUDE SQLDA ;
/* Let the maximum number of expected values to be       */
/* retrieved be N.                                       */
        SQLSIZE = N ;
        ALLOCATE SQLDA ;

        SQLSOURCE = 'SELECT * FROM SP WHERE QTY > 100' ;
EXEC SQL PREPARE SQLOBJ FROM :SQLSOURCE ;

EXEC SQL DESCRIBE SQLOBJ INTO SQLDA ;

/* Now SQLDA contains the following information (among   */
/* other things):                                        */
/*  - actual number of values to be retrieved in SQLN    */
/*  - data type and length of ith value in SQLVAR(i)     */

/* Using the information returned by DESCRIBE, the       */
/* program can now allocate a storage area for each      */
/* value to be retrieved, and place the address of the   */
/* ith such area in SQLVAR(i). Then:                     */

EXEC SQL OPEN X ;
        DO WHILE ( more-records-to-come ) ;
            EXEC SQL FETCH X
                    USING DESCRIPTOR SQLDA ;
                . . . . .
        END ;
EXEC SQL CLOSE X ;
```

Explanation: SQLSOURCE and SQLOBJ are basically as before; SQLSOURCE will contain the source form of a SQL statement (a SELECT statement, of course, in this example), and SQLOBJ will contain the corresponding object form. X is a cursor for that SELECT; note that it is declared by a new form of the DECLARE CURSOR statement, as follows.

```
EXEC SQL DECLARE cursor-name CURSOR FOR statement-name ;
```

The declaration of the SQL Descriptor Area is brought into the program by the statement

```
EXEC SQL INCLUDE SQLDA ;
```

This statement generates a declaration for a PL/I based structure called SQLDA, also a declaration for a numeric variable called SQLSIZE. The program must set SQLSIZE to the value N (where N is an upper bound on the number of values to be retrieved per row by the SELECT statement), then allocate storage for

SQLDA (the amount of storage allocated will be a function of the value of SQLSIZE).

Next, the desired SELECT statement is constructed in source form in SQLSOURCE, and is then PREPAREd to yield the corresponding object form in SQLOBJ. Then the program issues a DESCRIBE against SQLOBJ to obtain a description of the values expected per row from the SELECT. That description consists of two parts: (a) the actual number of values to be retrieved (in a field of SQLDA called SQLN); (b) the data type and length of each of those values (in an array of entries within SQLDA called SQLVAR). Using that description, the program can then allocate storage for each of those values. It then places the addresses of the storage areas it allocates back into the SQLDA—actually into the SQLVAR array.

Finally, the program uses OPEN, FETCH, and CLOSE statements on cursor X to retrieve the actual data. Note, however, that a new form of the FETCH statement is used; instead of an INTO clause, it has a USING DESCRIPTOR clause, and the structure named in that clause (usually SQLDA) in turn identifies the target variables for the values to be retrieved.

It is also possible to PREPARE a SELECT statement that includes parameters (identified by question marks). For example:

```
SQLSOURCE = 'SELECT  *
            FROM    SP
            WHERE   QTY > ?
            AND     QTY < ?'  ;
```

```
EXEC SQL PREPARE SQLOBJ FROM :SQLSOURCE ;
```

Arguments are specified in the corresponding OPEN statement. For example:

```
EXEC SQL OPEN X USING :LOW, :HIGH ;
```

(EXECUTE does not apply to SELECT. The function of EXECUTE is performed by OPEN when the statement to be executed is a SELECT.)

## 12.4   CONCLUSION

This brings us to the end of our discussion of the facilities of dynamic SQL, and indeed to the end of our three chapters on SQL application programming. Of those three chapters:

- Chapter 10 describes all the major principles of the embedded SQL approach. The material of that chapter is thus relevant to all SQL programming, and should be of interest to anyone who is concerned in any way with application programming in DB2.

▪ Chapter 11 is also concerned with principles that are relevant to all users—
to be specific, it discusses the concepts of transaction management (concurrency and recovery), and it shows how those concepts are exposed in the
SQL language. However, the nature of SQL is such that users need to worry
explicitly about such matters only very rarely; most of the time, DB2's default
mechanisms are entirely adequate.

▪ The present chapter, by contrast, has been concerned with a very specialized
topic, namely that of how to write an online application in SQL. Such an
application requires the facilities of dynamic SQL—principally the PRE-
PARE and EXECUTE statements, and (if it is a SELECT statement that is
to be PREPAREd) also the DESCRIBE statement. *Note:* The other portions
of the language are sometimes referred to as *static* SQL, to distinguish them
from the dynamic facilities that we have been discussing in this chapter.

It should be pointed out that it is of course possible to use the facilities
of dynamic SQL whenever greater variability is required than is provided by
the conventional static statements. (In other words, it is not quite true to say
that online applications are the sole justification for dynamic SQL, though
that statement is really not very wide of the mark.) For example, the following statement:

```
EXEC SQL SELECT * FROM :TNV ;
```

(where TNV is not the name of a table but the name of a host variable whose
*value* is the name of a table) is not a valid SELECT statement in conventional
static SQL, but dynamic SQL can be used to achieve the desired effect.

To conclude the entire set of three chapters, we offer the following comment.
The fact that DB2 uses essentially the same language (SQL) for both interactive
and programmed access to the database has one very significant consequence: It
means that the database portions of an application program can be tested and
debugged interactively. Using the interactive interface, it is very easy for a programmer to create some test tables, load data into them, execute (interactive
versions of) the programmed SQL statements against them, query the tables and/
or the catalog to see the effect of those statements, and so on. In other words,
the interactive interface provides a very convenient *programmer debugging facility*. Of course, it is attractive for other reasons too; for example, the data definition
process is normally carried out through this interface, and so too is the process
of granting and revoking authorization. Also, of course, the interface provides a
rudimentary but serviceable *ad hoc* query facility.

# 13

# Storage Structure

## 13.1 INTRODUCTION

As explained in Chapter 3, the data definition statements of SQL can conveniently be divided into two classes, namely logical and physical —the logical statements having to do with objects that are genuinely of interest to users, such as base tables and views, and the physical statements having to do with objects that are more of interest to administrators (i.e., system administrators and database administrators). In this chapter we take a brief look at the latter class of objects. The data definition statements corresponding to those objects are somewhat complicated, however, involving (as they necessarily must) a great deal of low-level detail. For that reason, we will not describe those statements in detail here; we content ourselves with the observation that they fall into the same broad pattern as the logical statements, in the sense that, for each kind of object, there is a CREATE statement, an ALTER statement, and a DROP statement. (Even this simple remark is not 100 percent true, as a matter of fact—not all kinds of object permit all three kinds of operation. But we leave all discussion of the details to the IBM manuals.)

Fig. 13.1 is a schematic representation of the major storage objects and their interrelationships. The figure is meant to be interpreted as follows.

- The total collection of stored data is divided up into a number of disjoint databases—several user databases and several system databases, in general. One system database, the catalog database, is shown in the figure.

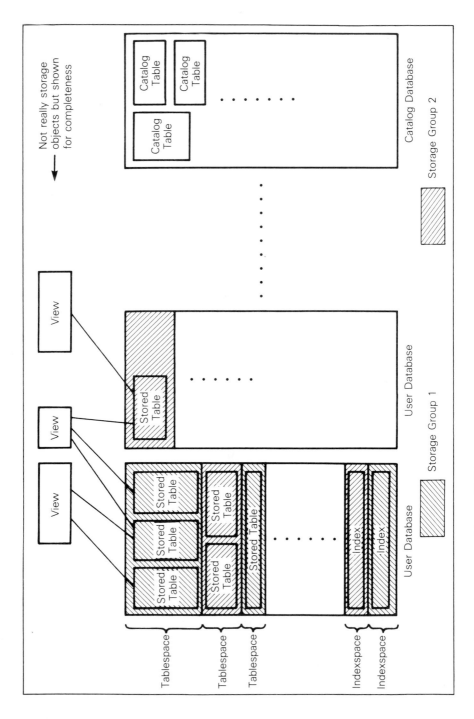

**Fig. 13.1** The major storage objects of DB2

- Each database is divided up into a number of disjoint "spaces"—several tablespaces and several indexspaces, in general. A "space" is a dynamically extendable collection of *pages*, where a page is a block of physical storage (it is the unit of I/O, i.e., the unit transferred between primary and secondary storage in a single I/O operation).

- Each tablespace contains one or more stored tables (frequently but not invariably just one). A stored table is the physical representation of a base table. A given stored table must be wholly contained within a single tablespace.

- Each indexspace contains exactly one index. A given index must be wholly contained within a single indexspace. A given stored table and all its associated indexes must be wholly contained within a single database.

- As explained in Chapter 8, views are not stored objects at all. They are mentioned in the figure just to illustrate the point that a given view can span multiple databases—that is, it can be based on multiple stored tables, and those stored tables do not necessarily all have to be from the same database.

- Each "space" (tablespace or indexspace) has an associated *storage group*.* A storage group is a collection of direct access volumes, all of the same device type. When a given space needs to be extended, storage is acquired from the appropriate storage group. The spaces in a given database do not all have to have the same storage group, nor do all the spaces that share a given storage group have to come from the same database. Note, therefore, that storage groups are in a sense the most "physical" of all the various storage objects in DB2; databases, tablespaces, etc., are all still somewhat "logical."

Before we go on to amplify the foregoing ideas, we make one further introductory remark concerning *system defaults*. The basic idea behind system defaults is as follows: The full array of storage objects—databases, tablespaces, storage groups, etc.—is somewhat complicated at first sight, and it would be rather unfortunate (indeed, it would be counter to the overall ease-of-use objective) if users had to understand all of those concepts in their entirety before they were able to do any useful work. For example, it should not be necessary to have to know about tablespaces in order just to be able to create and use a new table. Now, the complete CREATE TABLE statement includes a parameter that specifies the tablespace into which the new table is to go. However, it is always possible to omit that parameter (indeed, we have done exactly that in all examples in this book so far), in which case DB2 will automatically create a *default* table space and will place the new table in that. Thus it is indeed not necessary to be

---

*A partitioned space may have a different storage group for each partition. See Section 13.3.

familiar with the tablespace notion in order to be able to create a new table. Similar simplifications apply to most of the other data definition statements and most of the other storage objects. The full default mechanism is described in more detail in Section 13.8.

## 13.2  DATABASES

A database in DB2 is a collection of logically related objects—that is, a collection of stored tables that belong together in some way, together with their associated indexes and the various spaces containing those tables and indexes. It thus consists of a set of tablespaces, each containing one or more stored tables, together with a set of indexspaces, each containing exactly one index. As explained earlier, a given stored table and all its associated indexes must be wholly contained within a single database.

The database is *the unit of start/stop*, in the sense that the console operator can make a given database available or unavailable for processing via an appropriate START or STOP command. Note, therefore, that objects are grouped together into the same database primarily for operational reasons; users (in our sense of the term) need have no concern for databases at all, but can simply concentrate on the *data*, i.e., on tables (base tables and views). Tables can be moved from one database to another without having any impact on users. And finally (as suggested toward the end of the previous section), a database is not even a particularly "physical" kind of object; in particular, it is typically *not* a single disk, or single set of disks, but consists rather of portions of many disks, other portions of which may be allocated to other databases.

## 13.3  TABLESPACES

A tablespace can be thought of as a *logical address space* on secondary storage that is used to hold one or more stored tables ("logical" because it is typically *not* a set of physically adjacent areas). As the amount of data in those tables grows, so storage will be acquired from the appropriate storage group and added to that address space to accommodate that growth. One tablespace can be up to approximately 64 billion bytes in size (and there is no limit to the number of tablespaces in a database, nor to the number of databases).* The pages in a given tablespace are either all 4K bytes or all 32K bytes in size (K = 1024).

Fundamentally, the tablespace is the storage unit for reorganization and recovery purposes; that is, it is the unit that can be recovered (after a media failure) or

---

*As a matter of interest, 64 billion bytes (in 4K pages) is approximately equivalent to 128 volumes (i.e., 32 units) of IBM 3380 direct access storage.

reorganized via a command from the console operator. If the tablespace is very large, however, reorganization or recovery could take a very long time. DB2 therefore provides the option to *partition* a large tablespace into smaller pieces; for a partitioned tablespace, the unit of reorganization and recovery is the individual partition, rather than the entire tablespace.

Tablespaces thus come in two varieties, *partitioned* and *simple* (nonpartitioned). We discuss each in turn.

## Simple Tablespaces

A simple tablespace may contain more than one table, though one is perhaps the normal case. The advantage of having more than one is that stored records can be clustered together in such a way as to improve access times to logically related records. For example, if tables S and SP were stored in the same tablespace, then it would be possible (by judicious use of the load utility) to store all the shipment records for supplier S1 close to (i.e., on the same page as) the supplier record for S1, all the shipment records for supplier S2 close to the supplier record for S2, and so on. Queries such as "Get details of supplier S1 and all corresponding shipments" can then be handled efficiently, since the number of I/O operations will be reduced.

Note, however, that it is not easy to maintain such clustering in the face of arbitrary updates; moreover, neither the optimizer nor the reorganization utility would have any understanding of that clustering. Furthermore, sequential access may well be slowed down, inasmuch as the system will have to scan not only records of the table concerned, but also records of other tables that happen to be mixed in with the first table. In most situations, one table per tablespace is probably the most satisfactory arrangement.

Each table in the tablespace can have one or more indexes. If a table has any indexes at all, then exactly one is the *clustering index* for that table. Clustering indexes are discussed in detail in Section 13.6; for now, we content ourselves with the following brief explanation. In essence, a clustering index is an index that is used to control physical placement of the indexed records, such that the physical sequence of records in storage closely approximates the logical sequence of records as defined by the index. If a table has a clustering index, then records must be initially loaded into that table (via the load utility) in cluster order; they will be stored in the tablespace in order of arrival from left to right—i.e., in increasing address sequence—with periodic gaps to allow for future insertions. (Gap frequency is determined by the system, not by the user.) If a table has no indexes, then records can be initially loaded in any order; again they will be stored left to right, but without any gaps. Subsequent insertions to the table will be stored in a gap (if a clustering index exists and the record can be physically stored close to its logical position), otherwise at the right-hand end.

## Partitioned Tablespaces

A partitioned tablespace contains exactly one table. That table is partitioned in accordance with value ranges of a partitioning field or field combination. For example, if the shipments table SP were stored in a partitioned tablespace, then it could be partitioned by values of the S# field, such that all shipments for supplier S1 were stored in partition one, all shipments for supplier S2 were stored in partition two, and so on. A clustering index is required for the partitioning field or field combination; additional indexes are optional. The partitioning field (combination) cannot be UPDATEd. Records must be initially loaded (via the load utility) in cluster order; they will be stored from left to right (with gaps) within the appropriate partition.

As already indicated, individual partitions of a partitioned tablespace are independent of one another, in the sense that they can be independently recovered and reorganized. They may also be associated with different storage groups; thus, for example, it is possible to store some partitions on a faster device and others on a slower device (different storage groups can correspond to different device types).

## 13.4   STORED TABLES

A stored table is the stored representation of a base table. It consists of a set of stored records, one for each data row in the base table in question. Each stored record will be wholly contained within a single page; however, one stored table can be spread over multiple pages, and (in a simple tablespace) one page can contain stored records from multiple stored tables.

A stored record is *not* identical to the corresponding record of the base table. Instead, it consists of a byte string, made up as follows:

- a prefix, containing control information such as the internal system name for the stored table of which this stored record is a part; followed by

- up to $N$ stored fields, where $N$ is the number of columns in the base table. There will be fewer than $N$ stored fields if the stored record is varying length (i.e., if it includes any varying length fields) and one or more fields at the right-hand end are null; null fields at the end of a varying length record are not physically stored.

Each stored field, in turn, consists of:

- a length prefix (if the field is varying length), giving the length of the actual data (including the null indicator prefix, if there is one—see below);

- a null indicator prefix (if nulls are allowed), indicating whether the value in the data part of the field (a) is to be taken as a genuine data value or (b) is to be ignored (i.e., interpreted as null);

- an encoded form of the actual data value. Stored data is encoded in such a manner that the System/370 "compare logical" instruction (CLC) will always yield the appropriate response when applied to two values of the same SQL data type. For example, INTEGER values are stored with their sign bit reversed. Thus all stored data fields are considered simply as byte strings by the Stored Data Manager; any interpretation of such a string as, e.g., an INTEGER value is performed above the Data Manager interface. The advantage of such a scheme is that new data types can be introduced without any impact on the low-level components of the system. (As an exercise, the reader may like to try working out suitable encodings for the other SQL data types.)

All stored fields are byte-aligned. There are no gaps between fields. Varying length data occupies only as many bytes as are needed to store the actual value.

*Note:* The foregoing describes the standard representation of a stored record. For any given table, however, the installation has the option of providing an "edit procedure" which will be given control every time a record is stored or fetched. On "store," the edit procedure can convert the standard representation to any other form desired, and the record will be stored in that form. On "fetch," of course, the edit procedure must perform the opposite conversion. Thus, for example, the installation can decide to store data in a compressed or encrypted form; furthermore, it can make that decision on a table-by-table basis.

Internally, records are addressed by "record ID" or RID. For example, all pointers within indexes are RIDs. RIDs are unique within the containing database. Fig. 13.2 shows how RIDs are implemented. The RID for a stored record R consists of two parts: the page number of the page P containing R, and a byte offset from the foot of P identifying a slot that contains, in turn, the byte offset of R from the top of P. This scheme represents a good compromise between the speed of direct addressing and the flexibility of indirect addressing: Records can be rearranged within their page—e.g., to close up the gap when a record is deleted or to make room when a record is inserted—without having to change RIDs (only the local offsets at the foot of the page have to change); yet access to a record given the RID is fast, involving only a single page access.

*Note:* In rare cases it might involve two page accesses (but never more than two). This can happen if a varying length record is updated in such a way that it is now longer than it was before (e.g., the value in some varying length field has expanded), and there is not enough free space on the page to accommodate the increase. In such a situation, the updated record is placed on another ("overflow") page, and the original record is replaced by a pointer (another RID) to the new location. If the same thing happens again, so that the updated record has to be moved to still a third page, then the pointer in the original page is changed to point to this newest location.

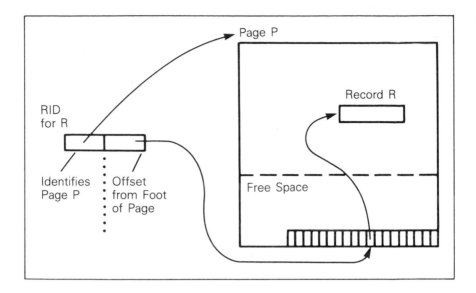

**Fig. 13.2** Implementation of RIDs

We conclude our discussion of stored tables with a note on "validation procedures." A validation procedure resembles an edit procedure in that it is a procedure that can be specified by the installation for a given base table. The validation procedure for a given table is given control each time a record of that table is stored. The purpose of the procedure is to perform validation checks on the newly inserted or newly updated record.

## 13.5 INDEXSPACES

An indexspace is to an index what a tablespace is to a table. However, since the correspondence between indexes and indexspaces (unlike that between tables and tablespaces) is always one-to-one, there are no data definition statements for indexspaces *per se*; instead, the necessary indexspace parameters are specified on the corresponding index definition statements. For example, there is no CREATE INDEXSPACE; instead, the indexspace is created automatically when the corresponding index is created, via CREATE INDEX, and that CREATE INDEX can include such parameters as the name of the associated storage group, etc.

The pages in an indexspace are always 4K bytes in size. The unit for locking purposes can be less than one page, however (another difference from tablespaces); it can, for example, be a quarter-page (1024 bytes).

Like tablespaces, indexspaces can be reorganized and recovered independently. An indexspace that contains the (required) clustering index for a partitioned tablespace is itself considered to be partitioned; all other indexspaces are simple (nonpartitioned). A partition of a partitioned indexspace can be reorganized independently. Individual partitions can be associated with different storage groups.

## 13.6 INDEXES

Indexes in DB2 are based on a structure known as the *B-tree*. A B-tree is a multilevel, tree-structured index with the property that the tree is always *balanced*; that is, all leaf entries in the structure are equidistant from the root of the tree, and this property continues to hold as new entries are inserted into the tree and existing entries are deleted. As a result, the index provides uniform and predictable performance for retrieval operations. Details of how this effect is achieved are beyond the scope of this book; however, Fig. 13.3 shows a simple example of what such an index might look like.

As you can see, the index consists of a root page, zero or more intermediate pages (at zero or more intermediate levels—there is one such intermediate level in the example), and a set of leaf pages. The leaf level contains an entry (indexed field value plus pointer) for every record in the indexed table; the leaf pages are chained together, so that the leaf pages alone can be used for fast *sequential* access to the indexed data (in index sequence). Each level above the leaf level, in turn, contains an entry (highest field value plus pointer) for every page of entries in the level below; thus the root page and intermediate pages together provide fast *direct* access to the leaf pages, and hence fast direct access to the indexed data also.

A given stored table can have any number of associated indexes, and thus any number of logical orderings imposed on it. (It always has exactly one physical ordering, of course.) To perform an exhaustive search on a table according to a given index, the Stored Data Manager will access all records in the table in the sequence defined by that index; and since that sequence may be quite different from the table's physical sequence, a given data page may be accessed many times. (On the other hand, data pages not containing any records of the table will not be accessed at all.) Thus exhaustive search via an index could potentially be much slower than exhaustive search via physical sequence—*unless* the index concerned is a clustering index. As explained earlier, a clustering index is one for which the sequence defined by the index *is* the same as, or close to, the physical sequence. A table can have at most one clustering index; that index should be the first one created for the table, and ideally should be created before any data has been loaded into the table. Clustering indexes are extremely impor-

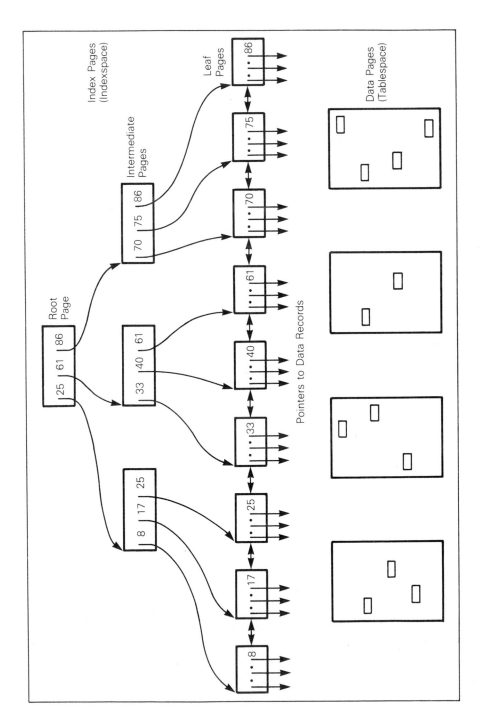

**Fig. 13.3**  Example of an index

tant for optimization purposes: Bind will always try to choose an access path that is based on a clustering index, if one is available. As a practical matter, every table should have a clustering index unless it is extremely small (and maybe even then).

## 13.7  STORAGE GROUPS

A storage group is a named collection of direct access volumes, all of the same device type. Each simple tablespace, simple indexspace, partition of a partitioned tablespace, and partition of a partitioned indexspace normally has an associated storage group.* When storage is needed for the space or partition, it is taken from the specified storage group. Storage groups thus provide a means for the installation to control data separation and data affinity—for example, they can force two tables to be stored on different volumes—while at the same time they allow most of the details of allocating data sets, extents, etc., to be handled automatically by the system.

Within each storage group, spaces and partitions are stored using VSAM entry-sequenced data sets (many data sets per space or partition, in general). DB2 uses VSAM for such things as direct access space management and data set cataloging. However, space management within pages (i.e., VSAM control intervals) is handled by DB2, not by VSAM, and VSAM indexing is not used at all. Thus, as mentioned in Chapter 9, DB2's data sets are not conventional VSAM data sets; their internal format is not what VSAM expects, and it is not possible to access those data sets using conventional VSAM. For the same reason, it is not possible to use the facilities of DB2 (e.g., the SQL language) to access existing VSAM data sets.

## 13.8  CONCLUDING REMARKS

This has been a brief overview of the storage objects supported by DB2. As explained in Section 13.1, it is not our intent in this book to give all the details of the corresponding data definition statements; however, we mention the following points.

- The tablespace for a given table is specified in the CREATE TABLE statement for that table.

---

*For a given space or partition, the installation always has the option of not using a storage group at all. If it does not, then it must use the Access Method Services utility of VSAM to define, extend, and delete data sets as necessary. The details of this option are beyond the scope of this book.

- The database for a given tablespace is specified in the CREATE TABLE-SPACE statement for that tablespace; the database for a given indexspace is implied by the table over which the index is defined (an indexspace must be part of the same database as the corresponding tablespace).

- Details of the partitioning (value ranges, etc.) for a partitioned tablespace are specified in the CREATE INDEX statement for the (required) clustering index. Details of the partitioning for the corresponding indexspace are also specified in that CREATE INDEX statement.

- The storage group for a given space or partition is specified in the statement (CREATE TABLESPACE or CREATE INDEX) that defines that space or partition.

- The volumes that make up a given storage group are specified in the CREATE statement that creates that storage group.

In addition to all of the above (and as mentioned in Section 13.1), DB2 provides a comprehensive system of *defaults* that are designed to make it easy to "get on the air." The full default mechanism is as follows:

- CREATE TABLE can specify a database instead of a tablespace. If it does, then DB2 will automatically create a tablespace within that database for the new table; that tablespace will automatically be dropped when the table is dropped. It is not even necessary to specify a database; if neither a database nor a tablespace is specified, DB2 will create a tablespace for the new table within the *default database*, which is a database that is defined for such purposes when the system is installed.

- If CREATE TABLESPACE does not specify a database, the new tablespace will be assigned to the default database.

- A storage group can be specified at any or all of the following levels:
  - the database level (in CREATE DATABASE)
  - the space level (in CREATE TABLESPACE and CREATE INDEX)
  - the partition level (in the partition specification within CREATE TABLE-SPACE and CREATE INDEX)

  If no storage group is specified at the partition level for a given partition, the storage group that applies to that partition is the storage group that applies to the containing space. If no storage group is specified at the space level for a given space, the storage group that applies to that space is the storage group that applies to the containing database. If no storage group is specified at the database level for a given database, the storage group that applies to that database is the *default storage group*, which is a storage group that is defined for such purposes when the system is installed.

From all of the above, it follows that the data definition statements shown in Chapter 3 are indeed adequate for "getting on the air." In most realistic situations, however, the installation will probably wish to exercise the tighter control that is possible without the use of defaults. The purpose of the defaults is primarily to allow users to learn to use the system quickly, rather than to serve as an appropriate set of specifications for a production environment.

We conclude with a brief mention of *buffer pools*. The buffers in main storage are grouped together into a number of pools. A given space can use only one such pool; the buffer pool for a given space is specified via yet another parameter in the appropriate CREATE statement (as usual, of course, a default is assumed if the parameter is omitted). In this way, the installation can control to some degree the separation and affinity of data in main storage. For example, a given indexspace and its corresponding tablespace might be assigned to different buffer pools, thus increasing the likelihood that index entries and data records might be present in main storage simultaneously.

# 14

# The DB2
# Interactive
# Interface (DB2I)

## 14.1 INTRODUCTION

Almost all of the function of DB2 is available online through the interactive interface DB2I. That interface provides, not only the ability to execute SQL statements interactively and to invoke prewritten application programs, but also (for example) the ability to issue operator commands, the ability to invoke utilities, and the ability to prepare application programs for execution (i.e., precompile and compile them, bind them, and so on). With regard to this last point, in fact, preparing programs interactively via DB2I is intended as the normal mode of operation (although of course it is always possible to use batch if you prefer; see Section 14.9). Note, however, that programs can be invoked for execution via DB2I only if they do not contain any IMS or CICS calls, because DB2I runs under TSO, and a program containing IMS or CICS calls must run under IMS or CICS (whichever is applicable).

Fig. 14.1 shows the TSO environment; in particular, it shows how DB2I relates to TSO. In the TSO environment, as explained in Chapter 11, TSO itself serves as the transaction manager. "TSO batch" programs (see Section 14.9) execute under the TSO monitor program directly. "TSO online" programs execute

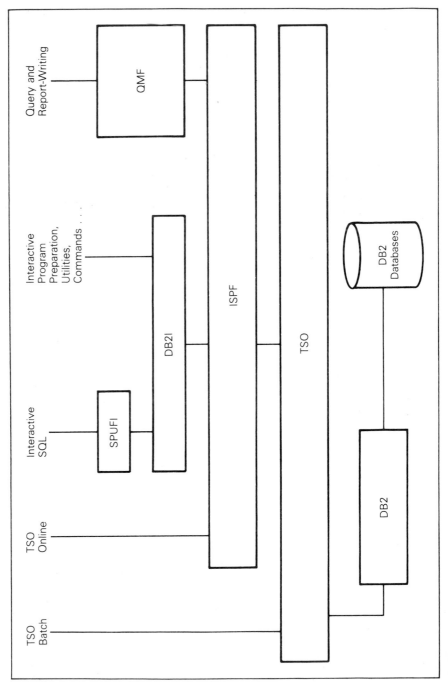

**Fig. 14.1** The TSO environment

under the control of the Interactive System Productivity Facility (ISPF), which is a screen/dialog manager for TSO. Two particular TSO online programs are DB2I and QMF (Query Management Facility); DB2I is discussed in the present chapter and QMF is discussed in Chapter 15. Finally, DB2I in turn provides (among other things) the ability to execute SQL statements interactively by means of a program called SPUFI (SQL Processor Using File Input; the acronym is usually pronounced "spoofy"). SPUFI is discussed in Section 14.2.

The following is the sequence of events for invoking DB2I:

■ Log on to TSO in the normal way and enter ISPF.

■ From the ISPF primary option menu, select the "DB2I" option.

■ The DB2I main menu will appear, offering the following options (see Fig. 14.2):

- SPUFI

- DCLGEN

- BIND/REBIND/FREE

- program preparation

- run

- DB2 commands

- utilities

Selecting one of these options will lead you through a series of prompts and menus to perform the corresponding task. (As usual, of course, you will only be allowed to perform a given task if you have the necessary authorization for that task.) Each of those sets of prompts and menus is backed by a set of help and tutorial panels, so that in most cases you should have no need of the printed manuals; most of the reference material you will require is available online. See Fig. 14.3.

We now proceed to discuss the DB2I options in more detail.

## 14.2  SPUFI

SPUFI stands for "SQL Processor Using File Input." As explained in Section 14.1, SPUFI supports interactive execution of SQL statements from a TSO terminal. The basic idea is that you can create a file containing one or more SQL statements, using the ISPF editor, then execute that file of statements via SPUFI, and then use the ISPF editor again to browse through the results of those statements (which will have been written to another file). Note, therefore, that SPUFI is a DP professional's tool rather than an end-user's tool; *QMF* is the corresponding end-user facility (see Chapter 15). SPUFI is intended primarily for application programmers who wish to test the SQL portions of their programs or adminis-

```
DSNEPRI                        DB2I MENU

===>_

SELECT ONE OF THE FOLLOWING DB2 FUNCTIONS:

    1  SPUFI                   Process SQL statements
    2  DCLGEN                  Generate SQL and host declarations
    3  BIND/REBIND/FREE        Issue BIND, REBIND, or FREE for plans
    4  PROGRAM PREPARATION     PRECOMPILE, BIND, COMPILE, LINK, RUN
    5  RUN                     RUN a SQL program
    6  DB2 COMMANDS            Issue DB2 commands
    7  UTILITIES               Invoke DB2 utilities
    X  EXIT                    Leave DB2I

PRESS: ENTER to process    END to exit    HELP for more information
```

**Fig. 14.2**  The DB2I main menu

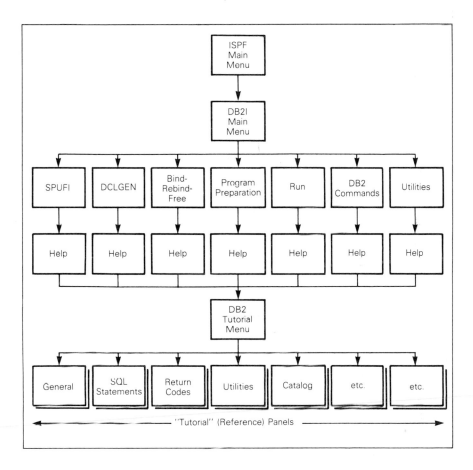

**Fig. 14.3**  DB2I menus and online documentation

trators who wish to perform SQL definitional operations (though in fact QMF can also be used to perform both of those functions).

Among other things, the SPUFI menus allow (or in some cases require) the user to specify the following parameters:

- The file to contain the SQL statement(s); this file must already exist, though it may currently be empty.

- Whether that file is to be edited via the ISPF editor before it is ready to be executed (normally YES).

- The file to receive the result(s) from executing the SQL statement(s); this file need not already exist (if it does not, then SPUFI will create it).

▪   The isolation level (RR or CS); see Chapter 11.

▪   Whether "autocommit" is YES or NO (normally YES). YES means that SPUFI will automatically issue a COMMIT after execution of the input file if no errors have occurred, or a ROLLBACK otherwise. NO means either that the input file itself includes COMMIT statements or (if it does not) that the user is to be asked interactively after execution which of COMMIT and ROLLBACK is to be issued.

If the input file contains multiple SQL statements, SPUFI will stop execution of those statements as soon as it encounters an error in any one of them. The output file will contain a sequence of results, one for each statement (including the SQLCODE value returned), followed by a summary of the overall execution (including, in particular, an indication as to which of COMMIT and ROLLBACK occurred). Fig. 14.4 shows an example of a SPUFI output file.

### 14.3   DCLGEN

The DCLGEN menu allows the user to invoke the declarations generator program. As noted in Chapter 10, DCLGEN is a program that creates EXEC SQL DECLARE TABLE statements and corresponding PL/I or COBOL structure declarations from table descriptions in the catalog. The output from DCLGEN is stored as a member of a partitioned data set, from which it can be brought into an application program by means of an EXEC SQL INCLUDE statement.

### 14.4   BIND/REBIND/FREE

This menu allows the user to issue the BIND, REBIND, and FREE commands.

1. The BIND command creates an application plan from one or more Database Request Modules (DBRMs—see Sections 2.1 and 2.2). The following parameters can be specified (among others):

   ▪  Whether the new plan is to replace an existing one.

   ▪  The isolation level (RR or CS) for the new plan.

   ▪  Whether the plan is to be validated at bind time or at run time. Validation is the process of checking that references to tables, columns, etc., are syntactically correct and that the user issuing the BIND command is authorized to execute the SQL operations in the DBRM(s) being bound. Validation is normally performed at bind time. In some cases, however, it may not be possible to perform such checks at bind time; for example, the plan may include references to a table that does not yet exist (maybe the plan itself creates that table), or it may include operations for which the user does not yet have the required authority. In such cases runtime validation

```
BROWSE-- CJDATE.RESULT ---------------------------------COLUMNS 001 072
COMMAND INPUT ===>                                       SCROLL ===> PAGE
+----+----+----+----+----+----+----+----+----+----+----+----+----+----+
SELECT *                                                 00010000
FROM   P                                                 00020000
WHERE  WEIGHT IN ( 12, 16, 17 )                          00030000
ORDER  BY P# ;                                           00040000
+----+----+----+----+----+----+----+----+----+----+----+----+----+----+
P#     PNAME   COLOR  WEIGHT CITY
P1     Nut     Red    12     London
P2     Bolt    Green  17     Paris
P3     Screw   Blue   17     Rome
P5     Cam     Blue   12     Paris
+----+----+----+----+----+----+----+----+----+----+----+----+----+----+
DSNE610I NUMBER OF ROWS DISPLAYED IS 4.
DSNE616I STATEMENT EXECUTION WAS SUCCESSFUL  SQLCODE IS 100.
+----+----+----+----+----+----+----+----+----+----+----+----+----+----+
DSNE617I COMMIT PERFORMED, SQLCODE IS 0.
```

**Fig. 14.4**  SPUFI output file (example)

must be requested. Note, however, that runtime validation is comparatively expensive, because it must be performed (for a given statement) every time that statement is executed.

2.  The REBIND command rebinds an existing plan. It differs from the "replace" version of the BIND command in that its input is a plan, not a set of DBRMs. REBIND would be used after the physical structure of the database has changed sufficiently—for example, new indexes have been created—that a reevaluation of access strategy is warranted (for the plan in question).

3.  The FREE command drops an existing plan.

## 14.5    PROGRAM PREPARATION

The program preparation menus allow the user to perform any or all of the following:

-   precompilation
-   compilation or assembly
-   linkage editor processing
-   bind processing
-   program execution

All of the necessary parameters to the Precompiler, Bind, etc. can be supplied via the menus. Note that the source program itself must already have been created via an appropriate text editor, such as the ISPF editor.

## 14.6    RUN

The RUN menu is effectively just the "run" portion of the program preparation menu set. It allows the user to execute a previously prepared application program—provided that, as mentioned previously, that program is a TSO application, not an IMS or CICS application.

## 14.7    OPERATOR COMMANDS

This menu allows the user to enter console operator commands such as START DATABASE, STOP DATABASE, etc.

## 14.8    UTILITIES

This menu allows the user to invoke the DB2 utilities. Those utilities include the following, among others:

- *LOAD*. The LOAD utility loads data from a SAM data set into one or more DB2 tables. *Note:* That SAM data set can consist of data unloaded from a VSAM data set, or from an IMS database, or from a DB2 or SQL/DS table. See Section 15.4.

- *COPY*. The COPY utility creates a full or incremental image copy of a tablespace or partition. An incremental copy is a copy of just the data that has changed since the previous copy—full or incremental—was taken.

- *MERGE COPY*. The MERGE COPY utility merges a full copy and one or more incremental copies to produce an up-to-date full copy, or a set of incremental copies to produce an up-to-date incremental copy (for a given tablespace or partition).

- *RECOVER*. The RECOVER utility uses the most recent full copy, any subsequent incremental copies, and the log to recover a tablespace or partition after a media failure has occurred on that tablespace or partition.

- *REORG*. The REORG utility reorganizes a tablespace or partition to reclaim wasted space and to reestablish clustering sequence (if applicable).

- *RUNSTATS*. The RUNSTATS utility computes various statistics concerning such things as the number of records in each table, and writes them to the system catalog. Bind uses those statistics in its process of optimization.

## 14.9  BYPASSING DB2I

As mentioned in the Introduction (Section 14.1), the use of DB2I is not mandatory. It is possible to invoke a DB2 application interactively without using DB2I by issuing the TSO command "DSN" (which invokes DB2), followed by the command

```
RUN PROGRAM ( program-name ) PLAN ( plan-name )
```

It is also possible to invoke a DB2 application in "batch" mode through JCL statements that (a) specify the TSO terminal monitor program (TMP) as the program to be run, and (b) pass the DSN and RUN commands as input to that monitor program.

# 15

# The Query
# Management Facility
# (QMF)

## 15.1  INTRODUCTION

The Query Management Facility, QMF, is a separately priced front-end product
that supports both DB2 (under TSO) and SQL/DS (under VM/CMS and DOS/
VSE). It provides a sophisticated set of *ad hoc* query and report-writing features
for those two systems. In this book, of course, we concentrate on the use of QMF
with DB2 specifically, but most of the concepts apply with little change to the
SQL/DS version also.

QMF is superficially similar to SPUFI, in that both provide an interactive
SQL interface to DB2 databases. However, the two are not really very much
alike. The following are some of the more significant differences between them:

- SPUFI is an integral part of the DB2 base product, whereas QMF is an
  optional front-end to that base product.

- QMF is aimed at genuine end-users, whereas SPUFI is aimed more at data-
  processing professionals. QMF is intended to be easy to use by comparatively
  unskilled users; for example, extensive help facilities are included, and there
  is an emphasis on "pushbutton operation" (most QMF commands can be

entered via program function keys). SPUFI, by contrast, is intended specifically, as a tool for DP professionals; it is a key component of DB2I, and DB2I in turn (as explained in Chapter 14) provides a full range of support for those professionals—not just the interactive SQL facilities of SPUFI, but also facilities for online program development, online utility invocation, and so forth.

- QMF provides a Query-By-Example interface in addition to the regular SQL interface. Query-By-Example (abbreviated QBE) is another relational language, comparable in some ways to SQL but "forms-based" rather than "statement-based" (i.e., the user operates by filling in forms on the screen rather than by typing in statements). *Note:* The QBE language was previously supported by IBM as the interface to an "Installed User Program" (IUP) running on the VM operating system; however, that IUP has nothing to do with QMF as such.

- SPUFI does not include any report-writing facilities at all.

In this chapter we discuss the major features of QMF, without however getting into as much detail as we did in earlier chapters (since this is basically a book on DB2, not on QMF). Section 15.2 is an introduction to the QMF report-writing facilities, and Section 15.3 is a description of the Query-By-Example interface (QBE). Section 15.4 briefly describes the product DXT (Data Extract), which—although an independent and separately priced product—can probably best be regarded as an adjunct to QMF in practice.

## 15.2 REPORT WRITING

A report in QMF is the displayed (or printed) output from a QMF query. Reports are formatted in accordance with a set of report specifications called a *form*. When a given query is executed, the user has the option of specifying the corresponding form explicitly; if no such explicit specification is given, then QMF will automatically create a default ("system") form and will display the output from the query in accordance with that. The user can subsequently revise that form and display the output again in accordance with the revised version, and this cycle can be repeated as many times as necessary until the user is satisfied. Thus a typical interactive session with QMF might go as follows (see Fig. 15.1):

1. The user constructs a QMF query (using either SQL or Query-By-Example), using the full-screen editing functions of QMF to do so. The query is kept in a temporary working area called QUERY.

2. The user issues the RUN QUERY command (probably via a program function key) to execute the query in QUERY. The result from that execution is kept in another temporary working area called DATA.

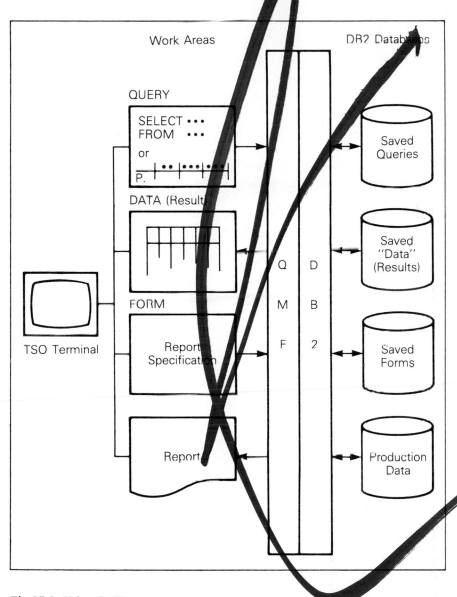

**Fig.15.1** Using QMF

3. QMF creates a default ("system") form for the data in DATA, and displays that data in accordance with that default form. It keeps the form in yet another temporary working area, called FORM.

4. After inspecting the report produced in the previous step, the user issues the DISPLAY FORM command (again, probably via a program function key) to display the current contents of FORM.

5. The user revises the current contents of FORM, using the QMF full-screen editing functions again.

6. The user issues the DISPLAY REPORT command to produce a revised report corresponding to the revised form. Note that it is not necessary to run the original query again; the output from that query has been kept in DATA, and DISPLAY REPORT uses the current contents of FORM to format and display the current contents of DATA.

7. Steps 4 – 6 are repeated as many times as necessary, until the user is satisfied with the final result.

8. Optionally, the user issues the PRINT REPORT command (once again, probably via a program function key) to obtain a hard copy of the final result.

Let us examine an example to see how this sequence of events might look in practice. Suppose the original query is:

```
SELECT S.CITY, S.STATUS, SP.S#, SP.P#, SP.QTY
FROM    S, SP
WHERE   S.S# = SP.S#
ORDER   BY S.CITY, SP.S#, SP.P#
*** END ***
```

(Queries in QMF are terminated by *** END *** instead of by a semicolon. The user does not have to type that terminator, however—it is built into the QMF query display.) QMF executes the query and stores the result in DATA. It then creates a system form for the query (which we will look at in a moment) and stores it in FORM. Finally, it formats and displays the contents of DATA in accordance with the form in FORM. The report appears as shown in the first box on page 235.

The automatically generated system form for this query (stored in FORM) is as shown in the second box on page 235.

This form is interpreted as follows.

1. DATA contains five columns. These columns are to appear in the report with column headings CITY, STATUS, S#, P#, and QTY, respectively.

2. The column widths are 15, 6, 5, 6, and 11 characters, respectively, and each column is to appear two character positions to the right of the one preceding it (INDENT is 2 in each case).

3. The total width of the report is 53 characters.

```
CITY            STATUS  S#   P#            QTY
------------    ------  --   ------   ------------
London          20      S1   P1            300
London          20      S1   P2            200
London          20      S1   P3            400
London          20      S1   P4            200
London          20      S1   P5            100
London          20      S1   P6            100
London          20      S4   P2            200
London          20      S4   P4            300
London          20      S4   P5            400
Paris           10      S2   P1            300
Paris           10      S2   P2            400
Paris           30      S3   P2            200
*** END ***
```

```
Column Descriptions:           Page width is now: 53
  NUM   COLUMN HEADING                 USAGE   INDENT   WIDTH   EDIT
  ---   -------------------------      ------  ------   -----   ----
   1    CITY                                     2       15      C
   2    STATUS                                   2        6      L
   3    S#                                       2        5      C
   4    P#                                       2        6      C
   5    QTY                                      2       11      L
*** END ***

Control Break Text:            Do you want outline? ===> YES
   1 ===>                    4 --=>
   2 ===>                    5 ===>
   3 ===>                    6 ===>

PAGE HEADING ===>
PAGE FOOTING ===>
```

4. CITY, S#, and P# are to be displayed "as is," i.e., as simple unedited character strings (EDIT is C). STATUS and QTY are to be displayed as decimal integers (EDIT is L).

5. No control breaks are specified (see below), and therefore no control break text is specified either. OUTLINE YES has no effect in the absence of control breaks.

6. No page heading or page footing is specified.

Suppose now that we DISPLAY this form and edit it as follows.

1. The column headings for CITY, S#, P#, and QTY are changed to the more informative headings SUPPLIER CITY, SUPPLIER, PART, and QUANTITY, respectively. For the first of these, a break character is specified to indicate that the two words in the heading are to appear on separate lines in the report (CITY is to appear centered under SUPPLIER). No new heading is specified for STATUS, because STATUS values are going to be suppressed anyway (see paragraph 4 below).

2. The column widths for SUPPLIER CITY, SUPPLIER, PART, and QUANTITY are changed to 8, 8, 4, and 8, respectively. INDENT is changed from 2 to 3 in every case.

3. USAGE for SUPPLIER CITY is set to BREAK1. *Note:* The original query must have specified CITY as the major ordering field for this specification to make sense. BREAK1 means that a "control break" is to occur each time the value in the SUPPLIER CITY column changes. The purpose of specifying control breaks is to enable QMF to compute and display subtotals or similar partial results when the report is produced—see paragraph 5 below.

4. USAGE for STATUS is set to OMIT. No STATUS values are to appear in the report.

5. USAGE for QUANTITY is set to SUM, indicating that QUANTITY values are to be totaled for each control break (i.e., for each city) and also for the report as a whole (i.e., for all cities). Averages, counts, etc. can be requested in a similar fashion.

6. Control break text for control break 1 (the only control break, in this example) is specified as

```
*** Total for &1
```

The specification "&1" refers to the current value in column number 1 of the report (namely, SUPPLIER CITY). It is thus a *variable* that enables QMF to display a different line of text each time a control break actually occurs. See the resulting report below for the effects of this specification.

7. OUTLINE is left as YES. The effect of this specification is to suppress the display of duplicate values for control break columns; again, see the resulting report below.

8. Finally, the page heading is set to

SHIPMENTS BY SUPPLIER CITY

and the page footing to

DETAIL REPORT

The revised form thus appears as shown below. The corresponding report (produced by DISPLAY REPORT) now appears as on page 238. Note that date, time, and page numbers are automatically included in the report.

The foregoing example gives some idea as to how easy it is to produce customized or tailored reports using QMF, but of course it does not illustrate the full range of QMF's report-writing capabilities. A brief survey of additional capabilities follows:

- Scrolling facilities (UP, DOWN, LEFT, RIGHT) are available for viewing reports (and other objects, such as forms) that are too large to fit in their entirety on to a single screen.

- Additional edit codes (over and above the C and L shown in the example) permit such things as the incorporation of editing symbols (e.g., dollar signs, decimal points) into numeric output and the display of floating point values in scientific notation.

---

```
Column Descriptions:          Page width is now: 40
  NUM  COLUMN HEADING              USAGE  INDENT  WIDTH  EDIT
  ---  --------------------------  ------ ------  ---    ----
   1   SUPPLIER_CITY               BREAK1  3        8     C
   2   STATUS                      OMIT    3        6     L
   3   SUPPLIER                            3        8     C
   4   PART                                3        4     C
   5   QUANTITY                    SUM     3        8     L
*** END ***


Control Break Text:          Do you want outline? ===> YES
    1 ===> *** Total for &1  4 ===>
    2 ===>                   5 ===>
    3 ===>                   6 ===>

PAGE HEADING  ===> SHIPMENTS BY SUPPLIER CITY
PAGE FOOTING  ===> DETAIL REPORT
```

```
                    SHIPMENTS BY SUPPLIER CITY


        SUPPLIER
          CITY      SUPPLIER   PART   QUANTITY
        ---------   --------   ----   ---------
        London      S1         P1          300
                    S1         P2          200
                    S1         P3          400
                    S1         P4          200
                    S1         P5          100
                    S1         P6          100
                    S4         P2          200
                    S4         P4          300
                    S4         P5          400
                                      ---------
        *** Total for London               2200

        Paris       S2         P1          300
                    S2         P2          400
                    S3         P2          200
                                      ---------
        *** Total for Paris                 900
                                      =========
                                           3100


   83/06/29 10:46            DETAIL REPORT              PAGE 1
```

- Page headings and footings (like control break text) can include references to variables of the form "&n" (standing for the current value in column number n).

- Multiple levels (up to 6) of control breaks can be specified, with different summary functions and different control break text at each level. For instance, we could extend our example to break on supplier (level 2) within city (level 1) by specifying a USAGE for SUPPLIER of BREAK2, and hence produce (for example) subtotals of quantity per supplier as well as per city. The display of duplicate supplier numbers would also be suppressed, assuming that "outline" is still specified as YES. *Note:* Whenever control breaks are specified, an appropriate ordering specification must appear in the original query, or the report will not make much sense. In our example, an ORDER BY clause specifying CITY as the major ordering field and S# as a minor ordering field would have to have been included—as indeed it was.

- Reports can consist of summary information only—e.g., totals or averages only—as well as of summary plus detail information as in the example. (Once again, the original query should include an appropriate ordering specification if such a report is to be meaningful.) Summary reports can be produced in "across-the-page" format as well as in the more conventional "down-the-page" format. For instance, we could revise our example to generate an across-summary report showing cities *down* the page and suppliers *across*; for each city, there would be a line across the page showing the total quantity for supplier S1, the total quantity for supplier S2, ..., and the total quantity for all suppliers (in that city).

- A SAVE command is provided to save the current contents of DATA, QUERY, or FORM (as specified) under a user-chosen name. The RUN command can specify a saved (named) query for execution and a saved (named) form for formatting the result. Similarly, the DISPLAY command can specify a saved (named) table to be displayed in accordance with the form currently in FORM; that named table can be one that was created via SAVE DATA, or it can be any other table in the underlying database. A saved query may include parameters; if it does, QMF will prompt the user for actual values to replace those parameters when the query is invoked for execution.

Finally, we should mention *procedures*. A procedure is a sequence of QMF commands (RUN, DISPLAY, SAVE, etc.) that is itself saved under some specified name. It is executed via a variation on the RUN command.

## 15.3  QUERY-BY-EXAMPLE

As stated in Section 15.1, QMF provides a Query-By-Example interface as well as a SQL interface. Query-By-Example (QBE) is a relational query language that is in some respects more "user-friendly" than SQL, at least for users who have no training in DP professional skills. It is certainly true that SQL is more "user-friendly" than older languages such as DL/I, but it still assumes a certain amount of programming expertise; it is still basically a programming language in the traditional sense, albeit one at a very high level. QBE, by contrast, is a language in which all operations are formulated simply by *making entries in empty tables on the screen*—in effect, by filling in forms. This "fill-in-the-blanks" style is very easy to learn and understand, and is frequently more attractive than the SQL style to users who have received little or no formal DP training.

Through the QBE interface of QMF, the user can issue QBE analogs of the SQL data manipulation operations SELECT, UPDATE, DELETE, and INSERT (but no others—data definition and data control operations, such as CREATE and GRANT, can be issued only via the SQL interface). The operations available in QBE are P., U., D., and I., corresponding respectively to the SQL operations SELECT, UPDATE, DELETE, and INSERT. (*Note:* "P." stands for "print," but it does not actually cause any printing to occur. The QMF PRINT command is provided for that purpose, as explained in Section 15.2.)

The basic idea behind QBE is very simple, and is illustrated by the following example. Consider the query "Get supplier numbers for suppliers in Paris with status > 20" (Example 4.2.5 from Chapter 4). This query can be represented in QBE as follows:

```
S    | S# | SNAME  | STATUS  |  CITY   |
-----|----|--------|---------|---------|
     | P. |        |  > 20   |  Paris  |
```

Explanation: First, by issuing the command DRAW S, the user causes QMF to display a blank version of table S (i.e., a version showing the table name and column names only, without any data values). Then the user constructs the query by typing entries in three positions in the body of that table, namely "P." in the S# position (to indicate the target of the query, i.e., the value(s) to be "printed" or displayed), and "> 20" and "Paris" in the STATUS and CITY positions (to indicate the condition(s) that those target values must satisfy).

It is also possible to specify "P." against the entire row, e.g., as follows:

```
S    | S# | SNAME  | STATUS  |  CITY   |
-----|----|--------|---------|---------|
P.   |    |        |  > 20   |  Paris  |
```

which is equivalent to specifying "P." in every column position in the table:

```
S    | S# | SNAME  | STATUS  |  CITY    |
-----|----|--------|---------|----------|
     | P. | P.     | P. >20  | P. Paris |
```

Note, incidentally, that character string values such as Paris can be specified without being enclosed in quotes. It is never wrong to supply the quotes, however, and sometimes they are required (e.g., if the string includes any blanks).

In the rest of this section we illustrate some of the highlights of the QBE interface by showing a number of further examples. For convenience we give references (where applicable) to the SQL versions of the examples in Chapters 4, 5, and 6. We do not however go into as much detail as we did with SQL. Before we get started, a couple of preliminary remarks:

- A QMF command allows the user to specify whether queries will be formulated in SQL or in QBE. It is possible to switch dynamically between the two within a single QMF session.

- Editing commands are available to tailor blank tables on the screen by the addition or removal of columns and rows and by the widening and narrowing of columns. Tables can thus be edited to fit the requirements of whatever operation the user is trying to formulate; in particular, columns that are not needed for the operation in question can be eliminated. For example, in the first of the sample queries shown earlier, the SNAME column could have been eliminated:

```
S    | S#  | STATUS  |  CITY   |
-----|-----|---------|---------|
     | P.  |  > 20   | Paris   |
```

We shall usually not bother to show such details in what follows.

### 15.3.1   Retrieval with Ordering

Get supplier numbers and status for suppliers in Paris, in ascending supplier number order within descending status order. (Extended version of Example 4.2.6)

```
S    |    S#    | SNAME |  STATUS  |  CITY   |
-----|----------|-------|----------|---------|
     | P.AO(2). |       | P.DO(1). | Paris   |
```

"AO." stands for ascending order, "DO." for descending order. The integers in parentheses indicate the major-to-minor sequence for ordering columns; in the example, STATUS is the major column and S# the minor column.

### 15.3.2   Retrieval Involving OR

Get supplier numbers and status for suppliers who either are located in Paris or have status > 20 or both. (Modified version of Example 4.2.5)

Conditions specified within a single row are considered to be "ANDed" together, as the examples so far have illustrated. To "OR" two conditions, they must be specified in different rows, as here:

```
S    | S#  | SNAME | STATUS  |  CITY   |
-----|-----|-------|---------|---------|
     | P.  |       |         | Paris   |
     | P.  |       |  > 20   |         |
```

*Note:* If a given supplier satisfies both of the conditions in this example, the corresponding supplier number will still appear only once in the output.

Another approach to this query makes use of what is known as a *condition box*. A condition box allows the specification of conditions of any degree of complexity. For example:

```
S    | S#  | SNAME  | STATUS  |  CITY   |
-----|-----|--------|---------|---------|
     | P.  |        |   _ST   |  _SC    |
```

```
|           CONDITIONS           |
|--------------------------------|
|  _SC = Paris OR _ST > 20       |
```

Explanation: __ST and __SC are "example elements." In fact, they are really *variables*, standing for the status and city, respectively, of some potential target supplier. The condition box specifies a predicate that those variables must satisfy in order that the corresponding target supplier appear among those retrieved. The name of an example element is arbitrary, except that it must begin with an underscore character.

Another editing command, DRAW COND, is provided to cause QMF to display a blank condition box. Conditions in a condition box can involve AND, OR, NOT, IN (the simple list-of-values form only), LIKE, and NULL, very much as in SQL. (*Note:* IN, LIKE, and NULL can also be used in entries in a blank table as well as in a condition box.) But it is frequently easier to formulate queries without making any use of a condition box, and we shall usually ignore the possibility from this point on.

### 15.3.3   Retrieval Involving Multiple Conditions on the Same Column ANDed Together

Get parts whose weight is in the range 16 to 19 inclusive. (Example 4.2.7)

```
P    | P#  | PNAME  | COLOR  | WEIGHT | WEIGHT |  CITY   |
-----|-----|--------|--------|--------|--------|---------|
     | P.  |        |        | >= 16  | <= 19  |         |
```

Editing commands are used to add another column to the blank table and to name it WEIGHT before the query is formulated.

### 15.3.4   Retrieval of Computed Values and Constants

For all parts, get the part number and the weight of the part in grams. Weights are given in table P in pounds. (Example 4.2.3, extended version)

```
P    | P#  | WEIGHT |                        |              |
-----|-----|--------|------------------------|--------------|
     | P.  |  _PW   | P.  'Weight in grams =' | P. _PW * 454 |
```

### 15.3.5 Retrieving (Specified Fields from) a Join

Get all supplier-number/part-number combinations such that the supplier and part concerned are "colocated." (Example 4.3.4)

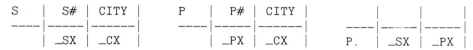

| S | S# | CITY | | P | P# | CITY | | | | |
|---|----|------|---|---|----|------|---|---|----|----|
| | _SX | _CX | | | _PX | _CX | | P. | _SX | _PX |

Explanation: Three blank tables are needed for this query, one each for S and P (only relevant columns shown) and one for the result (no table name or column names may be specified). Notice how example elements are specified to link these three tables together. The entire query can be paraphrased:

"Display supplier-number/part-number pairs, SX/PX say, such that SX and PX are both located in the same city CX."

### 15.3.6 Joining a Table with Itself

Get all pairs of supplier numbers such that the two suppliers concerned are colocated. (Example 4.3.6)

| S | S# | CITY | | S | S# | CITY | | | | |
|---|----|------|---|---|----|------|---|---|----|----|
| | _SX | _CZ | | | _SY | _CZ | | P. | _SX | _SY |

A condition box can be used to specify the additional condition _SX < _SY, if desired (see Chapter 4 for a discussion of this point).

### 15.3.7 Retrieval Involving Existential Quantification

Get supplier names for suppliers who supply part P2. (Example 5.3.1)

| S | S# | SNAME | | SP | S# | P# |
|---|----|-------|---|----|----|-----|
| | _SX | P. | | | _SX | P2 |

The row in table SP is *implicitly* quantified by the existential quantifier "there exists." The query can be paraphrased:

"Display supplier names for suppliers SX such that there exists a shipment showing supplier SX supplying part P2."

### 15.3.8 Retrieval Involving Union

Get part numbers for parts that either weigh more than 16 pounds or are supplied by supplier S2 or both. (Example 5.5.1)

```
P     | P#  | WEIGHT  |    SP   | S# |  P# |              |       |       |
------|-----|---------|    -----|----|-----|     ---- |------|
      | _PX |  > 16   |         | S2 | _PY |     P.       |  _PX |
                                                 P.       |  _PY |
```

### 15.3.9  Single-Record Update

Change the color of part P2 to yellow, increase its weight by 5, and set its city to null. (Example 6.2.1)

```
P     | P#  | PNAME  |  COLOR   | WEIGHT  |   WEIGHT     |  CITY  |
------|-----|--------|----------|---------|--------------|--------|
      | P2  |        | U.Yellow |   _WT   | U._WT + 5    | U.NULL |
```

### 15.3.10  Multiple-Record Update

Set the shipment quantity to zero for all suppliers in London. (Example 6.2.3)

```
SP    | S#   | QTY  |    S    | S#   |  CITY   |
------|------|------|    -----|------|---------|
      | _SX  | U.0  |         | _SX  | London  |
```

### 15.3.11  Multiple-Record Delete

Delete all suppliers in Madrid. (Example 6.3.2)

```
S     | S#  | SNAME  | STATUS  |  CITY  |
------|-----|--------|---------|--------|
D.    |     |        |         | Madrid |
```

Note that "D." applies to the entire row and so appears beneath the table name, whereas "U." applies to individual fields and so appears in the body of the table (i.e., within individual columns).

### 15.3.12  Single-Record Insert

Add part P7 (city 'Athens', weight 2, name and color at present unknown) to table P. (Example 6.4.1)

```
P     | P#  | PNAME  | COLOR  | WEIGHT  |  CITY  |
------|-----|--------|--------|---------|--------|
I.    | P7  |        |        |    2    | Athens |
```

"I.", like "D.", appears beneath the table name.

To conclude this section, we note that there are certain queries that can be formulated in SQL that cannot be expressed in QBE (at least as implemented in QMF). To be specific, QBE does not include any analog of the NOT EXISTS construct in SQL. This omission is perhaps not very serious in practice, since NOT EXISTS is needed only for rather complex queries.

## 15.4   DATA EXTRACT (DXT)

Data Extract (DXT) is not part of QMF as such, nor part of DB2—it is another separately priced product. In practice, however, an installation using DXT to extract data will probably also use QMF to query and update, and/or produce reports from, that extracted data, so it is convenient to include a brief discussion of DXT in the present chapter.

The purpose of DXT is to extract a copy of specified data from a DL/I database or from a SAM or VSAM data set and to construct a file containing that extracted copy in the format required by the DB2 load utility. (*Note:* DXT can also generate files in the format required for SQL/DS. But in this book we are primarily concerned with DB2.) The data can then be loaded into a DB2 table, where it can be used as the basis for *ad hoc* query/update and/or report-writing activities. Thus the intent is basically to provide online SQL (or QBE) access to data that was originally stored in some nonrelational form. Since that online access is directed to an extract, i.e., to a separate copy of the data, it does not interfere with other uses of that data; in particular, it does not affect the performance of any planned, regularly scheduled activities against that data.

*Note:* Even for a DB2 database it may be desirable for performance or other reasons to direct some or all online query/report-writing activity to an extract instead of to the original database. In such a case, however, the extraction process can be implemented using the regular facilities of DB2 itself (basically a CREATE TABLE plus a multiple-record INSERT); no "DXT-like" product is needed.

DXT consists of two major components, one that enables users to create extraction requests and one that actually executes those requests. The first of these, the User Input Manager, can be executed interactively under TSO (the simpler method) or as a regular batch MVS job. (The dialog manager that controls interactive execution under TSO is actually shipped as part of the QMF product, not as part of DXT itself.) The second, the Data Extraction Manager, executes as one of the following:

- an IMS batch application (to extract data from DL/I batch databases and optionally from SAM and VSAM data sets)

- an IMS "batch message processing" (BMP) application (to extract data from DL/I online databases and optionally from SAM and VSAM data sets)

- a batch MVS job (to extract data from SAM and VSAM data sets)

An optional third DXT component, the Dictionary Access Program, can assist in the process of building extract requests by obtaining source data descriptions from the IBM DB/DC Data Dictionary (if installed).

In the case of a DL/I database, data can be extracted from any or all segments in a single hierarchical path for loading into a single DB2 table. Individual segment instances are included or excluded according to a predicate specified in the extract request. Specific fields can also be included or excluded as required.

## EXERCISES

In the following exercises you are asked to give Query-By-Example solutions to certain of the exercises from Chapters 4–6. Once again we repeat the structure of the database:

```
S    ( S#, SNAME, STATUS, CITY )
P    ( P#, PNAME, COLOR, WEIGHT, CITY )
J    ( J#, JNAME, CITY )
SPJ  ( S#, P#, J#, QTY )
```

To facilitate comparisons with the SQL versions, we show the number of the original exercise from Chapters 4–6 in each case.

**15.1** Get full details of all projects. (Exercise 4.1)

**15.2** Get supplier numbers for suppliers who supply project J1, in supplier number order. (Exercise 4.3)

**15.3** Get project numbers and cities where the city has an "o" as the second letter of its name. (Exercise 4.7)

**15.4** Get all supplier-number/part-number/project-number triples such that the indicated supplier, part, and project are all colocated. (Exercise 4.8)

**15.5** Get part numbers for parts supplied by a supplier in London. (Exercise 4.11)

**15.6** Get part numbers for parts supplied by a supplier in London to a project in London. (Exercise 4.12)

**15.7** Get part numbers for parts supplied to any project by a supplier in the same city as that project. (Exercise 4.14)

**15.8** Get project numbers for projects supplied by at least one supplier not in the same city. (Exercise 4.15)

**15.9** Get all pairs of part numbers such that some supplier supplies both the indicated parts. (Exercise 4.16)

**15.10** Get supplier numbers for suppliers supplying at least one part supplied by at least one supplier who supplies at least one red part. (Exercise 5.5)

**15.11** Get supplier numbers for suppliers with a status lower than that of supplier S1. (Exercise 5.6)

**15.12** Construct a list of all cities in which at least one supplier, part, or project is located. (Exercise 5.24)

**15.13** Change the color of all red parts to orange. (Exercise 6.1)

**15.14** Delete all projects in Rome and all corresponding shipments. (Exercise 6.4)

**15.15** Insert a new supplier (S10) into table S. The name and city are 'White' and 'New York', respectively; the status is not yet known. (Exercise 6.5)

## ANSWERS TO SELECTED EXERCISES

**15.1**
```
J    | J# | JNAME  |  CITY    |
-----|----|--------|----------|
P.   |    |        |          |
```

**15.2**
```
SPJ  |    S#     | P# | J# | QTY   |
-----|-----------|----|----|-------|
P.   |  P.AO(1). |    | J1 |       |
```

The "(1)" can be omitted if desired.

**15.3**
```
J    | J# | JNAME  |      CITY        |
-----|----|--------|------------------|
     | P. |        | P. LIKE '_o%'    |
```

**15.4**

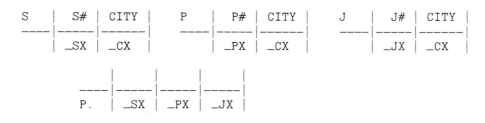

```
S    | S# | CITY |     P    | P# | CITY |     J    | J# | CITY |
-----|----|------|     -----|----|------|     -----|----|------|
     | _SX| _CX  |          | _PX| _CX  |          | _JX| _CX  |


           |      |      |      |
        ---|------|------|------|
        P. | _SX  | _PX  | _JX  |
```

**15.5**
```
SPJ  | S# | P# |        S    | S# |  CITY    |
-----|----|----|        -----|----|----------|
     | _SX| P. |             | _SX|  London  |
```

**15.6**

```
SPJ | • S# | P# |  J# |        S  | S# | CITY   |
----|------|----|------|        ---|----|--------|
    | _SX  | P. | _JX |           | _SX| London |

                                J  | J# | CITY   |
                                ---|----|--------|
                                   | _JX| London |
```

**15.7**

```
SPJ | S# | P# |  J# |           S  | S# | CITY |
----|-----|----|------|         ---|----|------|
    | _SX | P. | _JX |            | _SX| _CX  |

                                J  | J# | CITY |
                                ---|----|------|
                                   | _JX| _CX  |
```

**15.8**

```
SPJ | S# |   J#    |              S  | S# | CITY |
----|-----|--------|              ---|----|------|
    | _SX | P._JX  |                | _SX| _CX  |

                                J  | J# | CITY  |
                                ---|----|-------|
                                   | _JX| ¬_CX  |
```

**15.9**

```
SPJ | S# | P# |                     |    |    |
----|-----|-----|                ----|-----|-----|
    | _SX | _PY |                P.  | _PY | _PZ |
    | _SX | _PZ |
```

**15.10**

```
SPJ | S# | P# |              P  | P# | COLOR |
----|-----|-----|            ---|-----|-------|
    | P.  | _PX |               | _PY | Red   |
    | _SY | _PX |
    | _SY | _PY |
```

**15.11**

```
S  | S# | STATUS |
---|----|--------|
   | P. | < _Tl  |
   | Sl | _Tl    |
```

**15.12**

| S    | S#   | CITY   |
|------|------|--------|
|      | _SX  | _CX    |

| P    | P#   | CITY   |
|------|------|--------|
|      | _PY  | _CY    |

| J    | J#   | CITY   |
|------|------|--------|
|      | _JZ  | _CZ    |

|      |        |
|------|--------|
| P.   | _CX    |
| P.   | _CY    |
| P.   | _CZ    |

**15.13**

| P    | P#   | COLOR  | COLOR     |
|------|------|--------|-----------|
|      |      | Red    | U.Orange  |

**15.14**

First:

| SPJ  | S#   | P#   | J#   | QTY   |
|------|------|------|------|-------|
| D.   |      |      | _JJ  |       |

| J    | J#   | CITY   |
|------|------|--------|
|      | _JJ  | Rome   |

Then:

| J    | J#   | JNAME   | CITY   |
|------|------|---------|--------|
| D.   |      |         | Rome   |

**15.15**

| S    | S#   | SNAME   | STATUS   | CITY        |
|------|------|---------|----------|-------------|
| I.   | S10  | White   |          | 'New York'  |

# 16

# Summary and Conclusions

## 16.1 INTRODUCTION

In the chapters up to this point we have presented a detailed description of DB2, a state-of-the-art relational DBMS. The following topics have been discussed (among others):

- operating environments
- system structure
- data definition
- data manipulation
- the catalog
- views
- security and authorization
- application programming
- transaction management
- storage structure
- the interactive interface DB2I
- the associated products QMF and DXT

In this final chapter, we briefly consider a few aspects (of relational systems in general and DB2 in particular) that have not been discussed in any detail earlier in the book. To be specific, we summarize the advantages of a system like DB2, offer some opinions concerning the performance of such a system, and, finally, speculate as to possible future developments in the relational area. A word of warning: Please understand that this chapter, unlike previous chapters (which were by definition concerned purely with matters of fact), is bound to be somewhat subjective in nature. Other writers may disagree with any or all of the opinions expressed. Please note also that much of the discussion is applicable to any relational system, not just to DB2.

Before getting into those discussions, we make the following remarks concerning the SQL language. DB2 is just one of a family of mainstream products from IBM that support the SQL language (the others being QMF and SQL/DS, both DOS and VM versions). It follows that, in the IBM marketplace at least, SQL is likely to become widely used and hence to have a significant influence on product externals for some time to come. As a matter of fact, there are already at least ten or so products in the marketplace, in *addition* to the IBM products, that support some dialect of SQL; vendors of those products include both hardware manufacturers (e.g., Fujitsu, Honeywell) and software companies (e.g., ORACLE Corporation, Logica). The products concerned run on a wide variety of hardware, all the way from personal computers to large mainframes. Furthermore, the American National Standards (ANS) Database Committee X3H2, which has a charter to prepare proposals for a relational language standard, has adopted the IBM SQL definition as a startpoint for its activities. In some ways, therefore, the influence of SQL is likely to be even more pervasive over the next few years than the influence of DB2 *per se*.

## 16.2 ADVANTAGES

If the advantages of a relational system such as DB2 must be summed up in a single word, that word is *simplicity*—where by "simplicity" we mean, primarily, simplicity for the user. Simplicity, in turn, translates into *usability* and *productivity*. Usability means that even comparatively unskilled users can use the system to do useful work; that is, end-users can frequently obtain useful results from the system without having to go through the potential bottleneck of the DP department. Productivity means that both end-users and DP professionals can be more productive in their day-to-day activities; as a result, they can between them make significant inroads into the well-known application backlog problem (see the discussion under "Application Development" below). In this section we discuss some of the factors that contribute to the simplicity of a system such as DB2.

## Theoretical Base

The first point is that relational systems are based on a formal theoretical foun
dation, the *relational model* (discussed in detail in Appendix A). As a result,
they behave in well-defined ways; and (possibly without consciously realizing the
fact) users have a simple model of that behavior in their mind that enables them
to predict with confidence what the system will do in any given situation. There
are (or should be) no surprises.* This predictability means that the user interface
is easy to teach, learn, use, and remember.

Incidentally, we remark in passing that many critics of relational systems in
the past have objected to precisely this point. The objection seems to be that only
theoreticians are capable of understanding, or need to understand, something that
is based on theory. Our own position is exactly the opposite: Systems that are
not based on theory are usually very difficult for *anyone* to understand. It cannot
be stated too strongly that "theoretical" does *not* mean "not practical." On the
contrary, considerations that are initially dismissed as being "only theoretical"
(sic) have a nasty habit of becoming horribly practical a few years later on.

## Small Number of Concepts

The relational model is notable for the small number of concepts it involves. As
pointed out in Chapter 6, all data in a relational database is represented in one
and only one way, namely as column values within rows of tables, and hence
only one operator is needed for each of the four basic manipulative functions
(retrieve, change, insert, delete). For exactly the same reason, fewer operators
are also needed for all other functions—data definition, security and authorization, storage mapping, etc.—than are needed in a nonrelational system. In the
case of authorization specifically, it is the simplicity and regularity of the data
structure that makes it possible to define such a sophisticated data protection
mechanism (one in which, to repeat from Chapter 9, value-dependent, value-

---

*It cannot be denied that most systems today, even relational systems, do nevertheless
display rather ad hoc and unpredictable behavior in some areas; as an example, consider
the treatment of view updating in DB2, which does display a certain amount of unpleasant
arbitrariness (see Section 8.4). But such arbitrariness tends to occur precisely at those
points where the implementation has departed from the underlying theory. For example,
a crucial component of the relational model is the concept of *primary key* (see Appendix
A). However, DB2 does not support that concept, and it is that omission that is the direct
cause of the arbitrariness referred to above. DB2 is not the only offender in this regard,
of course—similar criticisms apply to most other systems at the time of writing—but it
does serve to illustrate the undesirable consequences of disregarding the prescriptions of
the underlying model.

independent, context-dependent, and other constraints can be easily defined and conveniently enforced).

A separate but related point is the following: In the relational model, distinct concepts are cleanly separated, not bundled together. By contrast, the owner-member (or parent-child) link construct found in many nonrelational systems bundles together several fundamentally distinct notions: It is simultaneously a representation of a one-to-many relationship, an access path (or collection of access paths), a mechanism for enforcing certain integrity constraints, and so on. As a result, it becomes difficult to tell exactly what purpose a given link is serving (and it may be used for a purpose for which it was not intended). For example, a program may come to rely on an access path that is really a side effect of the way the database designer chose to represent a certain integrity constraint; if that integrity constraint needs to be changed, then the database will have to be restructured, with a strong likelihood that the program will then have to be rewritten— even if that program is completely uninterested in the integrity constraint *per se*.

## Set-Level Operators

Relational data manipulation operations such as SELECT, UPDATE, etc., in SQL are *set-level* operations. This fact means that users simply have to specify *what* they want, not *how* to get to what they want. For example, a user needing to know which parts are supplied by supplier S2 simply issues the SQL query:

```
SELECT  P#
FROM    SP
WHERE   S# = 'S2'  ;
```

DB2 decides how to "navigate" through the physical storage structure on the disk in order to respond to this query. (For this reason, as mentioned in Chapter 1, systems such as DB2 are frequently described as "automatic navigation" systems. By contrast, systems in which users have to do that navigation for themselves are described as "manual navigation" systems.) By taking this burden off the user's back, DB2 is freeing the user to concentrate on solving the real problem—i.e., on finding an answer to the query, in the case at hand, and using that information for whatever purpose it is needed in the outside world. In the case of end-users, in fact, it is automatic navigation that makes it possible for the user to use the system in the first place. It is not difficult to find a simple SQL query for which an equivalent COBOL program would be ten or twenty pages long, and writing such a program would be out of the question for most users (and maybe not worth the effort involved even when not).

Furthermore, application programmers can take advantage of the automatic navigation feature of the system as well, just as end-users can. Application programmers too can be more productive in a relational system.

## Dual-Mode Language

In DB2 the same language, SQL, is used for both programming and interactive access to the database. This fact has two immediate consequences:

1. Different categories of user—system and database administrators, application programmers, end-users from any number of different backgrounds—are all using essentially the same language and are thus better able to communicate with one another. It is also easy for one person to switch between categories—e.g., to perform data definition (administrative) functions on one occasion and ad hoc query (end-user) functions on another.

2. Application programmers can debug the SQL portions of their programs through the interactive interface (SPUFI or possibly QMF). This point was discussed in some detail in Section 12.4.

## Data Independence

Data independence is the independence of users and user programs from details of the way the data is stored and accessed. It is critically important for at least two reasons:

1. It is important for application programmers because, without it, changes to the structure of the database necessitate corresponding changes to application programs. In the absence of such independence, one of two things happens: Either it becomes almost impossible to make required changes to the database because of the investment in existing programs, or (more likely) a significant portion of the application programming effort is devoted purely to maintenance activity—maintenance activity, that is, that would be unnecessary if the system had provided data independence in the first place. Both of these factors are significant contributors to the application backlog problem mentioned in the introduction to this section.

2. It is important for end-users because, without it, direct end-user access to the database would scarcely be possible at all. Data independence and very high level languages such as SQL go hand in hand.

Data independence is not an absolute—different systems provide it in differing degrees (to put it another way, few systems if any provide no data independence at all; it is just that some systems are more data-dependent than others). Furthermore, the term "data independence" really covers two somewhat distinct notions, namely physical data independence (i.e., independence of the physical arrangement of the data on the storage medium) and logical data independence (i.e., independence of the logical structure of the data as tables and fields). DB2 is fairly strong on both aspects, though there is undoubtedly still room for improvement in both areas (for example, it is unfortunate that the logical notion of enforcing uniqueness is bundled with the physical notion of an index). Basically, DB2 provides physical data independence by virtue of its automatic navigation and automatic bind features (see Section 2.2 if you need to refresh your memory concerning "automatic bind"); likewise, it provides logical data independence by virtue of its view mechanism (see Section 8.5 for details).

## Application Development

Systems like DB2 facilitate the application development process in a variety of ways:

1. First, the ad hoc query and report-writing capabilities mean that it may not be necessary to develop an application program (in the traditional sense of the term) at all. It is difficult to overemphasize the importance of this point. One relational installation (it is not possible to name it here, but it is not an insignificant one) has *exactly one* traditional application program; everything else is done through the system's query and report-writing front-end.

2. Second, the high degree of data independence provided and the high level of the data manipulation operations together mean that when it *is* necessary to write a program, then that program is easier to write, requires less maintenance, and is easier to change when it does require maintenance, than it would be in an older, nonrelational system.

3. Third, and largely as a consequence of the previous point, the application development cycle can involve a great deal more *prototyping* than it used to: a first version can be built and shown to the intended users, who can then suggest improvements for incorporation into the next version, and so on. As a result, the final application should do exactly what its users require it to. The overall development process is far less rigid than it used to be, and the application users can be far more involved in that process, to the benefit of all concerned.

## Dynamic Data Definition

We have already discussed the advantages of dynamic data definition at some length in Chapter 3 (Section 3.4), and we will not repeat the arguments here. However, we make one additional point: The ability to create new definitions at any time without having to bring the system to a halt is really only part of a larger overall objective, which is to eliminate the need for *any* planned system shutdown. Thus, for example, utilities can be invoked from an online terminal, and they can run in parallel with production work; it is possible, for example, to take an image copy of the database even while transactions are simultaneously updating it. Ideally, the system should have to be started exactly once, when it is first installed, and should then run "forever." (We are not claiming that this objective has yet been achieved.)

## Ease of Installation and Ease of Operation

DB2 is designed to be as easy to install and easy to operate as possible. Various features of the system, some of them touched on in previous subsections, contribute to the achievement of this objective. Details of such features (other than details already given in earlier chapters) are beyond the scope of this book, but it is worth pointing out explicitly one very important consequence of them, namely the following: It requires only a comparatively small population of DP professionals (administrators, system programmers, console operators) to provide DB2 services to a very large population of users (application programmers and end-users). DB2 is an extremely cost-effective system.

## Database Design

Database design in a relational system is easier than it is in a nonrelational system for a number of reasons (though it may still involve some difficult decisions in complex situations). First, the decoupling of logical and physical levels means that logical and physical design problems can be separately addressed. Second, there are some sound principles (basically the principles of *normalization*) that can be brought to bear on the logical design problem. Third, the dynamic data definition feature and the high degree of data independence (again) mean that it is not necessary to do the entire design all at once, and neither is it so critical to get it right first time. Appendix B discusses the question of database design for DB2 in considerable detail.

## Integrated Catalog

As explained in Chapter 7, the catalog in DB2 is completely integrated with the rest of the data, in the sense that it is represented in the same way (as tables) and can be queried in the same way (via SQL). In other words, there is no artificial and unnecessary distinction between catalog data and other data, or between data and "data about the data" (or "metadata," as it is sometimes called). This integration brings with it a number of benefits, among them the following:

1. Looking something up in the database and looking something up in the catalog are one and the same process. To see the advantage here, consider the analogy of looking something up in a book and looking something up in the table of contents for that book. It would be very annoying if the table of contents appeared somewhere other than in the book itself, in a format that required some different manner of access (for example, if the table of contents was in Spanish and was

stored on a set of 3-by-5 cards, while the text of the book itself was in English). The role of the catalog with respect to the database is precisely similar to that of the table of contents with respect to a book.

2. The process of creating generalized (i.e., "metadata"–driven) application programs is considerably simplified. For example, suppose it is required to write a program that checks that every supplier number value appearing anywhere in the database also appears in the S# column of the suppliers table S—in itself a reasonable requirement—without making any prior assumptions about the structure of the database (i.e., the program must not rely on any builtin knowledge as to what tables exist or what their columns are). More generally, suppose it is required to write a program to check that every value of type X appearing anywhere in the database also appears in some specified column Y of some specified table Z (where X, Y, and Z are parameters), again without making any prior assumptions about the structure of the database. In both of these examples, the integrated catalog is crucial. *Note:* Such programs may very well be needed in practice. See Appendix B, Section B.7.

## 16.3    PERFORMANCE

A number of misconceptions have grown up in the DP world over the past few years concerning relational systems, many of them having to do with performance. Two very commonly heard opinions are the following:

> "Relational systems are all very fine for ad hoc query, but they will never achieve the performance needed for production systems (or transaction processing systems or …)."

> "Relational systems require a breakthrough in hardware technology (e.g., hardware associative memory) before they will be able to achieve acceptable performance."

The contrasting opinion (that of the present writer, needless to say) is as follows:

> "There is no intrinsic reason why a relational system should perform any worse—or indeed any better!—than any other kind of system."

Let us try and justify this position. First, note that the two principal factors in performance are the number of I/O operations and the pathlength (amount of CPU processing). We consider each in turn.

### Pathlength

DB2 is a compiling system. (So too is SQL/DS. At the time of writing, most other systems, relational or otherwise, are interpretive; but the advantages of compilation are widely recognized, and several other relational systems are known to be moving toward a compiling approach.) The advantage of compiling is precisely that it reduces the runtime pathlength: All of the following operations —

- parsing the original request
- detecting and reporting on syntax errors
- mapping logical-level names to physical-level addresses
- choosing an access strategy
- checking authorization
- generating machine code

—are removed from the runtime path. (Of these operations, perhaps the most significant is choosing an access strategy—in a word, optimization.) The runtime pathlength is thus considerably shorter than it would otherwise be. What is more, the generated code is tightly tailored to the original request, and may thus be more efficient than more generalized, interpretive code would be. Moreover, as explained in Chapter 2, the system achieves the performance benefits of compilation without any corresponding loss of flexibility in operation: If recompilation becomes necessary (e.g., if an index is dropped), then the system handles that recompilation automatically ("automatic bind").

We note in passing that compilation (as that term is understood in DB2, i.e., *optimized* compilation) would not be feasible in a record-level system, because the system would simply not be able to capture the user's intent in the same way. Thus it is conceivable that a relational system may ultimately require *shorter* pathlengths than a nonrelational system (if, e.g., the nonrelational system always has to parse requests at run time).

## I/O Operations

The number of I/O operations required to satisfy a particular request is a function of the *physical* structure of the database, not the logical structure. In other words, it has nothing to do with how the database is perceived by its users (as relations or as some other logical structure). We can therefore break the question of how much I/O is needed in a relational system down into two subsidiary questions:

1. Are the physical structures supported by the system capable of providing the kind of I/O performance needed?

2. If the answer to the first question is "yes," then is the system capable of accepting high-level relational requests (e.g., SELECT statements) and converting them into operations on those physical structures that are "as good as hand code" (i.e., as good as the code that would be produced by a skilled programmer working directly at the physical level)?

Regarding Question 1, most relational systems today support B-tree indexes (a few systems support hashes, etc., in addition, but DB2 is not one of them). In fact, there is little doubt that if a single physical structure has to be chosen, then B-tree indexes are the obvious choice. Now, B-tree indexes are certainly capable of providing adequate performance for many applications (this statement must be true, or nobody would use VSAM). On the other hand, it is also true that there are some applications that simply have to use hashing (say) to meet their performance requirements. Thus, the answer to the first question (so far as DB2 is concerned) is "yes" if indexes are acceptable for the application in hand, "no" otherwise. (In the latter case, of course, the answer may still be "yes" for some other relational system.)

Assuming that the answer to Question 1 is "yes," let us now consider Question 2 (can the system produce code that is as good as hand code?). The short answer is "yes, it can" (in many cases but not all). The function of the DB2 optimizer is precisely to convert SQL statements into optimized machine code—where "optimized" means, basically, that the generated code employs the best strategy it can for satisfying the original request. For example, given the sample query from Section 16.2—"Get part numbers for parts supplied by supplier S2"—it will use the supplier number index on the SP table instead of a sequential scan (assuming, of course, that such an index exists). Of course, the optimizer does *not* produce the best possible code for every possible request; but then nor do most human programmers. Note, moreover, that we are talking here about Release 1 of a new product. It is reasonable to expect continuing improvements in the area of optimization throughout the lifetime of that product. Indeed, the field of database optimization today is somewhat analogous to the field of programming language optimization as it was some fifteen or so years ago: Numerous researchers are investigating the problem, at universities and elsewhere, and the fruits of that activity will no doubt eventually find their way into implemented products. Moreover, such enhancements can be made without in any way affecting the form of the external interface (that is what data independence is all about).

As a matter of fact, it is even conceivable that the optimizer could produce code that is *better* than hand code. It may well be the case that the optimizer has information available to it—regarding, for example, physical data clustering, table sizes, index selectivities, and so on—that a hand coder would not have. Moreover, that information may change with time. If it does, then reoptimization may become necessary. Such reoptimization is trivial in a system like DB2 (it simply requires a REBIND operation); it would be very difficult in a hand-coding system.

One final point (related to the previous point) regarding optimization: There is another reason why a relational system may in fact outperform a nonrelational system in some cases. The point is precisely that a system like DB2 is an optimizing system. High-level relational operations are optimizable precisely because they are high-level—they carry a lot of semantic content, and the optimizer is thus able to recognize what it is that the user is trying to do and is able to respond in an optimal way. By contrast, in a nonrelational system, in which the user operates at the record level instead of at the set level, access strategies are chosen by the user; and if the user makes a wrong choice, then there is little chance that the system will be able to optimize that user's code. For example, suppose the user is (in effect) trying to compute the join of two tables A and B. There are two possible strategies: (a) For each record of A in turn, find all matching records in B; (b) for each record of B in turn, find all matching records in A. Depending on such considerations as the relative sizes of A and B and their physical clustering characteristics, one of these strategies is likely to outperform the other by several orders of magnitude; and (as stated previously) if the user chooses the wrong one, then there is really no way that the system can convert it into the other, because the user's choice is expressed as a sequence of low-level operations instead of as a single high-level operation.

From all of the foregoing, we conclude that there is absolutely no reason why a relational system that is implemented on perfectly conventional hardware using perfectly conventional software techniques should not perform perfectly acceptably. A hardware breakthrough is *not* required (though if, e.g., cheap large-capacity associative memory ever did become a commercial reality, it would certainly be easier to take advantage of it in a relational system than in a nonrelational one).

*Caveat:* Note carefully that all of the foregoing discussions are very general! We are *not* saying that DB2 specifically is able to perform as well as a long-established system such as IMS. It is too early in the life of DB2 even to give any kind of performance figures as yet, though it is a safe bet that any such figures would be substantially less attractive than the corresponding figures for IMS. There is little doubt that *for a given application*, where the data structures and the transaction patterns are very well understood ahead of time, an established system like IMS can be customized and configured to produce far more impressive performance than a system like DB2 can—today. On the other hand:

(a)  That customized system may not look so impressive when other applications are added to it. Implementing application B on a system that is customized to application A is like cutting wood against the grain—extraneous considerations keep getting in the way. And note that we are not talking only about performance here, but also about the logical level of the system (that is, application B will probably be more awkward to write as well). Logical data structures in a nonrelational system tend to be biased toward some applications and against others (precisely because they closely reflect the physical data structure). Logical data structures in a relational system, by contrast, are more neutral: The application bias shows, not in the logical data structure, but in the manipulative operations, which by definition are far more flexible than the comparatively static data structure. (The bias will of course also show in the *physical* data structure.)

(b)  One reason for the performance advantage of nonrelational systems is simply that those systems have been running for ten or fifteen years and have been constantly improved and tuned throughout that time. Relational systems will improve too over the next few years. Moreover, it is not clear that further significant improvements are even possible in a nonrelational system, whereas (as indicated earlier) the field is wide open for such improvements in the relational case.

(c)  Even if the nonrelational system provides superior runtime performance, the value of that benefit has to be balanced against the amount of time it takes to get the system operational in the first place. The installation's investment will be recovered more quickly with a relational system than with a nonrelational system, because applications will be running sooner. The ultimate return on investment may be higher too, if the application lifetime is less than the time it takes for the nonrelational version to "catch up," economically speaking, with the relational version.

But we repeat that all of the above is somewhat theoretical. The fact is, a system like DB2, today, is extremely unlikely to be able to achieve the performance level of a system like IMS, today. The tradeoff that must be considered today is *performance versus usability*—or, to put it another way, machine productivity versus people productivity. Now, it is a truism that people costs are rising (fast) and machine costs are falling (also fast); as a result, people productivity is very rapidly becoming the dominating factor in many applications (indeed, it already is so in many cases). For such applications, relational systems are obviously ideally suited, even at their present level of performance. However, there are also numerous applications in which raw machine performance is still the overriding concern. Thus, systems like IMS will have a major role to play for several years to come. And even if relational systems do eventually achieve parity in performance, the huge investment in nonrelational systems is sufficient to ensure the continued existence of those systems for the foreseeable future. This is clearly one reason why DB2 is viewed by IBM as complementing IMS, not replacing it, and why the two products are designed to work together as explained in earlier chapters.

## 16.4  FUTURE DEVELOPMENTS

Relational systems such as DB2 stress, to a much greater degree than nonrelational systems, the distinction between externals and internals, or (equivalently) between the logical and physical levels of the system. At the logical level, the emphasis is on *usability*: The system provides a simple data structure and simple operators for manipulating that structure, and that simplicity leads to high user productivity, as described in Section 16.2. At the physical level, the emphasis is on *freedom*: The decoupling of the two levels means that the installation is free to make nontrivial changes at the physical level without affecting the logical level (other than in performance, of course).

Turning now to DB2 specifically, we can expect to see significant developments at both levels in the near future. At the physical level, new kinds of access mechanism (hashing, pointer chains, etc.) are likely to be provided as alternatives to the existing index mechanism, and the optimizer will be enhanced to exploit those new structures. (Of course, such new mechanisms should not be directly visible at the logical level.) At the logical level, extensions to the SQL language to provide direct support for such functions as outer join are likely to be implemented. We can also expect to see improved support for integrity, especially referential integrity (see Appendices A and B).

More far-reaching developments can be expected in the longer term. In order to get some idea as to what those longer-term developments might look like, we can take a look at the activities currently proceeding in university laboratories and similar research establishments. There are in fact a large number of such activities, all of them building on a relational foundation. They include:

- distributed database systems
- shared database machines
- semantic modeling
- integration of new kinds of data (e.g., text, images)
- expert systems
- new kinds of interface, including natural language
- engineering and scientific database systems

and others. Of course, some of these expected developments are much less "long-term" than others; for example, database machines are available in the marketplace today, and so are natural-language systems; but the point is that research is continuing on all of these topics, and all of it is relational-based. Moreover, the fact that it is built on a relational base is significant in itself: Much of the research would scarcely even be feasible on any other kind of foundation. Thus we might add yet another advantage to the list given in Section 16.2, namely *extendability*: Users of today's relational systems should be in a better position to take advantage of new technologies as they appear (where by "better" we mean, of course, "better than if they were users of some other kind of system").

On the question of distributed systems specifically, it is interesting to note that the IBM San Jose Research Laboratory has been at work for some time on a prototype system called R* (pronounced "R star"). R* is a distributed version of an earlier prototype called System R, and (as mentioned in the Preface to this book) System R in turn was the base from which the products DB2 and SQL/DS were both developed. Thus it is not unlikely that the technology of R* will someday be incorporated into distributed versions of SQL/DS and DB2.

The fact that all of this research is based on the relational model is an indication of the general acceptance of that model in the academic world.† More recently, relational ideas have become generally accepted in the commercial world also. In support of this claim, we can point to the large number of recent product announcements in the area. It is a fact that almost every database product announcement these days is either for a brand-new relational system (such as DB2) or for "relational" enhancements to one of the older systems ("relational" in quotes because it is by no means always clear that those enhancements are in fact relational; see Appendix A for a discussion of this point). At a conservative count there are now well over forty relational systems on the market (including a large number for microcomputers), and no doubt that number will have significantly increased by the time this book appears in print. And the announcement of DB2 by IBM can do nothing but strengthen the influence of relational technology in the commercial world. It is becoming increasingly clear that, so far as database management is concerned, relational systems are the way of the future.

---

†Further evidence of that acceptance is provided by the fact that the Association for computing Machinery (ACM) presented its 1981 Turing Award to Dr. Codd, the original architect of the relational model, for his work on that model. The Turing Award is awarded annually for significant contributions to computer science. It is generally recognized as the most prestigious award in the entire field of computer science.

# The
# Relational Model

## A.1 INTRODUCTION

DB2 is a relational DBMS ("relational system" for short). The purpose of this appendix is to explain exactly what that statement means. Basically, a relational system is a system that is constructed in accordance with the relational *model* (or at least the major principles of that model); and the relational model is *a way of looking at data*—that is, a prescription for how to represent data and how to manipulate that representation. More specifically, the relational model is concerned with three aspects of data: data *structure*, data *integrity*, and data *manipulation*. We examine each of these in turn (in Sections A.2, A.3, and A.4, respectively), and then consider the question of what exactly it is that constitutes a relational *system* (in Section A.5).

*Note:* In this appendix we will (for the most part) be using formal relational terminology. for convenience, Fig. A.1 (next page) repeats from Chapter 1 the major relational terms and their informal equivalents.

## A.2 RELATIONAL DATA STRUCTURE

The smallest unit of data in the relational model is the individual data value. Such values are considered to be *atomic*—that is, they are nondecomposable so far as

| formal relational term | informal equivalents |
| --- | --- |
| relation | table |
| tuple | record, row |
| attribute | field, column |

**Fig. A.1**  Some terminology

the model is concerned. A *domain* is a set of such values, all of the same type; for example, the domain of supplier numbers is the set of all valid supplier numbers, the domain of shipment quantities is the set of all integers greater than zero and less than 10,000 (say). Thus domains are *pools of values*, from which the actual values appearing in attributes (columns) are drawn. The significance of domains is as follows: If two attributes draw their values from the same domain, then comparisons—and hence joins, unions, etc.—involving those two attributes probably make sense, because they are comparing like with like; conversely, if two attributes draw their values from different domains, then comparisons (etc.) involving those two attributes probably do not make sense. In SQL terms, for example, the query

```
SELECT  S.*, SP.*
FROM    S, SP
WHERE   S.S# = SP.S# ;
```

probably does make sense, whereas the query

```
SELECT  S.*, SP.*
FROM    S, SP
WHERE   S.STATUS = SP.QTY ;
```

probably does not. (DB2, however, has no notion of domains *per se*. Both of the foregoing SELECT statements are legal queries in DB2.)

Note that domains are primarily conceptual in nature. They may or may not be explicitly stored in the database as actual sets of values. But they should be specified as part of the database definition (in a system that supports the concept at all—but most systems currently do not); and then each attribute definition should include a reference to the corresponding domain. A given attribute may have the same name as the corresponding domain or a different name. Obviously it must have a different name if any ambiguity would otherwise result (in particular, if two attributes in the same relation are both based on the same domain; see the definition of relation below, and note the phrase "not necessarily all distinct").

We are now in a position to define the term "relation." A *relation* on domains D1, D2, ..., Dn (not necessarily all distinct) consists of a *heading* and a *body*.

The heading consists of a fixed set of *attributes* A1, A2, ..., A$n$, such that there is a one-to-one correspondence between the attributes A$i$ and the underlying domains D$i$ ($i$ = 1,2,...,$n$). The body consists of a time-varying set of *tuples*, where each tuple in turn consists of a set of attribute-value pairs (A$i$:v$i$) ($i$ = 1,2,...,$n$), one such pair for each attribute A$i$ in the heading. For any given attribute-value pair (A$i$:v$i$), v$i$ is a value from the unique domain D$i$ that is associated with the attribute A$i$.

As an example, let us see how the supplier relation S measures up to this definition (see Fig. 1.3). The underlying domains are the domain of supplier numbers (D1, say), the domain of supplier names (D2), the domain of supplier status values (D3), and the domain of city names (D4). The heading of S consists of the attributes S# (underlying domain D1), SNAME (domain D2), STATUS (domain D3), and CITY (domain D4). The body of S consists of a set of tuples (five tuples in Fig. 1.3, but this set varies with time as updates are made to the relation); and each tuple consists of a set of four attribute-value pairs, one such pair for each of the four attributes in the heading. For example, the tuple for supplier S1 consists of the pairs

```
( S#     : 'S1'      )
( SNAME  : 'Smith'   )
( STATUS : 20        )
( CITY   : 'London'  )
```

(though it is normal to elide the attribute names in informal contexts). And of course each attribute value does indeed come from the appropriate underlying domain; the value "S1", for example, does come from the supplier number domain D1. So S is indeed a relation according to the definition.

Note carefully that when we draw a relation such as relation S as a table, as we did in Fig. 1.3, we are merely making use of a convenient method for representing the relation on paper. A table and a relation are not really the same thing, though for most of this book we have assumed that they are. For example, the rows of a table clearly have an ordering (from top to bottom), whereas the tuples of a relation do not (a relation is a mathematical *set*, and sets do not have any ordering in mathematics). Likewise, the columns of a table also have an ordering (from left to right), whereas the attributes of a relation do not.

Notice that the underlying domains of a relation are "not necessarily all distinct." Many examples have already been given in which they are not; see, e.g., the result relation in Example 4.3.1 (Chapter 4), which includes two attributes both defined on the domain of city-names.

The value $n$ (the number of attributes in the relation, or equivalently the number of underlying domains) is called the *degree* of the relation. A relation of degree one is called *unary*, a relation of degree two *binary*, a relation of degree three *ternary*, ..., and a relation of degree $n$ *n-ary*. In the suppliers-and-parts database, relations S, P, and SP have degrees 4, 5, and 3, respectively. The number of tuples in the relation is called the *cardinality* of that relation; the cardinalities of relations S, P, and SP of Fig. 1.3 are 5, 6, and 12, respectively. The cardinality of a relation changes with time, whereas the degree does not.*

## A.3    RELATIONAL DATA INTEGRITY

One important consequence of the definitions in the previous section is that *every relation has a primary key*. Since a relation is a set, and sets by definition do not contain duplicate elements, it follows that (at any given time) no two tuples of a relation can be duplicates of each other. Let R be a relation with attributes A1, A2, ..., An. The set of attributes K = (Ai,Aj,...,Ak) of R is said to be a *candidate key* of R if and only if it satisfies the following two time-independent properties:

1.  Uniqueness:
At any given time, no two distinct tuples of R have the same value for Ai, the same value for Aj,..., and the same value for Ak.

2.  Minimality:
None of Ai, Aj,..., Ak can be discarded from K without destroying the uniqueness property.

Every relation has at least one candidate key, because at least the combination of all of its attributes has the uniqueness property. For a given relation, one candidate key is (arbitrarily) designated as the *primary* key. The remaining candidate keys (if any) are called *alternate* keys.

Example: Suppose that supplier names and supplier numbers are both unique (no two suppliers have the same number or the same name). Then relation S has two candidate keys, S# and SNAME. We choose S# as the primary key; SNAME then becomes an alternate key. Note, however, that DB2 has no knowledge of either primary or alternate keys as such (although it is possible to enforce uniqueness via CREATE UNIQUE INDEX—see Section 3.3).

Continuing with the example, consider attribute S# of relation SP. It is clear that a given value for that attribute, say the supplier number S1, should be permitted to appear in the database only if that same value also appears as a value of the primary key S# of relation S (for otherwise the database cannot be considered to be in a state of integrity). An attribute such as SP.S# is said to be a *foreign key*. In general, a foreign key is an attribute (or attribute combination) of one relation R2 whose values are required to match those of the primary key of some relation R1 (R1 and R2 not necessarily distinct). Note that a foreign key

---

*An operation such as ALTER TABLE in SQL can be regarded, not as changing the degree of a relation from $n$ to $n + 1$, but rather as creating a new relation of degree $n + 1$ from one of degree $n$.

and the corresponding primary key should be defined on the same underlying domains.

We can now state the two integrity rules of the relational model. *Note:* These rules are *general*, in the sense that any database that conforms to the model is required to satisfy them. However, any specific database will have a set of additional specific rules that apply to it alone. For example, the suppliers-and-parts database may have a specific rule to the effect that shipment quantities must be in the range 1 to 9999, say. But such specific rules are outside the scope of the relational model *per se*.

1.  Entity integrity:
No attribute participating in the primary key of a *base* relation is allowed to accept null values.

2.  Referential integrity:
If base relation R2 includes a foreign key FK matching the primary key PK of some base relation R1, then every value of FK in R2 must either (a) be equal to the value of PK in some tuple of R1 or (b) be wholly null (i.e., each attribute value participating in that FK value must be null). R1 and R2 are not necessarily distinct.

A *base relation* corresponds to what we have been calling a base table in the body of this book: It is an independent, named relation (see Chapter 3 for further discussion). The justification for the entity integrity rule is as follows:

1.  Base relations correspond to entities in the real world. For example, base relation S corresponds to a set of suppliers in the real world.

2.  By definition, entities in the real world are distinguishable—that is, they have a unique identification of some kind.

3.  Primary keys perform the unique identification function in the relational model.

4.  Thus, a primary key value that was null would be a contradiction in terms — in effect, it would be saying that there was some entity that had no *id*entity (i.e., did not exist). Hence the name "entity integrity."

As for the second rule ("referential integrity"), it is clear that a given foreign key value must have a matching primary key value in some tuple of the referenced relation if that foreign key value is nonnull. Sometimes, however, it is necessary to permit the foreign key to accept null values. Suppose, for example, that in a given company it is legal for some employee to be currently assigned to no department at all. For such an employee, the department number attribute (which is a foreign key) would have to be null in the tuple representing that employee in the database.

We shall have more to say about primary and foreign keys in Appendix B.

## A.4   RELATIONAL DATA MANIPULATION

The manipulative part of the relational model consists of a set of operators known collectively as the *relational algebra*, together with a relational assignment operator which assigns the value of some arbitrary expression of the algebra to another relation. We discuss the algebra first.

Each operator of the relational algebra takes either one or two relations as its operand(s) and produces a new relation as its result. Codd originally defined eight such operators, two groups of four each: (1) the traditional set operations union, intersection, difference, and Cartesian product (all modified slightly to take account of the fact that their operands are relations, as opposed to arbitrary sets); and (2) the special relational operations select, project, join, and divide. The eight operations are shown symbolically in Fig. A.2. We give a brief definition of each operation below; for simplicity, we assume in those definitions that the left-to-right order of attributes within a relation *is* significant—not because it is necessary to do so, but because it simplifies the discussion.

### Traditional Set Operations

Each of the traditional set operations takes two operands. For all except Cartesian product, the two operand relations must be *union-compatible*—that is, they must be of the same degree, *n* say, and the *i*th attribute of each ($i = 1,2,...,n$) must be based on the same domain (they do not have to have the same name).

- Union
  The union of two (union-compatible) relations A and B is the set of all tuples *t* belonging to either A or B (or both).
      SQL example:

```
SELECT S# FROM S
UNION
SELECT S# FROM SP ;
```

- Intersection
  The intersection of two (union-compatible) relations A and B is the set of all tuples *t* belonging to both A and B.
      SQL example:

```
SELECT S# FROM S
WHERE  EXISTS
     ( SELECT S# FROM SP
       WHERE  SP.S# = S.S# ) ;
```

- Difference
  The difference between two (union-compatible) relations A and B is the set of all tuples *t* belonging to A and not to B.

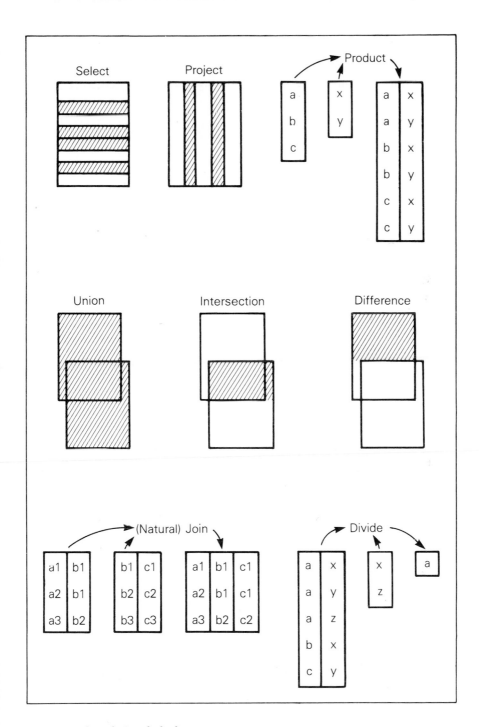

**Fig. A.2** The relational algebra

SQL example:

```
SELECT S# FROM S
WHERE  NOT EXISTS
     ( SELECT S# FROM SP
       WHERE  SP.S# = S.S# ) ;
```

- Product
  The product of two relations A and B is the set of all tuples *t* such that *t* is
  the concatenation of a tuple *a* belonging to A and a tuple *b* belonging to B.
  SQL example:

```
SELECT S.*, SP.*
FROM   S, SP ;
```

## Special Relational Operations

- Selection
  Let *theta* represent any valid scalar comparison operator (for example, =, ¬=,
  >, >=, etc.). The theta-selection of relation A on attributes X and Y is the
  set of all tuples *t* of A such that the predicate "*t*.X *theta* *t*.Y" evaluates to
  *true*. (Attributes X and Y should be defined on the same domain, and the
  operation *theta* must make sense for that domain.) A constant value may be
  specified instead of attribute Y. Thus, the theta-selection operator yields a
  "horizontal" subset of a given relation—that is, that subset of the tuples of
  the given relation for which a specified predicate is satisfied. *Note:* "Theta-
  selection" is often abbreviated to just "selection." But note that "selection"
  is not the same as the SELECT operator of SQL.
  SQL example:

```
SELECT *
FROM   S
WHERE  CITY ¬= 'London' ;
```

- Projection
  The projection operator yields a "vertical" subset of a given relation—that
  is, that subset obtained by selecting specified attributes and then eliminating
  redundant duplicate tuples within the attributes selected, if necessary.
  SQL example:

```
SELECT DISTINCT COLOR, CITY
FROM   P ;
```

- Join
  Let *theta* be as defined under "Selection" above. The theta-join of relation
  A on attribute X with relation B on attribute Y is the set of all tuples *t* such
  that *t* is the concatenation of a tuple *a* belonging to A and a tuple *b* belonging

to B and the predicate "*a*.X *theta b*.Y" evaluates to *true*. (Attributes A.X and B.Y should be defined on the same domain, and the operation *theta* must make sense for that domain.)

SQL example:

```
SELECT S.*, P.*
FROM    S, P
WHERE   S.CITY > P.CITY ;
```

If *theta* is equality, the join is called an equijoin. It follows from the definition that the result of an equijoin must include two identical attributes. If one of those two attributes is eliminated (which it can be via projection), the result is called the *natural* join. The unqualified term "join" is usually taken to mean the natural join.

- Division

In its simplest form (which is all that we consider here), the division operator divides a relation of degree two (the dividend) by a relation of degree one (the divisor), and produces a result relation of degree one (the quotient). Let the dividend (A) have attributes X and Y, and let the divisor (B) have attribute Y. Attributes A.Y and B.Y should be defined on the same domain. The result of dividing A by B is the relation C, with sole attribute X, such that every value *x* of C.X appears as a value of A.X, and the pair of values (*x,y*) appears in A for *all* values *y* appearing in B.

SQL example:

```
SELECT DISTINCT S# FROM SP SP1
WHERE   NOT EXISTS
          ( SELECT P# FROM P
            WHERE   NOT EXISTS
                      ( SELECT * FROM SP SP2
                        WHERE   SP2.S# = SP1.S# AND SP2.P# = P.P# ) ) ;
```

Here we are assuming for simplicity that (a) relation SP has only two attributes, namely S# and P# (we are ignoring QTY), and (b) relation P has only one attribute, namely P# (we are ignoring PNAME, COLOR, WEIGHT, and CITY). We divide the first of these two relations by the second and obtain a result, namely a relation with one attribute (S#) that lists supplier numbers for suppliers that supply all parts.

It is worth mentioning that, of these eight operations, only five are primitive, namely selection, projection, product, union, and difference. The other three can be defined in terms of those five. For example, the natural join is a projection of a selection of a product. In practice, however, those other three operations (especially join) are so useful that a good case can be made for supporting them directly, even though they are not primitive.

Turning now to the relational assignment operation, the purpose of that operation is simply to allow the value of some algebraic expression—say a join—to be saved in some more or less permanent place. It can be simulated in SQL by means of the INSERT . . . SELECT operation. For example, suppose relation XYZ has two attributes, S# and P#, and suppose also that it is currently empty (contains no tuples). The SQL statement

```
INSERT INTO XYZ ( S#, P# )
       SELECT S.S#, P.P#
       FROM   S, P
       WHERE  S.CITY = P.CITY ;
```

assigns the result of the SELECT (namely, a projection of a join) to the relation XYZ.

By way of conclusion, Fig. A.3 summarizes the major components of the relational model.

**Data structure**
   domains (values)
   n-ary relations (attributes, tuples)
   keys (candidate, primary, alternate, foreign)
**Data integrity**
   1. primary key values must not be null
   2. foreign key values must match primary key values (or be null)
**Data manipulation**
   relational algebra
     union, intersection, difference, product
     select, project, join, divide
   relational assignment

**Fig. A.3**  The relational model

## A.5   RELATIONAL SYSTEMS

We are now (at last) in a position to define exactly what we mean by a *relational database management system* (relational DBMS, or relational system for short). The point is, *no* system today supports the relational model in its entirety (several come close, but most systems fall down on the integrity rules if nowhere else). On the other hand, it would be unreasonable to insist that a system is not relational unless it supports every last detail of the model. The fact is, not all aspects of the model are equally important; some of course are crucial, but others may be regarded merely as features that are "nice to have" (comparatively speaking). We therefore define a system as *relational* if it supports at least the following:

- Relational databases (i.e., databases that can be perceived by the user as tables, and nothing but tables);
- At least the operations select, project, and join of the relational algebra (without requiring any predefinition of physical access paths to support those operations).*

Note carefully that a system does not have to support the select, project, and join operators *explicitly* in order to qualify as relational. It is only the functionality of those operators that we are talking about here. For example, DB2 provides the functionality of all three of those operators (and more besides) within its own SELECT operator. More important, note that a system that supports relational databases but not these three operators does not qualify as a relational system under our definition. Likewise, a system that allows (say) the user to select tuples according to values of some attribute X only if that attribute X is indexed also does not qualify, because it is requiring predefinition of physical access paths.

We justify our definition as follows:

1. Although select, project, and join are less than the full algebra, they are an extremely useful subset. There are comparatively few practical problems that can be solved with the algebra that cannot be solved with select, project, and join alone.

2. A system that supports the relational data structure but not the relational operators does not provide the productivity of a genuinely relational system.

3. To do a good job of implementing the relational operators *requires* the system to do some optimization. A system that merely executed the exact operations requested by the user in a comparatively unintelligent fashion would almost certainly not have acceptable performance. Thus, to implement a system that realizes the potential of the relational model in an efficient manner is a highly nontrivial task.

DB2 is a relational system according to our definition (even though there are several aspects of the relational model that it does not support). So too is SQL/DS. But there are a number of systems on the market today that advertise themselves as "relational" that do not meet the criteria defined above. As we have tried to suggest, those criteria are useful as a means of drawing a sharp line between systems that are indeed genuinely relational and systems that are merely "relational-like." "Relational-like" systems do not truly provide the benefits of the relational model. The distinction is thus worth making, as it ensures that the label "relational" is not used in misleading ways.

---

*By "join" here we mean either the natural join or the equijoin.

# Relational Database Design

## B.1 INTRODUCTION

Database design is a big subject; it is not really possible to do it justice in an appendix of just a few pages. All that we can hope to do is present an overall approach that can be useful in the design of relational databases in general and DB2 databases in particular. Many detailed questions will be left unanswered. However, we hope that the overall approach will be useful as a framework within which users can attempt to answer those more detailed questions for themselves.

We assume that the reader is familiar and comfortable with such terms as "entity," "relationship," and "property." We define those terms (informally) as follows:

- An *entity* is *any distinguishable object*—where the object in question can be as concrete or as abstract as we please. Examples of entities are persons, places, airplanes, flights, jazz, the color red, and so on. In a database context, of course, the entities we are principally interested in are those objects about which we wish to store information in the database.

- A *relationship* is *a connection among two or more entities*. Examples of relationships are the assignment of employees to departments (a many-to-one relationship) and the shipment of parts by suppliers (a many-to-many relationship).

- A *property* is *a single-valued fact about an entity.* Examples of properties are employee salaries, part weights, shipment quantities, etc.

In the next section we present a classification scheme for entities that forms the basis of our design methodology. That discussion is then followed by a discussion of the crucial role played by primary and foreign keys in database design, a checklist of the major steps involved in the design procedure, a suggestion as to how design decisions should be formally recorded, some "recipes" for mapping those decisions into formal DB2 constructs, a discussion of the basic concepts of normalization, and a brief list of miscellaneous tips and hints.

One final introductory point: The reader will probably have realized already that we are using the term "database design" to refer to *logical* design. This fact does not mean that we think that physical design is unimportant—merely that it is a separate problem that can and should be separately addressed, after the logical design has been done. Indeed, it is one of the major contributions of relational technology that the twin activities of logical and physical design can be cleanly separated in this manner.

## B.2   AN ENTITY CLASSIFICATION SCHEME

We classify entities into three basic types: *kernels*, *associations*, and *characteristics*. Briefly, a kernel is an independent entity (it has independent existence); an association is a many-to-many (or many-to-many-to-many, etc.) relationship among two or more other entities; and a characteristic is an entity whose sole purpose (within the universe of discourse) is to describe or qualify some other entity.

Examples:

| | |
|---|---|
| kernels | suppliers, parts, employees, departments |
| associations | shipments |
| characteristics | order lines (whose sole purpose is to describe a "superior" entity, namely a purchase order) |

Associations and characteristics are not independent entities, because they presuppose the existence of some other entity or entities to be associated or "characterized."

The foregoing classification scheme has its origin in the fact that *relationships* fall naturally into two different categories, namely many-to-many relationships, which we call associations, and many-to-one relationships, which we call designations. More precisely:

■   An *association,* as already explained, is a many-to-many(-to-many, etc.) relationship among two or more entities. *Associations are considered as entities in their own right:* They can have properties, participate in other associations, etc., just like kernel entities. For example, shipments (which are associations) have "quantity" as a property.

■   A *designation* is a many-to-one relationship between two entities. Designations are *not* normally considered as entities in their own right (although there is nothing wrong in doing so); instead, properties (etc.) of a designation are generally regarded as properties (etc.) of the designat*ing* entity. For example, there is a designation from employees to departments; the property "commencement date" (the date the employee joined the department), which strictly speaking is a property of the designation (i.e., the employee-department relationship), can equally well be regarded as a property of the employee alone. *Note:* A one-to-one relationship is regarded merely as a special case of a many-to-one relationship. It does not receive any special treatment in our methodology.

A *characteristic* is a designating entity that is *existence-dependent on the entity it designates*. Employees are not characteristics of departments, because employees have independent existence; if a department is deleted, it does not follow that employees in that department must be deleted too. By contrast, order lines *are* characteristics of purchase orders; it is not possible for an order line to exist in the absence of a corresponding purchase order, and if a purchase order is deleted, then all order lines for that purchase order must be deleted too.

The need for characteristics arises from the fact that real-world entities may sometimes have multivalued properties. Suppose, for instance, that parts come in multiple colors; suppose, for example, that part P1 is available in red, white, and blue. Since the relational model does not support repeating groups, the following is invalid:

```
P   P#   PNAME   COLOR                    . . .
    --   -----   --------------------     ---
    P1   Nut     { Red, White, Blue }     . . .
```

Instead, we must represent the situation as follows:

```
P   P#   PNAME   . . .          PC   P#   COLOR
    --   -----   ---                 --   -----
    P1   Nut     . . .               P1   Red
                                     P1   White
                                     P1   Blue
```

Here table P represents a kernel (the "part" entity type), and table PC represents a characteristic (the "part color" entity type) that is existence-dependent on that kernel. For example, if P1 is deleted from table P, then all records for P1 must also be deleted from table PC.

Since a characteristic is an entity, it can of course have properties, participate in associations, designate other entities, and have (lower-level) characteristics of its own.

Finally, we (re)define kernel entities as entities that are neither associations nor characteristics. Kernel entities are "what the database is all about." Kernel entities have independent existence (though they may still designate other entities, as employees, for example, designate departments; any entity, regardless of whether it is kernel, characteristic, or associative, may be designative in addition).

## B.3   PRIMARY AND FOREIGN KEYS

The single most important aspect of entities in the real world is their *distinguishability*. Hence, when we consider the problem of representing entities in the database, the single most important question to answer is "How are the *representatives* of those entities distinguished from one another?"—i.e., how are entities identified in the database?

Now, in the design procedure sketched in the next section, each entity type (suppliers, employees, shipments, purchase orders, etc.), regardless of whether it is kernel, characteristic, or associative, will map into a DB2 base table. Properties of the entity type will map into fields within that base table. Since the identification function is performed in the relational model by *primary keys* (see Appendix A for a definition of this term), it follows that each such base table should have a primary key, representing the identifying property for the entity type concerned. The following are the primary keys for the suppliers-and-parts database:

- table S    field S.S#
- table P    field P.P#
- table SP   the composite field SP.(S#,P#)

For each base table in the design, therefore, the database designer should specify the field or field combination constituting the primary key for that base table. See Section B.5 below for some suggestions as to how to write such a specification.

Next, if entities are represented by base tables, then connections among entities are represented by *foreign keys* in those base tables (again, see Appendix A for a definition of this term). More precisely:

- If entities of type B designate entities of type A, and if the corresponding base tables are TB and TA respectively, then TB will include a foreign key matching the primary key of TA.

- Likewise, if entities of type C are associations between entities of type A and entities of type B, and if the corresponding base tables are TC, TA, and TB, respectively, then TC will include a foreign key matching the primary key of TA and a foreign key matching the primary key of TB.

Shipments provide an example of this latter case, where the foreign keys are SP.S# (matching the primary key S# of S) and SP.P# (matching the primary key P# of P). As an example of the former case, suppose again that employees designate departments. Then the employees table (EMP, say) will include a foreign key (EMP.DEPT#, say) matching the primary key (DEPT#, say) of the departments table (DEPT, say).

Thus, in considering the problem of how associations and designations are to be represented in the database, the basic question to be answered is "What are the foreign keys?" but that is not the end of the story. For each foreign key it is necessary to consider three further questions:

1. Can that foreign key accept null values? In other words, is it possible for an instance of the entity type to exist for which the target of the foreign key reference is unknown? In the case of shipments it probably is not possible—a shipment for an unknown supplier or an unknown part does not make much sense. But in the case of employees it might well make sense—it might well be possible for some employee to be currently assigned to no department at all. Note clearly that the answer to this question (as to whether nulls are allowed for a given foreign key) depends, not on the whim of the database designer, but on the policies in effect in the piece of the real world that is to be represented in the database. Similar remarks apply to questions 2 and 3 below, of course.

2. What should happen on an attempt to delete the target of a foreign key reference?—for example, an attempt to delete a supplier for which there exists at least one matching shipment? For definiteness let us consider this case explicitly. In general there are three possibilities:

- CASCADES    The delete operation "cascades" to delete those matching shipments also
- RESTRICTED  The delete operation is "restricted" to the case where there are no such matching shipments (it is rejected otherwise)
- NULLIFIES   The foreign key is set to null in all such matching shipments and the supplier is then deleted (of course, this case could not apply if the foreign key cannot accept null values)

3. What should happen on an attempt to update the primary key of the target of a foreign key reference?—for example, an attempt to update the supplier number for a supplier for which there exists at least one matching shipment? For definiteness, again, we consider this case explicitly. In general there are the same three possibilities as for DELETE:

- CASCADES        The update operation "cascades" to update the foreign key in those matching shipments also

- RESTRICTED    The update operation is "restricted" to the case where there are no such matching shipments (it is rejected otherwise)

- NULLIFIES       The foreign key is set to null in all such matching shipments and the supplier is then updated (of course, this case could not apply if the foreign key cannot accept null values)

For each foreign key in the design, therefore, the database designer should specify, not only the field or field combination constituting that foreign key and the target table that is identified by that foreign key, but also the answers to the foregoing three questions (i.e., the three constraints that apply to that foreign key). Again, see Section B.5 below for some suggestions as to how to write such specifications.

We conclude this section with a brief note on characteristics. By definition, a characteristic is a designating entity that is existence-dependent upon the entity type it designates. The designation will of course be represented by a foreign key in the table corresponding to the characteristic; but the three foreign key constraints for that foreign key *must* be specified as

```
NULLS NOT ALLOWED
DELETE (of target) CASCADES
UPDATE (of target primary key) CASCADES
```

(using the syntax of Section B.5 below) to represent the existence-dependence.


## B.4    THE DESIGN PROCEDURE: A CHECKLIST

We are now in a position to present a checklist of the major steps in the design procedure. *Note:* For brevity, in what follows we use "entity" to mean entity *type.*

1. Represent each kernel (independent entity) as a base table. Specify the primary key of that base table.

2. Represent each association (many-to-many, or many-to-many-to-many, etc., relationship among entities) as a base table. Use foreign keys within that table to identify the participants in the association. Specify the constraints associated with each of those foreign keys. Specify the primary key of the table (probably the combination of all participant-identifying foreign keys).

3. Represent each characteristic (designating entity that is existence-dependent on the corresponding designated entity) as a base table with a foreign key identifying the entity described by the characteristic. Specify the foreign key constraints for existence dependence. Specify the primary key of the table (probably the combination of the foreign key and the property that guarantees "uniqueness within entity described").

4. Represent each designation (many-to-one relationship between two entities) not already dealt with under 3. above as a foreign key within the base table representing the designating entity. Specify the constraints associated with each such foreign key.

5. Represent each property as a field within the base table representing the entity most immediately described by that property.

6. Apply the recipes for primary and foreign keys (see Section B.6 below).

7. Apply the procedures discussed in Section B.7 below to ensure that the design does not unintentionally violate any of the normalization guidelines.

8. Iterate until the design is complete.

## B.5   RECORDING DESIGN DECISIONS: PSEUDODDL

As you proceed through the design process, it is of course necessary to record the decisions you make, preferably in some more or less formal manner. The question is, what formalism should be used in this activity? There are many possible answers to this question, none of them obviously preferable to all the rest; to some extent it is purely a matter of taste. However, one strong candidate is *data definition language statements* (DDL statements); after all, such statements eventually have to be produced anyway, when the design is converted into a database definition. Unfortunately, DDL statements alone are inadequate for the task in DB2, for the important reason that they do not support certain concepts—specifically, primary and foreign keys—that (as we have seen) are absolutely crucial to the design process. We therefore propose a formalism that might be called "pseudoDDL." PseudoDDL is based on the regular SQL DDL but includes direct support for those missing concepts. Consider the kernel entity type "suppliers," for example. We have already said that each entity type will map into a DB2 base table. Thus, we might write the pseudoDDL statement

```
CREATE TABLE S        /* suppliers (kernel) */
       PRIMARY KEY ( S# )
       FIELDS ( S# ... ) ;
```

to record the fact that a base table called S exists, it represents the kernel entity type "suppliers," and it has primary key S# (which is of course a field in the table).* Later on we will come back to add further specifications to this statement to record further facts about this entity type. Ideally all such pseudoDDL statements would be kept in the form of a text file, and a text editor used to maintain that file as design proceeds. Ultimately we will convert those statements into an appropriate set of genuine DB2 DDL statements, for input to the database definition process.

Here is a sample pseudoDDL statement for shipments, showing a possible set of foreign key specifications:

```
CREATE TABLE SP    /* shipments - associate S and P */
       PRIMARY KEY ( S#, P# )
       FOREIGN KEY ( S# IDENTIFIES S
                     NULLS NOT ALLOWED
                     DELETE OF S RESTRICTED
                     UPDATE OF S.S# CASCADES )
       FOREIGN KEY ( P# IDENTIFIES P
                     NULLS NOT ALLOWED
                     DELETE OF P RESTRICTED
                     UPDATE OF P.P# RESTRICTED )
       FIELDS ( S# ... , P# ... , QTY ... ) ;
```

General syntax for the pseudoDDL PRIMARY KEY and FOREIGN KEY clauses:

```
primary-key-clause
   ::=  PRIMARY KEY ( primary-key )
```

where "primary-key" is either a single field-name, such as S#, or a list of field-names separated by commas and enclosed in parentheses, such as (S#,P#).

```
foreign-key-clause
   ::=  FOREIGN KEY ( foreign-key IDENTIFIES target
                      NULLS [ NOT ] ALLOWED
                      DELETE OF target effect
                      UPDATE OF target-primary-key effect )
```

where (a) "foreign-key" is the same as "primary-key" above—i.e., it is either a single field-name or a list of field-names separated by commas and enclosed in parentheses; (b) "target" is a table-name; (c) "target-primary-key" specifies the "primary-key" for "target"; and (d) "effect" is CASCADES or RESTRICTED or NULLIFIES.

---

*The statement also includes a comment and the keyword FIELDS, neither of which is part of the real DB2 DDL.

*Note:* PRIMARY KEY and FOREIGN KEY clauses along the foregoing lines would be highly desirable extensions to the genuine DB2 DDL.

## B.6   A RECIPE FOR PRIMARY KEYS

As already pointed out, the DB2 DDL does not support the notion of primary or foreign keys. We therefore present, in this section and the next, recipes by which you can enforce the primary and foreign key discipline for yourself. First, primary keys. For each primary key in your design:

- Specify NOT NULL for each field in the primary key (see Section 3.2).
- Create a UNIQUE index over the combination of all fields in the primary key (see Section 3.3).
- Ensure that this index is in existence whenever a record is inserted into the table or the primary key of a record in the table is updated (i.e., create the index before you initially load the table, and "never" drop it).
- Keep the PRIMARY KEY specifications from the pseudoDDL as a comment in the catalog (see Section 7.3).

## B.7   A RECIPE FOR FOREIGN KEYS

For each foreign key in your design:

- Specify NOT NULL for each field in the foreign key, if and only if NULLS NOT ALLOWED applies to that foreign key.
- Consider the merits of creating an index (probably not UNIQUE) over the combination of all fields in the foreign key. (Such an index usually will be desirable for performance reasons—you will frequently find yourself performing join operations over the foreign key and its matching primary key—but performance considerations are strictly beyond the scope of this appendix.)
- Use the authorization mechanism to prohibit all online operations that could violate the constraints that apply to this foreign key. (By "online operation" here we mean a SQL operation, such as INSERT or DELETE, that is issued by an end-user [via SPUFI or QMF] rather than by an application program.) Specifically, prohibit online:
    - DELETE on the referenced table
    - UPDATE on the referenced table primary key
    - INSERT on the referencing table
    - UPDATE on the referencing table foreign key
- Take the foreign key constraints as part of the requirements specification for database maintenance programs. Ideally, have exactly one such program for

each foreign key (this does not mean that one program cannot deal with multiple foreign keys, only that one foreign key should not be maintained by multiple programs). Use the authorization mechanism to prevent all other programs from executing any operations that could violate those constraints (see previous paragraph).

▪ Keep the FOREIGN KEY specifications from the pseudoDDL as a comment in the catalog.

Finally, as an independent (and conservative) measure:

▪ Write a utility program to be run periodically to check for and report on any constraint violations.

## B.8   NORMALIZATION

By following the design procedure outlined in the previous sections, we will always finish up with a design that conforms to the following simple pattern:

---

Each table consists of:

(a) a primary key, representing the unique identifier for some particular entity type;

together with

(b) zero or more additional fields, representing additional properties of the entity type identified by the primary key (and not of some other entity type).

---

Such a design is *clean*, in the sense that each table contains information about one entity type, and one entity type only. That design will be easier to understand, easier to use, and (most important) easier to extend when new information is added to the database later on, than a design in which information about multiple entity types is bundled together into a single table. In other words, the design will be *stable* and will be a good foundation for future growth.

Another way of expressing the clean design objective is: *One fact in one place*. Each fact (for example, the fact that a certain supplier has a certain status) appears at exactly one place in the design. Yet another way of characterizing it (very informally) is: *Each field represents a fact about the key, the whole key, and nothing but the key* (where "key" is shorthand for "entity identified by the primary key of the table that contains the field in question").

Clean design is also the objective of the discipline of *normalization*. In fact, the methodology discussed in this appendix so far and the normalization discipline are complementary, in the sense that you will probably find yourself employing them both in practice. However, normalization is frequently discussed in the literature as if it were the only design tool necessary; our feeling, by contrast, is that (as already suggested) its principal usefulness is as a final check on the design methodology already presented. It is certainly not a panacea. That is why we devote only a comparatively small part of this appendix to it. (For a fuller discussion of the topic, see some of the references mentioned in the Bibliography.)

In brief, the idea of normalization is as follows. As explained in Chapter 1, every table in a relational database satisfies the condition that, at every row-and-column position within the table, there is always a single atomic value, never a set of such values. Any table satisfying this condition is said to be *normalized* (in fact, *un*normalized tables—equivalently, tables containing repeating groups—are not even allowed in a relational database). Every normalized table is automatically considered to be in *first normal form*, abbreviated 1NF. (That is, "normalized" and "1NF" mean the same thing, strictly speaking. But in practice the term "normalized" is often taken to have the narrower meaning of "fully normalized," in the sense that the design does not violate any of the normalization guidelines discussed below.)

Now, it is possible to define further levels of normalization, over and above 1NF—second normal form (2NF), third normal form (3NF), and so on. Basically, a table is in 2NF if it is in 1NF and also satisfies a certain extra condition (which will not be spelled out here); it is in 3NF if it is in 2NF and also satisfies yet another extra condition; and so on. Thus each normal form is in a sense more restrictive than the one before. More significantly, each normal form is generally more *desirable* than the one before, too. This is because "(N+1)st normal form" does not possess certain unattractive features that "Nth normal form" does. The whole point of the extra condition imposed on (N+1)st over Nth is precisely to eliminate those unattractive features. For example, here is a table—table SPSC, primary key the combination (S#,P#)—that is in first normal form and not in second:

```
SPSC   S#   P#   QTY   SCITY
       --   --   ---   ------
       S1   P1   300   London
       S1   P2   400   London
       S2   P1   200   Paris
       S2   P2   400   Paris
```

The "unattractive feature" of SPSC is obvious: Field SCITY (supplier city) contains a lot of redundancy. That redundancy in turn will lead to update and consistency problems (e.g., supplier S1 might be shown as having city London in one record and city Paris in another, unless appropriate controls are exercised). Intuitively, field SCITY is in the wrong place. A better design is:

```
SP   S#   P#   QTY              SC   S#    CITY
     --   --   ---                   --    ------
     S1   P1   300                   S1    London
     S1   P2   400                   S2    Paris
     S2   P1   200
     S2   P2   400
```

These tables are in 2NF (in fact, they are also in 3NF and 4NF and 5NF; 5NF is the "ultimate" normal form, in a very specific sense which it is unfortunately beyond the scope of this appendix to discuss).

The overall purpose of the further normalization discipline is to eliminate redundancies such as that illustrated in this example. That discipline provides a set of guidelines by which a table that contains such redundancies can be broken down into smaller tables that do not. The ultimate objective, as already stated, is to come up with a design in which each fact appears in one and only one place.

We discuss the normalization guidelines only very briefly here. First we need to introduce the notion of *functional dependency* (FD). Field B of table T is said to be functionally dependent on field A of table T if and only if it is the case that, for each distinct value of field T.A, there is necessarily exactly one distinct value of T.B (at any given time). For example, in table SPSC above, field SCITY is functionally dependent on field S#—for each supplier number, there must be exactly one city (e.g., every time S1 appears as the supplier number, London must appear as the city). Note that fields T.A and T.B are allowed to be composite in this definition: For example, in table SPSC again, field QTY is functionally dependent on the composite field (S#,P#). We write:

```
S#          -->   SCITY

(S#,P#)     -->   QTY
```

Now comes the crucial point. If the database design satisfies the "one fact in one place" objective, *the only functional dependencies in any table will be of the form K → F, where K is the primary key and F is some other field.* Note that it follows from the definition that K → F always holds for all fields F in the table. "One fact in one place" says that no *other* functional dependencies hold. The purpose of the normalization discipline is to get rid of all "other" FDs, i.e., FDs that are not of the simple form K → F.

There are basically two cases to consider:

1. The table has a composite primary key, of the form (K1,K2) say, and also includes a field F that is functionally dependent on part of that key, say on K2, instead of on the whole key. (This was the case illustrated in the SPSC example

above.) In this case the guidelines recommend forming another table containing K2 and F (primary key K2) and removing F from the original table:

```
Replace    T(K1,K2,F),   primary key (K1,K2), with FD K2 --> F

by             T1(K1,K2),   primary key (K1,K2)
        and T2(K2,F),    primary key K2
```

2. The table has primary key K, a field F1 that is (of course) functionally dependent on K, and another field F2 that is functionally dependent on F1. The solution here is essentially the same as before—we form another table containing F1 and F2 (primary key F1), and remove F2 from the original table:

```
Replace    T(K,F1,F2),   primary key K, with FD F1 --> F2

by             T1(K,F1),    primary key K
        and T2(F1,F2),   primary key F1
```

Given any table as input, repeated application of these two rules will (in almost all practical situations) eventually yield a set of tables that are in the "ultimate" normal form and thus do not contain any FDs not of the simple form $K \rightarrow F$.

To recap, the normalization discipline involves reducing large tables to smaller ones. Loosely speaking, it assumes that you already have some small number of large tables as input, and it manipulates that input to produce a large number of small tables as output. But it does not say anything about how you arrive at the large tables in the first place. The design procedure sketched earlier in this appendix, by contrast, addresses exactly that problem. That is why we claim that the two approaches complement one another. Our overall suggested design methodology thus consists of:

1. Using the procedures of Sections B.1–B.7 to generate tables representing kernels, associations, etc.; and then

2. Using the procedures of the present section to verify that those tables do not unintentionally violate any of the normalization guidelines.

To conclude this section, a couple of final remarks on normalization:

- The lower normal forms such as 2NF are not particularly important in themselves other than as stepping-stones to the final normal form.

- Tables that are in 3NF but not in 4NF or 5NF, though theoretically possible, are very unlikely to occur in practice. This is why you hear people talking about third normal form, rather than fourth or fifth, as if it were the only and final goal; in practice this is usually a justifiable simplification.

## B.9   MISCELLANEOUS TIPS AND HINTS

We conclude this rather lengthy appendix with a short list of miscellaneous tips and hints. Space precludes very much detailed discussion of these points.

### Composite Keys

Composite (multiple-field) primary keys can be very clumsy. Whenever you find you have a table in your design with a composite key, consider the merits of introducing a new, noncomposite field to serve as the primary key instead. For example, introduce a shipment number (SHIP#) into the SP table.

### Entity Subtypes

Sometimes a given entity can be of multiple types simultaneously. For example, the same person may simultaneously be an employee, a stockholder, and a customer. Furthermore, some entity types are *subtypes* of others (for example, all managers are employees). *Entity type Y is said to be a subtype of entity type X if every instance of Y is necessarily an instance of X.* All properties, designations, etc., applying to X also apply to Y, but the converse is not true. For example, managers have salaries because all employees have salaries, but they also have budgets, which nonmanagers do not. Such a situation can conveniently be represented as follows (pseudoDDL again):

```
CREATE TABLE EMP              /* employees (kernel) */
       PRIMARY KEY ( EMP# )
       FIELDS ( EMP# ... , SALARY ... ) ;

CREATE TABLE MGR     /* managers -- subtype of EMP */
       PRIMARY KEY ( EMP# )
       FOREIGN KEY ( EMP# IDENTIFIES EMP etc. )
       FIELDS ( EMP# ... , BUDGET ... ) ;
```

One advantage of this design is that it avoids the need for the null values that would otherwise be required to represent BUDGET values for nonmanagers (if the two tables were combined into one).

### Domains

Although DB2 does not support the notion of domains, they can still be useful in the design process (and can still be represented in pseudoDDL). For example:

```
CREATE DOMAIN S# CHAR(5) ;      /* supplier numbers */

CREATE TABLE S
       FIELDS ( S# DOMAIN ( S# ), ... ) ;
```

```
CREATE TABLE SP
          FIELDS ( S# DOMAIN ( S# ), .. ) ;
```

Recommendation: Whenever possible, give every field the same name as the underlying domain. When it is not possible, give the field the name of the domain prefixed by some qualifier to make it unique (within its containing table). Thus, for example, use S# or S__S# or SP__S# (etc.) as names of fields containing supplier numbers; do *not* use (e.g.) S# in one table and SNO in another and SNUM in a third (etc.). One reason for this rule is that it makes life easier for the user (fewer distinct names to remember, less arbitrariness). Another, perhaps more significant, is that it allows you to discover all uses of a given domain by querying the catalog: for example,

```
SELECT NAME, TBNAME
FROM   SYSIBM.SYSCOLUMNS
WHERE  NAME LIKE '%S#' ;
```

## Null Values

Be very careful over null values. Null values exhibit very arbitrary and inconsistent behavior and can be the source of a lot of difficulties. For example:

- Two null values are considered to be duplicates of each other for the purposes of DISTINCT and UNIQUE and ORDER BY but not for the purposes of WHERE or GROUP BY.

- The builtin functions COUNT, SUM, and AVG are not guaranteed to satisfy the requirement that the average is equal to the sum divided by the count (in the presence of null values).

- If F1 and F2 are fields, the expression SUM(F1) + SUM(F2) is not guaranteed to be equivalent to the expression SUM(F1+F2) (in the presence of null values).

As a result, you should consider very carefully whether you want to allow null values for any fields at all. It may well be that using certain nonnull but "illegal" values, such as $-1$ for an HOURS__WORKED field, will serve your purposes better. (Of course, if you do choose to go this way, then the primary and foreign key recipes given earlier will require some revision.) Note, however, that there are three points at which the notion of null is woven into the very fabric of the SQL language. To be specific, SQL:

- *insists* on allowing nulls for any field added to a table via ALTER TABLE

- *generates* null as the result of applying a function such as AVG to an empty set

- *generates* null for any unspecified field on INSERT

## Vectors

Represent vectors column-wise rather than row-wise. For example, represent last year's sales figures for items x, y, . . . as

```
SALES   ITEM   MONTH   QTY
        ----   -----   ---
         x     Jan     100
         x     Feb      50

         .      .        .
         x     Dec     360
         y     Jan      75
         y     Feb     144

         .      .        .
         y     Dec      35

         .      .        .
```

instead of as

```
SALES   ITEM   JAN_QTY   FEB_QTY   ...   DEC_QTY
        ----   -------   -------   ---   -------
         x        100        50    ...       360
         y         75       144    ...        35

         .          .         .    ...         .
```

One reason for this recommendation is that it makes the writing of generalized (parameterized) queries much simpler. Consider, for example, what is involved in comparing the sales figure for item $i$ in month $m$ with that for item $j$ in month $n$ (where $i$, $j$, $m$, and $n$ are parameters).

## Field Overloading

Do not overload fields with more than one meaning. For example, the "purchase-order quantity" field clearly applies to purchased parts only, so it *could* be used to represent "work-in-progress quantity" for parts that are manufactured in-house. But such a design leads to programming complexity, difficulty in understanding system documentation, and severe problems if it is ever decided both to manufacture and purchase the same part.

## Normalization (again)

Finally, a few more words on the topic of normalization.

- First, the normalization guidelines *are* only guidelines. There is no mandatory requirement that all tables be in (say) third normal form. The only requirement is that they be in at least first normal form. In a sense, the normalization discipline optimizes update performance at the expense of retrieval performance (redundancy, which is what that discipline tries to eliminate, is bad for update, but it may be good for retrieval). Another way of saying this is the following: The normalization guidelines recommend "one fact in one place"; but sometimes there are good reasons for having two facts in one place, or one fact in two places. So you may choose to violate the guidelines on occasion; but if you do, please carefully document your reasons!

- Second, all of our discussions have been concerned with base tables. There is no requirement that *views* be in 3NF, even if the base tables are, and indeed they frequently will not be. The design procedure we have been advocating in this appendix is, to a large extent, *application-independent*; we have simply been saying "Decide what entities you are interested in, decide what relationships exist among them, and so on," and we have totally ignored the question of how that information is going to be used. It is possible (to some extent) subsequently to tailor, restructure, and slant that application-independent design to meet the needs of individual applications, via the view mechanism. However, that tailoring activity is very much a secondary consideration. The primary objective is to get the independent design right in the first place.

# Syntax of SQL Data Manipulation Operations

## C.1 INTRODUCTION

We give a BNF grammar for the four data manipulation operations of SQL (SELECT, UPDATE, DELETE, and INSERT) described in this book. The grammar makes use of the following convenient shorthand:

- If "xyz" is a syntactic category, then "xyz-commalist" is a syntactic category consisting of a list of one or more "xyz"s in which each pair of adjacent "xyz"s is separated by a sequence of characters consisting of zero or more spaces, followed by a comma, followed by zero or more spaces.

The categories "identifier," "constant," and "integer" are terminal with respect to this grammar.

*Note:* Aspects of the four statements not described in the body of the book (e.g., the comparison operators >ANY, =ALL, etc.) are ignored. In the interests of clarity and brevity, moreover, the grammar does not accurately reflect the dialect of SQL supported by DB2 but is instead slightly permissive, in the sense that it allows the generation of certain constructs that are not legal in DB2. For example, it allows the argument to a function such as AVG to consist of a reference to another function such as SUM, which DB2 does not permit.

## C.2   NAMES

```
table-name
    ::=     base-table-name
          | view-name
          | alias
          | synonym

base-table-name
    ::=  [ user-name . ] identifier

user-name
    ::=  identifier

view-name
    ::=  [ user-name . ] identifier

alias
    ::=  identifier

synonym
    ::=  identifier

column-name
    ::=  [ table-name .] identifier
```

## C.3   SCALAR EXPRESSIONS

```
scalar-expression
    ::=  scalar-term [ arithmetic-operator scalar-expression

scalar-term
    ::=  [ + | - ] scalar-value

scalar-value
    ::=     column-name
          | function-reference
          | constant
          | USER
          | ( scalar-expression )
```

```
function-reference
    ::=    COUNT ( * )
         | function-name ( scalar-expression )
         | function-name ( DISTINCT column-name )

function-name
    ::=  COUNT | SUM | AVG | MAX | MIN

arithmetic-operator
    ::=  + | - | * | /
```

## C.4   SELECT-EXPRESSIONS

```
select-expression
    ::=   select-clause
          from-clause
          [ where-clause ]
          [ grouping-clause | having-clause ] ]

select-clause
    ::=  SELECT [ DISTINCT ] select-spec

select-spec
    ::=  * | select-item-commalist

select-item
    ::=    table-name . *
         | scalar-expression

from-clause
    ::=  FROM from-item-commalist

from-item
    ::=  table-name [ alias ]

where-clause
    ::=  WHERE predicate

grouping-clause
    ::=  GROUP BY column-name-commalist

having-clause
    ::=  HAVING predicate
```

## C.5   PREDICATES

```
predicate
    ::=     condition
          | condition AND predicate
          | condition OR predicate
          | NOT predicate

condition
    ::=     compare-condition
          | between-condition
          | like-condition
          | in-condition
          | exists-condition
          | ( predicate )

compare-condition
    ::=     scalar-expression compare-operator scalar- expressi
          | scalar-expression compare-operator
                            ( column-select-expression )
          | scalar-expression IS [ NOT ] NULL

compare-operator
    ::=   = | ¬= | < | ¬< | <= | > | ¬> | >=

column-select-expression
    ::=   column-select-clause
          from-clause
          [ where-clause ]
          [ grouping-clause [ having-clause ] ]

column-select-clause
    ::=   SELECT [ DISTINCT ] scalar-expression

between-condition
    ::=   column-name [ NOT ] BETWEEN scalar-expression
                                   AND scalar-expression

like-condition
    ::=   column-name [ NOT ] LIKE scalar-expression

in-condition
    ::=   scalar-expression [ NOT ] IN ( set-of-scalars )
```

```
set-of-scalars
    ::=     constant-commalist
          | column-select-expression

exists-condition
    ::=  EXISTS ( select-expression )
```

## C.6  STATEMENTS

```
statement
    ::=     select-statement
          | update-statement
          | delete-statement
          | insert-statement

select-statement
    ::=  union-expression [ ordering-clause ] ;

union-expression
    ::=  select-expression [ UNION union-expression ]

ordering-clause
    ::=  ORDER BY order-item-commalist

order-item
    ::=  ordering-column [ ASC | DESC ]

ordering-column
    ::=  column-name | integer

update-statement
    ::=  UPDATE table-name [ alias ]
         SET column-assignment-commalist
         [ where-clause ] ;

column-assignment
    ::=     column-name = scalar-expression
          | column-name = NULL

delete-statement
    ::=  DELETE FROM table-name [ alias ]
         [ where-clause ] ;
```

```
insert-statement
    ::=    INSERT INTO table-name [ ( column-name-commalist )
                    source-values ;

source-values
    ::=    VALUES ( insert-item-commalist )
         | select-expression

insert-item
    ::=    constant | NULL
```

# System Requirements

## D.1 DB2

DB2 can run on any CPU supported by MVS Version 1 Release 3 (MVS/370) or Version 2 Release 1.1 (MVS/XA). The hardware cross memory extension feature is recommended for the 3033 CPU. DB2 uses direct access storage for:

- database data sets (optionally mass storage subsystem, MSS)
- catalog data sets
- active log data sets
- archive log data sets (optionally tape or MSS)
- image copy data sets (optionally tape or MSS)
- utility work data sets (optionally tape or MSS)
- bootstrap data set

*Note:* The bootstrap data set is used in system restart.

Virtual storage: Under MVS/370, the minimum requirement for common storage area (CSA) is approximately 512K bytes. The practical minimum private virtual storage requirement is approximately 4.5M–5M bytes. For MVS/XA, most DB2-required areas reside in the extended CSA; most DB2 code, control blocks, and buffers reside in the extended private area.

The following support software is required:

- MVS/SP-JES2 or - JES3, Version 1 Release 3 or Version 2 Release 1.1 (or a subsequent release)
- MVS/370 Data Facility Product Release 1 or MVS/XA Data Facility Product Release 1.1
- MVS TSO Command Package Release 1.1 or MVS TSO Extensions (TSO/E) Release 1
- OS/VS Sort/Merge Release 5
- (optional, but required to run DB2I) Interactive System Productivity Facility (ISPF) and ISPF / Program Development Facility (ISPF/PDF or PDF)
- System Maintenance Program (SMP) Version 1 Release 4

The following are optional:

- Query Management Facility (QMF) Release 1
- Data Extract (DXT) Release 1
- Information Management System / Virtual Storage (IMS/VS) Version 1 Release 3
- Customer Information Control System / OS / Virtual Storage (CICS/OS/VS) Version 1 Release 6
- Resource Access Control Facility (RACF) Release 5
- OS/VS COBOL Compiler and Library Release 2.3
- TSO Assembler Prompter Release 1
- TSO COBOL Prompter Release 1
- OS PL/I Optimizing Compiler Release 4
- VS FORTRAN Release 1.1
- OS Assembler H Release 5
- Assembler H Version 2 Release 1

## D.2   QMF

To work with DB2, QMF requires:

- DB2
- ISPF Release 1.1
- Graphical Data Display Manager, Release 2

## D.3   DXT

To work with DB2, DXT requires:

- DB2
- ISPF/PDF Release 1.1
- OS/VS DB/DC Data Dictionary, Release 4 (optional)

# Bibliography

We present a short list of selected further reading.

*IBM Database 2 General Information*. IBM Form No. GC26-4073.

*IBM Database 2 Introduction to SQL*. IBM Form No. GC26-4082.

> These two manuals provide overviews of the DB2 product and the DB2 dialect of the SQL language, respectively. They also include references to numerous other IBM manuals on the DB2 system.

*Query Management Facility: General Information*. IBM Form No. GC26-4071.

*Data Extract: General Information*. IBM Form No. GC26-4070.

> These two manuals provide overviews of QMF and DXT, respectively, and (like the two DB2 manuals mentioned above) include many references to other relevant IBM documentation.

*SQL/Data System for VSE: A Relational Data System for Application Development*. IBM Form No. G320-6590.

> An introductory manual on SQL/DS.

M. M. Astrahan et al. "System R: Relational Approach to Database Management." *ACM Transactions on Database Systems 1*, No. 2 (June 1976).

> The paper that first described the overall architecture of System R, the prototype forerunner of DB2 (and SQL/DS).

M. W. Blasgen et al. "System R: An Architectural Overview." *IBM Systems Journal 20*, No. 1 (February 1981).

Describes the architecture of System R as it became by the time the system had been fully implemented.

D. D. Chamberlin et al. "A History and Evaluation of System R." *Communications of the ACM 24*, No. 10 (October 1981).

Discusses the lessons learned from the System R prototype.

D. D. Chamberlin, A. M. Gilbert, and R. A. Yost. "A History of System R and SQL/ Data System." Proceedings of the Seventh International Conference on Very Large Data Bases (September 1981). Obtainable from ACM, IEEE, and INRIA.

Includes a description of the major differences between System R and SQL/DS.

E. F. Codd. "A Relational Model of Data for Large Shared Data Banks." *Communications of the ACM 13*, No. 6 (June 1970). Reprinted in *Communications of the ACM 26*, No. 1 (January 1983).

This was the paper that (apart from some internal IBM documents) first proposed the ideas of the relational model.

E. F. Codd. "Extending the Relational Database Model to Capture More Meaning." *ACM Transactions on Database Systems 4*, No. 4 (December 1979).

Proposes an extended version of the relational model called RM/T. The entity classification scheme described in Appendix B is based on some ideas from this paper.

E. F. Codd. "Relational Database: A Practical Foundation for Productivity." *Communications of the ACM 25*, No. 2 (February 1982).

The paper that Codd presented on the occasion of his receiving the 1981 Turing Award. The definition of "relational system" in Appendix A of this book is taken from this paper.

W. Kent. "A Simple Guide to Five Normal Forms in Relational Database Theory." *Communications of the ACM 26*, No. 2 (February 1983).

An informal description of first, second, ..., fifth normal form (see Appendix B of this book).

C. J. Date. "A Practical Approach to Database Design." *IBM Technical Report TR 03.220* (December 1982).

The design methodology presented in Appendix B is largely based on this report. (See also Codd's paper on RM/T, referenced above.)

C. J. Date. *An Introduction to Database Systems*. *Volume I* (Third Edition), Addison-Wesley (1981); *Volume II* (First Edition), Addison-Wesley (1983)

These two books between them provide the basis for a comprehensive education in most aspects of database technology. In particular, they include a detailed tutorial on the relational approach.

# Index